"For millennia, Black and brown people's prophetic imagination has revived the Church—and with this book, Rev. Dr. Jason Villegas carries forward this powerful and holy lineage. Timely, wise, provocative, practical—and above all, faithful—*When Methods Die* reads like a love letter to a church that has lost its way. Jason invites readers who also love the church to cast off the shackles of certainty, control, and death avoidance—and join him in bringing death and resurrection into cosmic and practical unity. May all who have ears to hear, hear!"

— CHRISTENA CLEVELAND
Author of *God Is a Black Woman*

"This young Latinx pastor brings the voice of a new American apostolate—with a sober eye on the legacy of the church and a heart for its future. He begins with a searing yet empathetic eulogy for a dying 'Method of Church,' then walks us through a labyrinth of decline and denial toward an expectancy of resurrection. A hip-hop poet exploring fraught terrain through language and metaphors both playful and poignant, Miller-Villegas serves the tradition he loves as hospice chaplain and midwife."

—ELAINE ENNS AND CHED MYERS
Authors of *Healing Haunted Histories: A Settler Discipleship of Decolonization*

"In this book, Rev. Dr. Jason Villegas, 'does not turn away' but looks straight into death and loss, both of the church and its fading ideologies. While expressing both grief and a longing hope, he expertly weaves story, scripture, and insight. This is a book to be read, for all of us, who are actively witnessing our churches pass away yet are longing for resurrection. Jason will walk you through the loss, the grief, and the beauty of hope and God's good care."

—FATIMAH SALLEH
Founder, A Certain Work

"*When Methods Die* is a stunning, honest, courageous love letter to the church and its people. Jason Miller-Villegas reflects deeply on the church's struggles and institutional brokenness with a yearning hope for resurrection. Through poetry and prose, with prophetic urgency and pastoral tenderness, he names our dying and weaves a hope-filled vision of renewal. This is a must-read for anyone longing to see the church reborn in love and justice."

—STEVE TAYLOR

Home missioner, Spring Forest New Monastic and Missional Community UMC

"Jason Miller-Villegas writes with tender clarity and fierce wisdom, drawing for us a deep and enduring vision for the future of the church. We need to hold room for real grief in institutional church spaces, and *When Methods Die* helps us do that through the lens of deep hope. This book is about facing death as a transition to life and honoring the power of resurrection in a hurting world. I highly recommend it!"

—KAITLIN B. CURTICE

Award-winning Potawatomi author of *Native and Living Resistance*

When Methods Die

When Methods Die

The Writing on the Wall for a Fading Church

JASON MILLER-VILLEGAS

WIPF & STOCK · Eugene, Oregon

WHEN METHODS DIE
The Writing on the Wall for a Fading Church

Copyright © 2025 Jason Villegas. All rights reserved. Except for brief quotations in critical publications or reviews, no part of this book may be reproduced in any manner without prior written permission from the publisher. Write: Permissions, Wipf and Stock Publishers, 199 W. 8th Ave., Suite 3, Eugene, OR 97401.

Wipf & Stock
An Imprint of Wipf and Stock Publishers
199 W. 8th Ave., Suite 3
Eugene, OR 97401

www.wipfandstock.com

PAPERBACK ISBN: 979-8-3852-3475-2
HARDCOVER ISBN: 979-8-3852-3476-9
EBOOK ISBN: 979-8-3852-3477-6

VERSION NUMBER 021425

Service of Death and Resurrection from *The United Methodist Book of Worship*, #s 141, 150 © 1992 The United Methodist Publishing House. Used by permission. All rights reserved.

All Scripture quotations, unless otherwise indicated, are taken from the Holy Bible, New International Version®, NIV®. Copyright ©1973, 1978, 1984, 2011 by Biblica, Inc.™ Used by permission of Zondervan. All rights reserved worldwide. www.zondervan.com The "NIV" and "New International Version" are trademarks registered in the United States Patent and Trademark Office by Biblica, Inc.™

Scripture quotations marked NRSV are from the New Revised Standard Version Bible, copyright © 1989 National Council of the Churches of Christ in the United States of America. Used by permission. All rights reserved worldwide.

Scripture quotations marked (ESV) are from The ESV® Bible (The Holy Bible, English Standard Version®), © 2001 by Crossway, a publishing ministry of Good News Publishers. Used by permission. All rights reserved.

Scripture quotations marked KJV are from The Authorized (King James) Version. Rights in the Authorized Version in the United Kingdom are vested in the Crown. Reproduced by permission of the Crown's patentee, Cambridge University Press.

Scripture quotations marked CEB are from the COMMON ENGLISH BIBLE. © Copyright 2011 COMMON ENGLISH BIBLE. All rights reserved. Used by permission. (www.CommonEnglishBible.com).

This book lives dedicated to anyone who walks as a faith leader in spaces where institutional death occurs, where nobody knows what new life will yet look like.

Are we death doulas and end-of-life chaplains?
Or are we midwives of a future awaiting its birth? Or both?

Contents

Preface | ix
Acknowledgments | xiii
List of Abbreviations | xiv
Introduction | xv

1. Funeral for the Methods of a Fading Church | 1
2. Recognizing the Ruins: Understanding the Crisis | 9
3. Silent Symptoms in the Shadows: Signs of Decline | 34
4. Lonely, Grieving, Leaving: The Emotional Toll | 44
5. Attitudes in Ashes: What Must Change | 63
6. Prophetic Whispers: Embracing Mystical Visions | 80
7. White Supremacy's Demise: A Necessary Death | 102
8. Strategies for Survival: Living amid Death | 118
9. Holy Saturday Silence: Waiting in the In-Between | 153
10. Resurrection's Dawn: A Step Toward Renewal | 168

Bibliography | 187

Preface

Right then the fingers of a human hand appeared and wrote on the plaster of the king's palace wall in the light of the lamp. The king saw the hand that wrote. The king's mood changed immediately, and he was deeply disturbed. He felt weak, and his knees were shaking.

—Dan 5:5–6 CEB

"The Writing on the Wall"

If you squint and close your eyes, I wonder, can you see it, the writing on the wall, the 20-year-old fingerprints turned to gray smudges from the last children who were in the building, never washed off, because when the children left, the church could not afford a janitor, and the blessing of the fingerprints, like the young people who left them, was accidentally overlooked by the people suffering an identity crisis, thinking that the building and not they were the church?

Can you see it, the writing on the wall, the cracks between cinder blocks, that started small and turned into words, like tectonic plates, creating new worlds, continental rifts, dividing and separating edifices, pulling parishioners asunder into different camps?

Can you hear it, the writing on the wall, the voices of ancestors, whose names exist in brass plaques, whose voices are bastardized to make modern-day points that maybe they could and maybe they couldn't have imagined in their own rhetoric?

Can you hear it, the writing on the wall, the graphite on loose leaf scrambled and scribbled by the young adult visitor who came in for worship and, through stealthy shallow breathing, sat nervously, mindlessly, drawing pictures of her safe space outside until the bell tolled and told everyone it was time to leave their hour-long weekly commitment?

Can you notice it, the writing on the wall, the "for sale" sign on all of the damned church buildings down the road, telling the tale of what happens when we don't wake up to reality, as we pray for divine intervention, believing that the rules of God's presence and presents should function differently for us than the Palestinian Christian at the bottom of a pile of bomb rubble, or the asylum seeking *campesino* from Central America crossing the Devil's Highway?

Can you witness it, the writing on the wall, the words of mourning and warning and wanting and waiting and wailing that the disciples wrote in their cabin of solitude, hiding on Holy Saturday, right before Jesus Christ walked through the walls to surprise the hell out of them?

And then, can you abide with it, the writing that you come to see on all your walls, drawing you liturgical pictures on old ivory paint jobs, like flowers blooming in the desert, showing that new ideas can come in places that the world sees only as whitewashed tombs?

Can you behold it, the writing in the walls, a Word so deep that its wisdom intertwines and exists with us, like DNA, coming forth to remind us what was so deep that it had been forgotten, like a buried seed, awakened by heat, coming through scorched earth, to start afresh on a new day?

Can you name it, the writing on the walls, telling of death and new life, even if with your child's mind, you cannot read what it says?

Can you dignify it, the writing on the walls, appearing in front of your eyes in a language, you can't understand, necessitating that we find a prophet like Daniel to tell us what God is saying?

Can you feel it, the writing on the walls of our heart, vibrating your being—the Tattoo Artist's gun, causing positive heartburn as the Word appears on the tablet of your inmost being, the Message that was and is and will be?

Can you hold it all, the writing on the walls, that began before you, that tells the story for you, and that will still be the story of God after you are dead?

Can you be held by it, the writing on the walls?

In the Hebrew Bible/Old Testament's book of Daniel, chapter 5, we see the story of some wealthy royals who have inherited stolen objects from a place of worship, suddenly terrified out of their comfort zone by a heavenly hand miraculously writing on the wall. It was a statement that the foundation on which the walls of that kingdom existed would be broken down. And it was a statement about the new life that would be inherited by someone else.

I could spend many pages writing about the social and religious differences between the royalty of Babylon and the church in the United States, but for all the differences, a couple of similarities pull my mind to this story as a starting point for this book.

Because of the connection between Christianity and the forces of empire created by the emperor Constantine in the early 300s, Christianity in the West has long benefited from wealth that empire has taken and built. And now we are at a place and time when that wealth is changing hands, when our social systems are experiencing death.

In a much different way, I think God is writing on the wall. It is a writing about how we have missed the mark and about what is dead, but, for us as people who believe in Jesus Christ, it is also a message about life and what will come next.

The main metaphor of this book is the funeral, the "service of death and resurrection." But also, as you read on, I hope you can encounter this message as I have—like inconvenient words, interrupting everyday life, written where they have not been invited, like graffiti from God's holy hand on the walls of the edifices we inhabit.

Acknowledgments

MANY THANKS: ELIZABETH, THANK you for being a constant companion and hearing many of these thoughts in verbal form before they were written down; to the Murfreesboro United Methodist Church for giving me space to write this; to Debbie for the idea of naming our method of church in a funeral service; to my doctor of ministry cohort for being conversation partners during a crucial part of this book; to Aunt Ruth for planting the seed of writing a book a decade ago when I had hope but not confidence as a writer; and thanks to all of my many mentors, pastors, parent figures, and guides along the way, especially Mari, Fatimah, Laura, Steve, and my friends in The Remnant, Stubborn Hope, Little Band, and the Church of (Star) Trek. Y'all, like me, have likely struggled with the burnout that comes from serving God, or the Greater Good as you understand it, and working with a people who experience the agony of institutional death and the longing for resurrection. An immeasurable thanks to those who have helped me with editing, especially Adam, who helped me complete my manuscript in May 2023; Ben, who swooped in to assist with citations; and Nicole from Wipf and Stock, who has shown immense patience with me throughout the editing process. I remain grateful to the Holy Spirit for her tenacity in all the aforementioned people reigniting my fire each time it has gone out.

List of Abbreviations

AARP	American Association of Retired Persons
AUMC	Ahoskie United Methodist Church
CEB	Common English Bible
MUMC	Murfreesboro United Methodist Church
NAACP	National Association for the Advancement of Colored People
NIV	New International Version
RHUMC	Rose Hill United Methodist Church
UMC	United Methodist Church

Introduction

"You know pastor, you are really good at funerals." This sentiment, echoed in various ways throughout my career, often catches me off guard. While sometimes about the sermon, other times about my aura, and yet other times about my pastoral care, it always nudges me toward a profound realization—our encounters with death reflect the most authentic manifestations of our faith. These moments of grief, intertwined with an enduring hope for the promise of resurrection, have time and again made me question, reflect, and wonder about the complexities of our mortal existence.

In the United Methodist Church, funerals symbolize the paradox of death and resurrection, mourning the loss while affirming the promise of new life. This duality has profoundly shaped my pastoral service and deeply influenced my perception of the church and my understanding of faith.

But as I've grown in my faith and service, I've come to realize that our encounters with death and resurrection aren't just personal experiences. They are deeply woven into our collective existence. In a broader sense, they influence our societal structures, cultural norms, and even the institutions that we cherish and hold dear. Among these institutions, the church, particularly the United Methodist Church, has held a central place in my life. As a faithful follower of Jesus Christ and a member of this church, I have felt increasingly called to contemplate this paradox in the context of the church itself.

The challenge of this contemplation is that it arrives at a crucial time for us. We find ourselves standing at the crossroads of a new era where the once familiar church landscape has dramatically shifted. We are faced with the stark reality that the church, in its traditional form, is grappling with a loss of efficacy. It struggles to resonate in an increasingly diverse, rapidly evolving society, struggling to maintain its relevance and influence. This predicament, however, is not unique to the church; it mirrors a broader societal transformation that we are witnessing today.

For example, we live in a time when racial dominance, a long-standing aspect of our societal fabric, is being challenged and transformed. The old structures that perpetuated this dominance are being critically reassessed, questioned, and dismantled. And the church is no exception to this broader societal upheaval. Yet, as people of faith, we should not view this transformation as a crisis but rather as an opportunity—a divine invitation—to reimagine our church.

There lies before us a unique prospect to break free from the shackles of an antiquated past and construct a more equitable, inclusive sanctuary for all of God's children. A place where every person, regardless of their race, color, or creed, can find solace, acceptance, and the love of Christ. More than a building, we have an opportunity to again become that place, to reimagine who we will be as the church of Jesus Christ.

Embracing this opportunity, however, is not a passive act. It is not a journey to be embarked upon with complacency. It is not going to happen to us or without us. Like my father used to say, "It's not a spectator sport." Instead, it's a journey fraught with complexities, questions, and, at times, discomfort. It demands from us a willingness to examine our traditions, question our assumptions, and embrace the reality that things have died and live in the possibility of a transformative resurrection. Our opportunity to live into death and resurrection calls us to recognize that our mission isn't just to those within our immediate congregations but extends to all of the people. The mission statement of my church has long been, "Making disciples of Jesus Christ for the transformation of the world." And the current moment requires of us that we live as disciples for the transformation of a church that cannot live into the future without transformation.

I am writing within the context of a historically white church. Robert Jones, in his well-researched book *The End of White Christian America*, uses broad data to dissect the decline of the white church's influence. Jones's work has springboarded this conversation, and I invite you to join it. This book reflects my ten-year pastoral career marked by witnessing the death of outdated methods and the potential for their transformation.

Through serving four churches and as a high-level youth director, from my master of divinity to receiving my doctor of ministry degree, the death and resurrection of attitudes, beliefs, and traditions within the church have profoundly influenced and embraced my pastoral journey. This embrace extends back to my three years, from 2010 to 2013 as a youth pastor, when my grief at death in the church began to grow, when I began to notice that the staid ways of inviting youth to come and be entertained in the church basement were not working.

INTRODUCTION

This book attempts to navigate the intricate tapestry of these experiences, beliefs, and attitudes that I've encountered in my service to God and the church. It revolves around one extended reflection about our service to God and the world through the church. The word *service* holds particular significance in my Christian tradition. It means "to serve," and it is also the name of the event of worshiping God, known as "a worship service." This dual meaning of service—serving God and the world and worshiping God—encapsulates the essence of this book.

Structured as a series of reflections and conversations, this book journeys through different phases of death and resurrection in the church. Because it is about the institutional church, I am not going to be talking about heaven and hell or the afterlife. It begins with a chapter that invites us into the attitude of lament, something for which my tradition has a good method but which we do not practice well when tragedy strikes.

The first chapter, titled "Funeral for the Methods of a Fading Church," focuses on grieving the death of traditional church practices rather than individual lives. The subsequent chapters delve into recognizing death in different aspects of our lives in the church, returning to mourning and lamenting, and considering these Christian postures in specific ways.

Further along, the book discusses attitudes that need to die in the church—dispositions that have themselves caused death. Once these attitudes are acknowledged, the book invites you to adopt a prophetic stance, a brave posture of truth-telling about death and resurrection in a time when it's often easier to create convenient countertruths. With this prophetic posture, the book revisits the theme of beliefs that need to die—white supremacy, which many Christians, myself included, view as the original sin of the church in the Americas.

The discussion on death and resurrection within the church cannot be complete without acknowledging the experiences of racially minoritized[1] people. Many have often experienced death from ideas like white supremacy, often at the hands of the white church. This experience resonates with

---

1. The term *minoritized* has emerged in recent years as a more nuanced way to describe individuals and groups who have been systematically positioned as minorities through social, political, and economic structures. Unlike the term *minorities*, which can imply an inherent identity or attribute of the individuals themselves, *minoritized* emphasizes the external processes and systems that actively marginalize and diminish the collective power of these groups. This shift in language seeks to highlight how historical and ongoing practices—such as colonization, enslavement, segregation, and discriminatory policies—have created and sustained these inequities. By using *minoritized*, I'm trying to acknowledge the agency of those affected while focusing on the structures and actions that perpetuate their marginalization. It broadens our understanding beyond numerical representation to consider the power dynamics at play.

the story of Jesus Christ's death during Holy Week. The period from Good Friday, his death, his remaining dead on Holy Saturday, and then his resurrection on Easter Sunday is a poignant reminder of the journey of minority people who often live in the space of "Holy Saturday," where they do not know if new life can come again.

The book further explores the "Holy Saturday Silence," offering a posture of waiting and hoping. Without rushing through our necessary grief, it finally arrives at the last chapter, which discusses "Resurrection's Dawn: A Step Toward Renewal." This chapter doesn't attempt to cast a robust vision of what resurrection will look like but instead tries to talk about postures for living into resurrection as the new life that God surprisingly brings amid death.

As we traverse the space between death and resurrection, different structures guide us. The structure of this book is akin to stepping stones, seemingly disjointed solid places that keep us from falling and being inundated by the chaos, which do not at first glance seem to be connected to each other. This structure invites you to consider that the process of transformation is not always linear; it's a sequence of moments that challenge us, enlighten us, and ultimately transform us.

In essence, this book serves as a mirror reflecting the beauty, the flaws, the challenges, and the potential of the church. It's a call to introspection, a guide to consider transformation, and an affirmation of faith. As we delve deeper into this shared journey, my hope is that we not just witness the death and resurrection within our church but actively participate in it. We are, after all, people of the resurrection—and that, I believe, is our highest calling.

1.

Funeral for the Methods of a Fading Church

Gathering[1]

Dying, Christ destroyed our death.
Rising, Christ restored our life.
Christ will come again in glory.
As in baptism Our Method of Church put on Christ,
so in Christ may Our Method of Church be clothed with glory.
Here and now, dear friends, we are God's children.
What we shall be has not yet been revealed;
but we know that when they—Father, Son, and Holy Spirit appear, we shall
 be like them,
for we shall see them as they are.
Those who have this hope purify themselves
as Christ is pure.

The Word of Grace

Jesus said, "I am the resurrection and I am life.

---

1. United Methodist Publishing House, *Book of Worship*, 141–50. The UMC Service of Death and Resurrection can also be found online at https://www.umcdiscipleship.org/book-of-worship/a-service-of-death-and-resurrection.

Those who believe in me, even though they die, yet shall they live,
and whoever lives and believes in me shall never die.
I am Alpha and Omega, the beginning and the end, the first and the last.
I died, and behold I am alive for evermore,
and I hold the keys of hell and death.
Because I live, you shall live also."

Greeting

Friends, we have gathered here to praise God
and to witness to our faith as we celebrate the life of Our Method of Church.
We come together in grief, acknowledging our human loss.
May God grant us grace, that in pain we may find comfort,
in sorrow hope, in death resurrection.

Opening Prayer

God of our ancestors,
You were there at the tower of Babel when homogenous humanity worshiped its own devices,
And you were there at Pentecost giving birth to your church from the dispersed and different.
You were there when a small group of renegade enthusiasts began banding together in England,
And you were there when their revival evangelized virtually all of the United States of America.
You were there each time we suffered a schism and became unglued over trifling trivialities,
And you were there each time we have mended and found meaning in your presence with us.
Be with us now, as we face the death of our certain way of being Christians,
That we might find you under the layers of "doing" that have covered us.
   Amen.

Eulogy

"... *that you may not grieve as others do who have no hope*" (1 Thess 4:13b NRSV; emphasis added).

Remembering What Was

As you think about this Service of Death and Resurrection, close your eyes and imagine that you are walking into your church building. As you walk through, certain things meet your eye that make this building uniquely yours and uniquely your community's. You see pictures celebrating potlucks, plaques with names of charter members. The wall of pastors commands attention—the first dozen being the exact same age and looking very similar, and as *then* moves toward the *now*, the age and color of the faces slowly changes.

As you move closer to the place called *the sanctuary*, you go past Sunday school rooms which the saints remember as being filled to overflowing with excitement and fervor for learning the Bible and living scriptural holiness. You go past a place called *the narthex*—a word that is so old that it predates our method of being Christian. As you come to the double doors going into the sanctuary, you are aware that the architect made more than one way in and out, but all attention is on that center aisle, a riverbed that connects the flow of worshipers into the space and directs their attention to one vital point.

In the center, the place where energy and focus are funneled, a cross stands like a lighthouse on a cliff. In some churches that cross is by an altar, and in some it is centrally embedded like the beating heart itself on a pulpit. For as long as we have met like this, our attention has pointed at that shape, but now some people who would have it tattooed on their arms don't even know why. It is everywhere, and some might even say "overused," perhaps because it appears without requiring anything of those who bear it.

As we look around the sanctuary we see that many times the cross exists alongside other artifacts and holy objects. Sometimes the cross has a flame erupting beside it, and sometimes there is a crown of thorns draped victoriously over it. In more traditional churches, sometimes we even see a crucifix, with a statue of the body of Jesus still on the cross. That image, which is ubiquitous in our society, used to mean so much more than it does now. And somehow, it also meant so much less, meaning only one thing.

As we ponder our church buildings, we can look around at the various pews, seeing places where the varnish is worn off by certain ordinary saints having seated themselves in the same sixteen inches for seventy-five years. In this place where the canonized Catholic saints are not venerated, the lives of ordinary people encapsulate the faithfulness of God, their long-form discipleship a testimony to God's work among particular people in history.

We can look at the communion rail and still see the water stains from the tears of bygone revivals. We can look at the stained glass windows and see pictures which would have been biblical education for the illiterate five hundred years ago. At the bottom of those same windows we see the names of recently deceased saints who left their legacy to build this edifice. We see our favorite hymnals beside pew cards and literature, all celebrating a certain hour of the week on Sunday morning.

When we show up in our favorite places of worship, we cannot help but get the feeling that something is off kilter, that something's not quite right. The rest of the world swirling by on the outside of those stained glass windows does not even stop to think about the church, because the world itself is changing so quickly. We hold on to the church, because it has been the one constant in the world that moves too quickly. And yet we feel the awkwardness of the emptiness in the sanctuary. Does the sanctuary offer a resting place for immigrants and asylum seekers with deportation orders? Or is it only a place of refuge for members of the church seeking the comfortable nostalgia of the past?

The faithful few still have memories of the past that are greater than their hopes for the future, and yet a shred of optimism holds out that tomorrow will come, and that it will be the same as yesterday because we are in the church building. So long as we can sing our songs and pray our prayers, we like to believe that doing church in this manner is enough. But there is a difference between doing church and being church. A big part of the reason that we feel the subtle awkwardness is because we have experienced a death in our midst, and many times we did not even realize it, some of us until we showed up to this funeral right now.

The welcome card asking for information from new visitors shows a date of thirty years ago, when it was printed. The page on the welcome book gathering information in the narthex has not been moved from its current location in some years. The few people who have been to visit were greeted warmly, but they did not understand why they subconsciously made up their minds four minutes after darkening the doorway that they would never come back. The Sunday school class which still bears the name "young adult" has members who have all begun receiving mail from the AARP. Even so, they are still twenty years younger than their peers in the "older adult" class. The library has classics that everybody still remembers as relevant, but each of these books have faded covers from prolonged exposure to the sun coming in the window, three hours a day, repeated over decades. All of these images give off a spiritual scent, the smell of a decaying body. Or perhaps we have not noticed the smell because of the mortician's perfume used to disguise the embalming fluid. The church has experienced a death. We are finally grieving it now.

Fifty years ago our method of church brought in scores of people who each looked and thought the same. The roots grew deeper and the steeple grew higher—a tower worshiping God, built on the ingenuity of an army of architects who all thought alike. Because Jesus was the center and because the community was full of joy, nobody thought of the building as the tower of Babel. It was a monument, similar but different to monuments around town and in neighboring towns, a monument of what God could do in a Christian society. Our method of church gave everybody a job, and it ensured that adept records were kept of the membership—of how old, how baptized, how new, and how active each person was. It was a well-oiled machine. The method did not only exist inside of the church building, but it existed in books that were scripture for the Methodists, and it again ensured that the best and brightest would be brought from the outside in as the insiders went out into the world: the mission of making disciples of Jesus Christ for the world's transformation.

Grieving What's Dead

Our method of church died, but the church either did not notice or did not choose to believe that it had, and so things continued without change. Like grape juice poured into the ground the spiritual vitality slowly seeped through small cracks, leaving the church dry. The bread of heaven stopped coming in as fresh, leaving a cupboard with crumbs, leaving people starving. Because there had been no funeral, the bygone method of church was not able to be grieved and buried. The outside of the building continued to be washed and painted, but without vitality it might as well have been a whitewashed tomb.

When our method of church died it still kept operating, because methods unlike people can become zombies and consumers, unable to give back what they once could. Whereas once the method of church enlivened young pastors, it moved in death to be an instrument of anxiety and depression. Whereas in life the method of church had provided an avenue of celebration for what happened yearly, in death the method only served to provide shame at the apparent scarcity. Whereas in life the method of church brought unity, in death it only uplifted difference and drove people to polarization, squabbling over differences which barely existed in the first place.

There is a great irony in the death of our method of church. It died on the altar which held and pointed to the cross. The cross was an ancient lynching tree, an ancient method of murder and humiliation. The cross was a tool of a cruel empire to subjugate and thwart individualism, creativity, and subversion. It was also the tool that was used to murder Jesus when he was alive. But the reason it is the central icon in the Christian faith is that the cross itself was emptied of power at the resurrection. If we allow the dead method of church to remain unburied and ungrieved, it is tantamount to wearing a cross around our neck and forgetting that the resurrection is possible.

We grieve the death and loss of our method of church, but we also realize that death does not have the final word. Whenever methods have been created in Christianity, they have been created for a specific need, with the enabling of the Holy Spirit. When John Wesley and a small group of young Oxford academics began living as followers of Jesus, when they were named "Bible Moths" and "Methodists," it was for a particular time with a particular reason. Jesus, through the power of the Holy Spirit, always deals in particularities. We see that Jesus was born into the first-century world to an unwed peasant mother, born with beautiful brown skin in Bethlehem, that oppressed, Palestinian town, born under the hegemony and oppression of a cruel empire. When the church was born, it was born from people gathered across the Jewish dispersion, born as an affront to the earthly kingdoms, born with the power of the Holy Spirit.

Our method of church has definitely died, but in every method that is born is the methodology of the Holy Spirit. In some ways, we cannot understand from whence it comes or to where it goes any more than we can understand a wisp of wind lifting our chin up on a hot summer day. But the church has always understood certain elements of the Holy Spirit's methodology. The Holy Spirit inspired Scripture, inspired tradition, and shows up in our experiences and our reason. Even though our old method of church has died, the same Spirit awaits eagerly to do something new.

Not Being Without Hope

I'm not gonna tell you that I'm happy that our method of church died, and indeed I grieve like the rest of the church. I grieve because it means that I will irrepressibly be thrust out of my comfort zone and actually have to live in movement and with faith. But that's not such a bad thing. As we step out into the unknown, like Peter stepping out of the boat into the torment of the waves, we will look around and see other people whose boats have already sunk, people who are desperately trying to cling to Jesus. We will see members of the body of Christ who crossed the desert, hoping for the opportunity of a new life, their church and their old lives having been destroyed. We will see people who are the most disadvantaged and historically oppressed who already have been living this thing called faith that we are trying to get back to. We will see that our method of church became a bit stale, that it both oppressed and minoritized people needlessly. And we will see that every method which lives too long may turn into an idol.

We grieve the death of our method of church, and we also see the possibility of something new. In some ways we are left naked, but Jesus is offering us a new cloak. In some ways our wardrobes have been emptied, but we still have something to call our own. In some ways we will be left with less of a home, but we will remember that our home *is* in heaven *and* on the streets in the reign of God. In some ways we will feel distant from our family, but we will remember that Jesus said, "I will not leave you orphaned" (John 14:18 NRSV).

We will constantly see the present pain of death, but even then we will long for what is next. I would be lying if I said that we would be able to experience the resurrection as soon as we mourn the death, but it simply doesn't happen that way. Between Good Friday and Easter Sunday is the impossibly cold and dank space of Holy Saturday. Some marginalized communities have been living there for longer than we can imagine, and their existence is proof that Jesus still shows up.

We grieve, but we do not grieve as those who have no hope. Our sorrow brings with it a sort of pregnancy, a longing within us for something new. So let us hope in the Spirit, receiving the prenatal care needed to nurture this new fetus as it awaits birth into God's wild reign. We are a resurrection people, and not the type who want to revert back or demand a resuscitation. Our beloved dead, we believe, will be clothed in imperishability, in Christ, after they die. This is not the same as the earthly body. Our method of church will not be reborn like it was, but its death makes way for God to do a new thing. May we grieve what is lost, knowing that the Holy Trinity will bring new life, that God will do whatever wild God will do. Amen.

Prayer of Thanksgiving[2]

God of love, we thank you
for all with which you have blessed us
even to this day:
for the gift of joy in days of health and strength
and for the gifts of your abiding presence and promise
in days of pain and grief.

---

2. United Methodist Publishing House, *Book of Worship*, 150 (adapted by the author).

We thank you for the Body of Christ
And every expression of it throughout time and space;
For the Methods of Church which we have loved,
And which we give back to you when they die.
We praise you for home and friends,
and for our baptism and place in your Church
with all who have faithfully lived and died.
Above all else we thank you for Jesus,
who knew our griefs,
who died our death and rose for our sake,
and who lives and prays for us.
And as he taught us, so now we pray.

The Lord's Prayer

Our Father who art in Heaven,
Hallowed be thy name.
Thy Kingdom Come, thy will be done,
On earth as it is in Heaven.
Give us this day our daily bread,
And forgive us our trespasses,
As we forgive those who trespass against us.
And lead us not into temptation,
But deliver us from evil.
For thine is the Kingdom,
And the power and the glory, forever. Amen.

Dismissal with Blessing

The peace of God which passes all understanding
Keep your minds and hearts open
As we together grieve what has died,
Live in the space of Holy Saturday
And together anticipate the resurrection. Amen.

2.

Recognizing the Ruins
Understanding the Crisis

"Seeing Death"

Hello, Death. You, the familiar menace, as close to my consciousness as my sanity, or the precarious absence thereof. How peculiar it is, that you and I are acquainted like this, in the quiet corners of existence where life's clamor grows silent.

Isn't it strange? I've come to know you better than the ones you've claimed. As if one could know the ruins better than the buildings that once stood tall before they crumbled into fragments of history.

Once, you were the specter in the shadows, the chill that tingled up my spine, the unseen phantom that tore at the edges of my being. But now? Now you've claimed all but me. You've gathered the threads of their lives, leaving me to unravel the tapestry of memories stitch by lonesome stitch.

Yet I do not tremble in your presence. No, it is not you who stirs the fear within me. It is the sight of those still fleeing from their own finitude, running headlong from the embrace of your inevitability. If only they could see you as I do—not as a monster in the night, but as an integral part of life's grand tapestry, neither good nor bad, simply . . . there.

How it aches to watch them exhaust their breaths in the chase, squandering the precious currency of time on frivolities that do not matter. To see them forget the living memories they leave behind, the people who will carry their names forward into tomorrow. To watch them ignore the whispers of ancestors, their stories untouched by your cold hands. To see them forget that they, too, will one day join the chorus of ancestral voices.

Perhaps, Death, you could lend me your persuasive eloquence. Help me convince them to lay down their weapons, to cease their futile battle against the inevitable. To embrace the transient beauty of what is, and, in doing so, open their hearts to the potential joy of what might be. For in acceptance, there is peace. And in peace, there is life, even in the shadow of death.

Secularity

In this chapter I will talk about what it is like to see and then name death around us.

As I say in the subtitle, this book is rooted in my witness and testimony. And also, before I share about my experience of naming and seeing death around us, I want to ground this chapter in a short conversation about secularity, which to church folk looks like the absence of religion and faith in society. I'll be using images shared by seminary professor Andrew Root at a conference I attended.[1] Alright, let's dive into why it seems like fewer folks are going to church these days. It's not just that people are less religious—it's more like there's this whole new space opening up where we're redefining what's sacred and what's not. A thousand years ago in Europe, these two realms were kept separate, but now it's like they're mingling. A powerful mix of sacred and profane is the music of Prophets of Rage—blending a sacred love of human dignity and rage at the injustices we face.

Dr. Root, drawing on the work of Canadian philosopher Charles Taylor, talked about going back in our memory to the sixteenth century. This man named Paulo Sarpi was pretty much the only guy in Italy who didn't believe in God. That moment was like "secular ground zero" when the first person stopped believing in God. People who did not believe or practice religion were ostracized and hunted for their lack of faith. The closest thing to that in modern imagination might be the book and show *The Handmaid's Tale*, where faith is imposed on everyone.

---

1. Root, "Why Are They Leaving?"

To get to this "ground zero," you need three things: a sense of magic or "enchantment," the idea that objects can carry divine powers (like the body parts of saints being treated as holy relics in Europe), and the belief that your self isn't closed off but can be influenced by outside forces. Five hundred years ago in Europe they took literally that Bible verse where Paul says, "For he that eateth and drinketh unworthily, eateth and drinketh damnation to himself, not discerning the Lord's body" (1 Cor 11:29 KJV). It was very serious, and they would not have understood my children running up to the communion table after worship to eagerly consume the rest of the bread and juice.

Fast forward to the first shift toward secularity, which was the separation of the public and private. At this point, around the time of the Protestant Reformation, the church began to be separated from the government. This first shift also changed how we see the world around us. For example, before secularity, people would see things like lunar eclipses or meteor showers and would've asked, What does this mean? But now, we're less likely to think God is sending us messages through natural events.

The second shift toward secularity is all about participation—or the lack thereof. Sundays aren't just for church anymore, and there's a ton of other stuff vying for people's attention. So churches start thinking like businesses, trying to attract and keep "customers." It becomes all about resources—like, can we afford a great children's ministry? How much energy did we pour into this question during the height of the COVID-19 pandemic? The "success" of a church in the second shift toward secularity starts to be judged by how many people show up.

Finally, we get to the third shift toward secularity, where all kinds of beliefs—including unbelief—are on shaky ground. This is a space where we prize what's in front of us, where everyone's living out their own truths as long as they're not stepping on anyone else's toes. This is a far cry from older, one-size-fits-all truth models, like Martin Luther's "at the same time sinner and saint" principle. In this stage of secularity, where we are now, you can't easily tell people they are "sinning," because they don't believe in the basis for your truth claims. In this stage of secularity, everything is fragile. But the irony is that even atheism is fragile. For example, even atheists can have a "spiritual" moment—at the birth of a baby or when something tells them to slow down driving and a tree falls in the road where they would have been.

That's a basic outline of these three big shifts toward secularity. Understanding these shifts is important as we think about how the church is dying all around us. Even though I am going to later name some of the things that cause death in the church, I also want to do so in light of this. Resisting secularity is like being a home owner on the end of a barrier island of the

Outer Banks of North Carolina that is starting to shift. You can put all the sandbags that you want around your house, but you cannot change the flow of this massive body of water that will soon have you either in a rowboat or conceding your place as you move to dry ground. I will say a few more words about secularity in chapter 7.

A Hospice Chaplain

"I have lived through the best times in history," Miss Annabel said to me, after having recounted what it was like to spend her first decade of life before the Great Depression. She was blind, so she could not tell that my sympathy smile only crept halfway up my face and that the crows feet at the end of my thirty-one-year-old eyes weren't squinting in a genuine smile. "Wonderful," I said, thinking about how she was the second geriatric member of one of the two congregations I was then serving who had told me that same sentiment within the past few days.

At that point of 2021, in my career I had been appointed to four different churches, and I had heard the same thing from white members of the greatest generation and the baby boomers—that fondness for the 1950s, for the so-called glory days. "Those good ole days died before I was born, and I can't remember anything except for decline," I want to say, but cannot bring myself to do so.

My pastor and wife, my best friend, has told me on more than one occasion that many of them remember being in one-horse towns which turned into minimetropolises with thriving downtowns boasting several service stations. They remember the first television in town, and now they have a cell phone that replaces every big electrical gadget they splurged on for the past thirty years. The world around them has changed, and the only thing which has seemed to remain steady is the church. And whenever I talk about the decline of the church, I am forcing them to realize that the one seemingly steady thing is weathering away.

In my conversation with Miss Annabel, I tried to be focused on her energetic, elderly face, but my spastic neurochemistry kept leading me back to this inconvenient truth. I am seen as a hospice chaplain for a dying church and a chaplain to its dying people. But, also, I am in training to be a midwife, giving birth to another way of existing as church.

Not a Hospice Chaplain

"Well you need to decide whether you want a hospice chaplain who helps this church transition, or whether you want a pastor who leads you in mission," my district superintendent and supervisor said as he clenched his jaw out of frustration. I was their seventh pastor in fourteen years, and they were a mix of people who really wanted to their church to grow—in as many ways as they could define that—and a few toxic souls who really wanted to control their pastor. In the end, the poison was getting the better of the congregation, by some counts forty-seven of them having left as a result.

Since that 2013 conversation in my first year of full-time ministry, I have often thought about what seems to be self-defeating in the United Methodist denomination I serve: that some churches want pastors who will ride the last ripple of the old Methodist momentum until the church finally stops in deceased stagnation. I have personally known a few pastors whom I would consider superheroes having boundless energy, hope, and excitement for the work of the Lord. But most pastors who I see in their last decade of ministry seem to be either burned-out, toxic themselves, or not caring. Many of us younger pastors are already burned-out.

In the end, maybe we are all a mix. Particularly as I think about the death of the old way of doing church, I become outraged at the idea of a hospice pastor. The "old way of doing church" refers to this complacency of being in our own echo chambers, sitting alongside people who look and act mostly like we do, without a care for the world that is different and beyond our walls. The hospice chaplain is a metaphor of course, that whenever people are dying, you just make them comfortable and allow their last few days to pass without anything exceptional happening. But congregations and denominations are not people, even though they are made up of individual humans.

I feel like those who would invite me to treat institutions and systems as if they had feelings are trying to sell me something. My sentiment comes from the capitalist world. Corporate bigwigs, looking for a bailout to continue their business malpractice, ask that you consider the feelings of the corporation as they try to humanize it. This is the same with giant corporations like Walmart. It is why every corporation wants to have a humanitarian kind of image—to humanize the corporation. But corporations are not humans, and they don't have feelings in the sentient way that we do.[2]

---

2. The term *sentient* comes from the Latin root for "feeling or perceiving." In this sense, institutions might definitely be considered as sentient. You will see that later on, I draw on this idea in depth, and in some ways put that idea in paradox with my argument here. But the underlying idea is that we should not prioritize institutions over the

Even the United Methodist Church, and even our many congregations are not human. So the idea that we would make them comfortable is not only bullshit, I think it is a heresy. To the extent that disciples of Jesus Christ live in these congregations, we should not allow ourselves to sit on our laurels, or lower roles, but we must be encouraged to make disciples of Jesus Christ. Even if we are an aged church, we must not simply rest until we have died, but we must live faithfully until the end. I have found that some of the most faithful disciples are people in their last third of life who realize they will die soon, who challenge the rest of us by fearless faithfulness. If we tell these people that they are allowed to be comfortable, it ruins the rest of us.

A chasm of difference exists between doing church and being church. In many ways, the method of being church has not changed, but the method of doing church must change. Our mode of being is tied up in our worship services, living liturgy and practice that are in some places over a thousand years old. I would argue that the content of our faith is often solid but our practice of love of neighbor through personal relationships is often squalid. Our worship service content is flavorful, but the content of our service in the local world around the individual congregations is sometimes foul.

Even as I write that, I realize that the church I serve has an outstanding amount of grants and partnerships in the world around us. When disaster strikes, we have the infrastructure to be some of the first ones on the scene, alongside the Latter Day Saints and teams from the American Baptist Men. And yet something about our service needs to change. Later in this book, I will argue that sinful beliefs, like the roots of white supremacy, harm us and the people we want to serve. I am proud of the geographic body that I am a part of, the North Carolina Conference of the United Methodist Church, which has for half a decade prioritized "antiracism" as one of its core priorities. Being present with the death of what has been in the church means that we will see the loss of what has worked as well as what has not worked. Our capacity has shrunk, but, thank God, so has our level of racism.

The church as an institution is not human, but I can see where it does have soulfulness. Susan Beaumont, in *How to Lead When You Don't Know Where You're Going*, talks about the soul of the institution, how we need to learn its characteristics in order to move with it. Part of the soul of the United Methodist Church, I have found, is that it is accustomed to being vibrant and powerfully in movement in the world. Like many of its faithful members, it does not know how to slow down and learn a new way of being. It has a hard time changing, evidenced by the slow process of general church

---

humans whom they serve, because doing so falls in line with an exploitative capitalist structure that allows certain powerful people controlling institutions to extract wealth from the exploited.

change. And that is not necessarily a bad thing, because it prevents us from being blown about by every wind of change. But, also, it is hard to know when the time for change has come and is coming through the death of our methods. Several church leaders have quoted the idea that we will not be able to corporately change until the pain of staying the same is greater than the pain of change. Perhaps, until we see that death and resurrection are parts of the life cycle of the church, we will not be willing to move through our pain.

Death Is a Part of Life

Death can bring beauty, even as it can also traumatize and wound us beyond words. The end of life for an octogenarian can bring a loving longing to rest with bygone family, even as it spawns a celebration of life for those who cared for the deceased. A bittersweet beauty. But for a single mother who just unexpectedly lost her child, death is a cutthroat and sadistic reality, creating trauma and unwanted change.

Death is part of life. When someone dies, it can feel like the angel of death is an unwanted specter that just keeps coming around. Sometimes we suffer from an analysis paralysis of the emotions, a numbing depression where they stop working for awhile. Other times we feel more profoundly than we knew possible.

As people of faith, we have a whole, mostly forgotten, category of prayer that weaves together our fears and sadness with the longing and hope of bygone saints. Lamentation is a time when we both pray and cry and when we find help that intercedes for us. The apostle Paul said that the Holy Spirit, when we do not know how to pray, intercedes for us with unexpressed groanings. When we do not know how to pray, words of lament, long ago written, get spelled out for us by the mouths of saints and sinners long since dead who in life cried the same type of tears.

We can yet see something irresistible and exquisite in lamentation. We may be drawn in like cold wanderers to a warm hearth by those who create containers for our pain—holding hands and reciting rituals that miraculously tell our scared nervous systems, "You are safe here. Breathe."

Death is a part of life, whether or not we find ways to reach the depths of meaning that it offers. Sometimes death comes to individuals, but, also, death comes to ways of life. Systems and social institutions, businesses and buildings, places of praise and prayer—none of them are immune from the reality of death.

When something or someone perishes, those who love the departed may feel shame that can cause an inability to grieve. We talk about loss in terms of "winning and losing," and when someone says, "My husband lost his battle with cancer," it can produce shame. It can shut us up.

Our inability to accept death lives in our language and also in our medical systems. We prolong death in an attempt to extend life. What ends up happening is we spend the majority of our healthcare expenses for our lives in the last five years that we still have beating hearts. We often do not want to see death, whether in our healthcare or in our spiritual care.

If we cannot name and talk about death, how will we ever find meaning in it? How will we lament? How will we celebrate the life of what is gone? Why is the idea of death bad?

We think that it is an enemy to be vanquished. That idea has some merit; we read in the Bible that Jesus is the one who will vanquish death at the end. But we end up trying to vanquish death ourselves, doing this by trying to leave our own legacy as a way to get out of life alive. We have bought into this atheist worldview that we only stay alive until the last person who remembers us dies. And so we become idolaters, worshiping the idea of legacy so that we might be remembered.

We should look at the natural cycles of the world. Death is a part of life.

We should respect but not live in fear of death. In the original language of the New Testament, the main word for fear is *phobos*. Thinking about this word, my mind goes back to a former professor saying, "Words don't mean things, people mean things using words." The word *fear* sometimes means dread or terror, and it sometimes means respect. When we can have respect for realities that connect us—like God and even the reality of death—we grow stable. When we do not have respect for these things, we grow unstable.

Our phobia and dread of death disrupts the natural order. We can look at the way that we guard and hang on to our dead bodies as an example. The funeral industry, with its insistence on creating caskets and putting them in cement vaults with formaldehyde-infused bodies, is bad for the environment. Some of the most dear people I have met as a pastor are funeral home workers who see death every day in a society that is afraid to accept it. I will celebrate though that nationwide there is a movement toward death positivity and many people are learning to have green funerals. But in the church where I have lived that is the exception.

I wish that it was normative for people to return to the earth instead of mummifying everyone's remains in our own private sarcophagi. The end result is that many rural churches are struggling and dying, while they have multimillion-dollar endowments for the graveyard which will continue to be preserved. In many years our descendents will have the problem of a landscape where church buildings used to be with graveyards being fed by endowments that cannot be touched, because we were afraid to let our bodies be returned to the earth. What's wrong with becoming food for worms and mushrooms and future plants?

In cement shrines our bodies cannot be returned to the ground and become one with the earth. In fear of returning to the ground, I have heard what I would name as harmful theology. Church folk have told me about how they are afraid that their bodies will not be resurrected to heaven in the end, because the resurrection of the dead will only happen to people whose bodies are still intact—this coming from a verse in a New Testament letter saying, "the dead in Christ shall rise" (1 Thess 4:16 KJV).

Rather than fear death or what happens to our bodies and legacies, we should name it as a part of life. Sure, it is the *last* part of life, but a necessary part nonetheless. I will talk about the experience of death that we individually experience, but the main focus of this book is the collective experience of death—when we see things of which we are a part come to an end. Again, I will discuss how our service to God and to the world, much like a funeral, signifies the death of old methods and the potential for renewal. Before we can get to the piece about resurrection, we first have to admit what has died. In the next few sections, I will look at several of the faces of death in the church, several places where we can notice that death has entered. I will wait until later in the book to talk about the specific, death-dealing attitudes and practices that I believe need to die. Below, I will talk about some places where I have noticed death encroaching, starting first with our idea of "legacy." I will then talk about money, the buildings, technology, and schism and division. Lastly, I will name a few symptoms and signs of death: bodily sickness, clergy stress, a worthiness contest, and dislocation.[3]

An Expiring Legacy

Enter any United Methodist Church edifice or any traditional or mainline denominational church, and you will be greeted not only by a host of people excited to see a new face but also by the saints who have gone on to glory and joined the great cloud of witnesses from the other side of the grave. With great intentionality, we have, as religious people in America, found a way to continue the propagation of monuments to our ministries. One of

---

3. My context of being a United Methodist Christian I also situate in the larger context of being part of "White Christian America." For a sociological and historical investigation into the demise of the church in the United States, see Robert Jones's book *The Death of White Christian America*.

the most outright methods of sustaining our mammoth monuments is with *mammon*.[4]

Mammon is simply a Greek word translated often as "wealth." Jesus uses this word when he says, "You cannot serve God and wealth" (Matt 6:24 NRSV). As soon as you come onto the campus of most United Methodist Churches, you see that they have been endowed with wealth—paved parking lots, stainless steeples, and stained glass stories of the Bible greet you, and that's before even walking inside. The church, throughout its history, has mostly agreed that a mark of faithfulness is how much we give of what we have to God. But what does that look like? Indeed, in our experience as Christians in the United States, we usually equate giving to the church with giving to God.

How easy it is to leave a legacy to our church and know that we will be remembered for it. I am part of a system that benefits from the legacy gifts offered to God through the United Methodist Church, and so it is excruciating and painful to even think about offering criticism. One of the two churches I served from 2019 to 2021 was once named for a family still there, because of their extreme generosity to God—through that place. My divinity school education would not have occurred if it was not for a multibillion-dollar endowment set up in part as a gift to God through the United Methodist Church.[5] And yet we should challenge ourselves to see exactly who the legacy benefits.

In the first church I served, the majority of my pastor's aid line item in the budget was funded by a small endowment given to help impoverished people who asked for aid from the church. It was distributed annually through an account at the Methodist Foundation. We congratulate

---

4. I use the term *mammon*, because it not only means "money" or "wealth," but also has been taken to have a spiritual factor. I would not be the first one to point out that because God is juxtaposed with mammon, it can be seen as a spiritual entity. Indeed, many have even gone so far as to say that there is a nefarious spiritual entity, a demon, known as Mammon. I won't argue one way or another on the matter, but I do think that, either way, we should listen to the words of Jesus to the rich young man, "It is easier for a camel to go through the eye of a needle than for someone who is rich to enter the kingdom of God" (Mark 10:25 NRSV).

5. I am speaking of course of the Duke Endowment. Many of the places where rural ministry thrives is directly due to the benevolence of the Duke Endowment, given through scholarships to rural church pastors, given through feeding programs and educational interventions, and through subsidiary and intermediary organizations. I greatly appreciate that at least everybody I know in the rural church division of the Duke Endowment are working hard to redistribute the legacy gifts of the Duke Endowment to people who otherwise would not have benefited from Methodist money. They are working to impact impoverished communities of color and challenging the church to do the same.

ourselves for carving out a place for the impoverished to receive, but most of our resources are internally spent.

As a pastor, whose salary is usually more than half of the budget in a rural church, I try to work toward repair of the historic inequity of resources by both spending a lot of my time working at the margins of the place to which I am appointed and also by searching for grant funding for this work to grow. Even if the church I serve does not directly give to marginalized communities, they can know that by paying me they are investing resources into someone who will challenge the church to leave its comfort zone.

Even though I try, through my work, to share the legacy of the church with people who have not been invited into it, so many markers show how the legacy of the church is tied to a few. As I mentioned in the Service of Death and Resurrection, we can walk into almost any historic church and see plaques dedicated by bygone people to their descendants.

At the root of our legacy issues is this: previous generations have given and given generously. However, their gifts are so targeted that they are in fact attempting to define the significance of the sacred space for subsequent generations. We might see hundreds of thousands of dollars worth of gifts in organs, hardbacked hymnals and pew bibles, and even the furniture itself. But these designated gifts are given with a stipulation—that they must be used as intended. I imagine that any pastor who has tried to remove a gift with a plaque on it has either been chastised or had a challenging time finding the offspring of the giver or convincing them to allow the church to change the gift.

Older folk want to have younger folk who will continue their legacy. In my experience, they do not realize this is what they are doing. In their minds they have continued the legacy of their forebears and want to pass the torch. However, they don't realize that the light has gone from being a torch with fire to an LED light. So passing the light means passing the ability to light the way. Continuing this metaphor, I've seen older folk trying to pass the fire torch and accidentally burning the younger people out and melting the container for the newer person's light, leading to a spiritual lack of luminosity or ability to bear the light.

Legacy is a loaded word for us United Methodists. When a congregation closes or merges with another one it becomes a "legacy congregation" meaning that the only thing left of it is its legacy. And so, seeing everything that we and our forebears have worked for at stake, we oftentimes want to fight even harder to protect it. Yes, in our conversations about legacy, I see the threat to the church in the United States, vulnerable to lose its legacy.[6]

---

6. Later on I will talk more at length about how parts of our legacy, like white

Consider this quick story about when I was part of a conversation to close a church, and how connected the conversation was with the capital assets of the church.

In early 2021, I found myself gearing up to make a series of phone calls to one of the two church communities I served. The objective was twofold: to check on them and to share the decision made the previous Wednesday for our congregation to become a "legacy" one—to permanently close down by merger with the other church I served. The task was an awkward one as so many on our rolls had only visited a few times and many were estranged. I was unsure where to begin until my partner Elizabeth imparted some wisdom, a theological vision that would guide my approach even if not explicitly voiced in each of my individual calls.

She brought to my memory the story of her grandmother's passing years earlier. At that time, her tears flowed not for her grandmother's death, but for the sale of the land on Great Neck Point at Virginia Beach. She felt a pang of guilt for her seemingly misplaced grief. However, I reminded her of the Israelites' profound sorrow when faced with exile and the potential loss of their land, their connection to God. Grieving the loss of a place, especially one imbued with personal significance, can be akin to mourning the loss of a sacred space. Her beloved Great Neck Point had offered her solace during the trials of her childhood, and losing it felt monumental.

To provide context, I reflected on the grand timeline of our planet as a twenty-four-hour clock within which modernity represents less than a minute. This modern era has seen the emergence of privatized land, a departure from the ways humanity had historically existed. Our hardwiring still craves a connection to land, yet many of us reside on borrowed territory. A few years prior, I'd learned that the largest purchaser of land in the United States was Bill Gates through his Foundation. In addition, modernity has witnessed nations pilfering land from others on a global scale. Of course, this isn't a new phenomenon—since premodern times, small groups have attempted to seize land from others, as seen with Alexander the Great's military campaigns in Asia and the Babylonian conquest of the Israelites.

So, as I readied myself to contact our congregation members, I was acutely aware of the magnitude of their impending loss of a holy place. I pondered the most suitable dispositions to adopt for these calls. I resolved to start with the easiest conversations, the individuals who I knew would be charitable in their responses, before gradually moving on to the more challenging ones.

---

supremacy and being isolated from others, need to die.

Conversations about legacy are often tied up with conversations about capital. "Do you want to give a legacy gift with your estate?" we might ask a saint of the church. A related marker of the demise of the church relates to capital, especially to money, and I will call it "fiscal" or "financial" trauma in what follows.

Fiscal Trauma

As far back as I can remember I have been concerned and even worried about money. Our brains are formed by the realities we see and as a child there was never enough money to do all of the things we wanted to do. My parents were able to find creative ways of giving us gifts and taking advantage of programs like "mystery shopper" (to receive vouchers for fast-food restaurants to bring the family to and enjoy the food before leaving a rating). Every time we went shopping we would compare prices, placing generic brands up against each other, buying in large quantities, and then making food from scratch. I remember the sad look on my mom's face when she told me we couldn't afford things I asked for, but, even so, I don't remember feeling like we were poor. The feelings of inadequacy came about in comparison.

Whenever I saw other people walking about with things that I did not have I was curious about those things. Was it possible for me to have the same name brand of clothing? Was it possible for me to have a new backpack? Could I go shopping somewhere that was not a secondhand store? These questions, steeped in insecurity, helped to form me to be a frugal person. As I looked around as a young adult, seeing that many of my friends were not asking the same questions as I was, I became aware that these friends in particular were not raised in a lower socioeconomic status.

As an adult now, a lot of my mindset and way of seeing the world has been formed by the necessary frugality of my childhood. I know that others, who have been formed in extreme poverty, have similar but different ways of looking at finances.

Talking with Fatimah, one of the wonderful humans that I consider to be my pastor, I learned a new term: fiscal trauma. She told me about how people who were raised in poverty have trauma associated with that poverty, not having enough to eat, possibly getting evicted from their home, having substandard clothing, shame being associated with their financial status, to name a few things. Financial trauma affects the body much in the same way that other types of trauma do, but, because it may not be easily recognizable, it may hide under the surface.

When multiple types of trauma converge in a person's body, that is when posttraumatic stress disorder becomes a threat. I learned from Fatimah that financial trauma might be one of the reasons why so many people came back from the Vietnam War with PTSD, numbers much greater than World War II. The majority of those who went to fight in the Vietnam War were impoverished. Many of them, coming from that relative instability, already had trauma living in their bodies, and when they added the trauma of war on top of it, it was more than their bodies could handle. Even though I have never wanted for food or faced housing instability, I have learned about the relative poverty that some of my ancestors lived in. I know that my grandfather, who fought in both World War II and the Korean War, probably suffered from PTSD and accidentally brought this trauma home to his family.

In the book *My Grandmother's Hands*, the wisdom of Resmaa Menakem teaches us about how ancestral trauma can be biologically passed down from generation to generation, being also passed down through character traits and ways of being in the world. When trauma is decontextualized from its original source it just looks like problematic character traits. At a time when the church and many other historic institutions are dying, I cannot help but wonder what historic trauma is tied up in the life and methods of the church.

I first wonder if financial trauma lives in the body politic of the church. When we look at churches, white churches especially, we can see immense resources that have been both gathered and hoarded. In a very systematic way we can see endowments that are bloated and living in financial institutions, money that is stored up as treasure on earth, the principal of which can never be touched. But we can also see a physical hoarding that takes place. The recently deceased patriarchs and matriarchs of the church, saints who lived through the Great Depression, experienced financial trauma. They told the stories of not having enough, of standing in soup lines, of having only two pairs of clothes. They talked about living on self-sustaining farms in which they never had money but had to barter for everything they owned, all of that being contingent upon the harvest doing well.

The institutions that the silent generation and the greatest generation helped to grow remind me of a child, raised as a dedicated church member, who I met a number of years ago.

He was a young child who had been adopted from a foreign country, from a life of extreme poverty, never knowing where his next meal would come from. As a result, his neurochemistry was affected. Even as a preteen, living in the home of his relatively wealthy adoptive family, this child became like an optimal feeder, a mammal who would continue to eat and eat as if unsure where the next meal would come from. His father told me that the doctors said there was something wrong with the part of his brain that governed when to stop eating. Another hypothesis was that it was due to being raised in poverty. This beloved child of God struggled to know when he had reached enough, and his body kept asking for more.

On a biological level, when we overeat it is stored in our bodies as fat, energy to be accessed when there are not enough resources. It makes sense for any of us who have been formed in profound lack to want to store up extra for the times of famine. We even see a biblical precedent for this in the story of Joseph leading in the years of plenty, preparing for the years of famine.

But now that impulse has gotten out of hand. Instead of seven years of plenty preparing for seven years of famine, as in the story of Joseph preparing Egypt in the book of Genesis, we want to hoard resources indefinitely for an indefinite future. We see doomsday preppers who have begun preparing to isolate and sustain themselves, disjointed and disconnected from any would-be communities. This same impulse exists in the church.

Having served as the pastor of several different churches, I often see pantries full of food that has been expired for a decade. Certain rooms contain technology that should have been given away or recycled decades prior. Cabinets in the kitchen are overflowing with Tupperware that has accumulated, containers and lids from all sections of the grocery store—none of which seem to match up. And I understand this. I have never met a mason jar or plastic container that I did not want to add to my collection.

I wonder if this impulse in our churches has become part of our church culture as a result of financial trauma experienced by very real problems encountered by our predecessors. Many of our churches have intentionally designed mechanisms for outreach into the world, ministries that receive a fixed percentage of missional income.

Going back to Resmaa Menakem, he talks about the phenomenon of people in power "blowing trauma through" from their bodies to the bodies of disempowered.[7] For example, where Europeans had just come through the Dark Ages and held immense trauma in their lives and practices they inflicted that same brutality onto Native Americans and enslaved Africans. In a similar way, I wonder if the church accidentally blows our financial trauma, from the poverty of generations ago, through to the disempowered people around us, even as we have a lot of capital but live in scarcity mindsets. Do we think we do not have enough, even while we turn people away who have far less?

---

7. Menakem, *My Grandmother's Hands*, chap. 4.

As our church structures actually do wane now and we move into a new space of "not enough," as our methods and systems start to die, will we be moved deeper into the self-protecting, hoarding mentality that comes from generational financial trauma? Will we, who every week pray, "give us this day our daily bread," become obsessed with storing bread in the freezer in case there is a famine? And the more pressing question, Are there neighbors of ours starving, who need the bread of heaven that is getting freezer burned in cryostasis in the church basement?

Our tendency to live with a scarcity mindset comes from somewhere. When we had excesses and overabundance, it was easy to be self-congratulatory as the overflow of our coffers and cups went to people needier than ourselves. But with our churches dying, and with the needs becoming more pronounced, we must come to a place where we name the need that we have. Perhaps we should take a look into the history and see the places from where we learned to hang on to resources. We can be grateful to our ancestors for being frugal, and we can lament that their frugality led to us building palaces, temples, and social clubs for our own expression of religion that accidentally kept out the people to whom we had been sent to love.

I am not an expert on trauma, and I am certainly not an expert on trauma living in institutions. But I know that one of the ways to live with trauma and not be controlled by it is to deeply feel it and name it in our body—whenever we are triggered or have an embodied reaction—to become radically in tune with the present moment. When we feel the piece of our culture that says there is not enough, and when we become tempted to guard our resources instead of sharing them, we should name that as an embodied traumatic reaction. And when we do that, we should take a moment to breathe in, hold the breath, let it permeate our being, and breathe out. We should allow the Holy Spirit to enter us, hold on to her, and then release her. Someone who holds on to breath, refusing to release it, is vulnerable to pass out. The natural flow of the body is to receive and give. We receive Spirit, it intravenously travels through us, and then we breathe out. The more profound our breath, the more profound our healing from anxiety.

Parts of healing from the trauma of historic financial trauma is looking around us and realizing that, even though so much of what we know church to be is dying, we are yet alive. That is to say that we may realize we are, as the apostle says, "pressed . . . but not crushed . . . persecuted but not abandoned; struck down but not destroyed" (2 Cor 4:8–9). For most of us, the feeling of persecution is just another traumatic reaction, even to problems caused within our bodies by accidents committed through the church by our ancestors.

In addition to breathing, we also practice being grounded—centered in what is in the present moment. We may be afraid of something else falling apart tomorrow, but if we stay focused in the present moment, today, we can celebrate what still is.

In bringing our individual bodies through traumatic reactions, we can plant our feet on the ground and name the sensation of being connected to the earth with all of our senses. Similarly, as church institutions financially feeling our way in the present moment, we can look at the fact that we have not been foreclosed upon, that though we may not have been able to pay all of our bills, and some accounts may have been closed, we are still alive and connected to a larger connection that is still alive as well.

If we can yet ground ourselves, we may find that we are able to share what we have instead of living in the traumatic space of hoarding and holding on to. In my experience, the most prolific ministries of the church are not the ones that require the most resources to prop up. A little bit of money goes a long way in setting a table for neighbors to come in and meet each other.

Ironically, some of the systems of the church and mechanisms that once brought in the most resources are now the greatest financial liabilities. In the past, launching a building program or renovation project was seen as a statement of growth and vitality. Today, with declining church attendance, many of these large, beautiful structures are underutilized and expensive to maintain. The same could be said for music programs or many other types of programs that used to cater to what no longer exists.

If we can learn to share with the community upstarts and outliers, and if we can learn to live in the possibility of what might be instead of the trauma of what has been, we might be able to direct our currency in a new direction that brings life. For example, if your church is one of those that bought a big, beautiful building that is going unused, you can creatively utilize underused spaces by forming partnerships with community organizations that align with your mission—such as renting spaces, hosting community events, or developing affordable housing. Your church could transform into a vibrant community hub offering services like coworking spaces or health clinics, working toward community engagement and also toward achieving financial sustainability. This is not easy though.

Organizationally, we are creatures of habit and we go with the flow as long as possible. This is even true of humans on a vascular level. I learned that even with heart bypass surgery sometimes the bypasses are ineffective if the clog is not severe enough. If a blockage is only 60 percent, the body may still choose to use that blockage, even at a reduced rate, because it is what is normal.

Money is called currency precisely because it flows with currents. I am not a financial strategist, but I understand that, especially in moments of disruption, we must evaluate the patterns of financial flow, trying to understand if we need to undertake fiscal bypass surgery.

The current moment in the life of churches and other institutions has caused a lot of heartburn. Certain members have become necrotic and died. And yet like a tree that has lost certain limbs, we can also hope for new ones to grow or be grafted on. Being a living branch taken from a dead tree and grafted onto a living one requires movement. It requires acknowledging and admitting that the place, whether physical or ideological, where we once lived has become untenable.

Perhaps the image of grafting branches is not the best one here. Maybe we should talk about the warren for rabbits that lived a cozy existence in the root system of an old oak tree, and then the oak tree was uprooted in a storm. They then have to be a group on the move, having been displaced. The church will feel displaced in the future. Or at least we will be on the move and the centrality of our physical place will be no more. As a decentralized people, we will find that our "place" is in action.

Death of the Centrality of Place: The Termites Are Coming

"You could stick your hand into the wall of the church," Mr. Ellis said, "and pull out dust." As he spoke the words, the ninety-five-year-old patriarch of his church reached out like he was grabbing part of the crumbling edifice. He talked about how the termites had eaten the walls to almost nothing. "Those old folks did not know what was good for them," he said, as if he was twenty-five again and arguing with his parents' generation about a wooden church that would go on to be demolished around the year 1950. "All they knew was that they did not want to lose their building." Perhaps any of us who have fallen in love with the majestic edifice of a place of worship would not be able to come to terms with the fact that it is dissipating.

Picture what Mr. Ellis was talking about: a once-grand church building now crumbling under the weight of time and neglect. The walls, once strong and proud, now crumbling like the faith of those who once gathered within them. Fear has a way of making us act irrationally, and, as we face this decline in our sacred spaces, we must confront our fears and embrace the change that lies ahead. I've come to realize that the transformation of the church in America is about more than just bricks and mortar. It's about the community that transcends these physical walls.

As we venture down this path, we begin to see a shift from the traditional gathered church, which hinged on one holy place, to a distributed church that harnesses the power of technology to unite people in faith. Yet I believe there's even more potential for us to evolve into a relational church focused on the connections between people rather than the physical structures that house them.

In the world of church buildings, questions of ownership, access, and cost take center stage. Meanwhile, the United States' true sacred spaces—sports stadiums and arenas—continue to thrive. These imposing structures dominate city skylines demanding significant financial offerings from their faithful followers. And yet, as these modern-day secular temples flourish, our church buildings crumble.

The story of Mr. Ellis and his church is a stark reminder that our faith is not built on stone and mortar but on the relationships and memories forged within these walls. Jesus spoke of the church as an indestructible gathering of believers, not a physical building. This tension between the tangible and intangible aspects of our faith has been a constant struggle throughout history.

Take, for example, the tale of Nehemiah. In this ancient story, God wanted his people to have a physical place of worship to keep them connected to their faith. Yet the true purpose of this space was to serve as a reminder of the God they served and the community they shared.

Today, we must remember that our church is about more than just the buildings in which we gather; it's about the connections we make and the memories we create. The story of the church on Main Street, consumed by termites, teaches us the importance of trust and unity as we navigate the ever-changing landscape of faith.

As we face the termites—both physical and spiritual—that threaten our churches, we must remember that our faith is about the God we serve and the community we build. By embracing a relational church model we can foster a sense of community that transcends any physical space.

So, as we Christians in the US church embark on this journey, which I believe is from a building-centric to community-centric practice of faith, let us remember that it is through unity and reliance on God that we can overcome the challenges ahead. Together we can continue to serve our congregations and communities regardless of the walls that may crumble around us. In a later chapter on belonging and staying alive amid death, I will continue this thought by talking about community-centric faith and "people as place."

Seeing Death: Technology as a Case Study

We tend to think about ourselves as pretty important as church people. We believe what Jesus says when he says, "I am the way, the truth, and the life. No one comes to the Father except through me" (John 14:6 NRSV). And we believe that we have a pretty important value proposition. We are offering people Jesus, and Jesus holds the keys of hell and death. But what we *don't* realize is that the world around us is secular and does not care. Whether we are Christians who fear for the eternal salvation of those who are non-Christians, or whether we are convinced that everyone will be confronted with the amazing love of Jesus after death and be unable to turn it down, we should realize just how far behind the rest of the world we are.

While we are writing books, the world has moved on to other forms of communication. While we are centered around the Bible as our book, the world has very few forms of long-form communication that it sees as valid and efficacious. While we are constrained by specific beliefs, the world around us tells everyone that they can decide what to believe for themselves. While we are offering one dish and calling it truth, the world around us is eating at a buffet and questioning why they should be so singularly focused when they can have a pluralistic meal.

We can look at constraints as a gift, realizing that working within them can bring creativity and new meaning to our lives. Indeed, some of the most brilliant innovations of technology and art have come through constraints of different types. However, as information technology and biological technology cruise toward each other, and as we face a future in which new people can be programmed, and living things can be 3-D printed, and the gift of even longer life will be extended to those who have more money, the small constraints that we have seem to be outclassed by a world of questions that we have not even begun to ask.

Because our best pastors are not also top scientists, we find a disconnect between the most valuable voices in the church and the ones considered most valuable by a world that is built by technocrats. When we look at the monumental presence of cathedrals that used to show the greatest wealth centralized in the hands of a few in the name of faith in the Middle Ages, we see how the most wealthy in the world, behind companies like Blackwater and Vanguard, do not even need to present themselves. We cannot see how the powerful hands of a few have already grabbed the reigns of artificial intelligence and are using it to grab even more wealth, even while the working poor are still fighting to get paid fifteen dollars an hour. The church finds itself slipping further behind, being unable to even measure the unfathomable depth that separates it from a world that has taken a different turn from it.

I lament to bring up technology knowing that some people in our churches are not familiar with so much of it—whether information technology or biological/medical technology. I remember, in the first church I served back in 2013, coming to be aware of something. I talked with members of the congregation who had been in that small, rural town for much longer than half a century. They could remember when the roads were dirt. They remembered when the roads became paved and cars started coming through. They remembered when the town got its first television. They remembered as the town grew that there were ten service stations in town. And then when the interstate came and bypassed them that number reduced to two. They had seen the rise and fall of their small town in a short half-century, and they had seen the rise of technology that put to death most of the technological family heirlooms they once held so dear—the first family television encased in oak, the radio around which they would sit and listen as a family. And now a small piece of technology that holds what they knew for most of their lives as a supercomputer sits in the back pocket of each of their grandkids—who each know how to use a touch screen better than they do. And in the span of all of that time the one thing they saw as consistent was the church.

With the church holding steady, or at least steady enough, many of the older members of the congregation did not want it to change. They fought for it to remain constant. With a Bible that tells us our God "is the same yesterday, today, and forever" (Heb 13:8 CEB), we want to have some form of consistency from our faith in a world that changes to be unrecognizable. And those who see unrecognizable changes as profane may be tempted even to leave the church to which they have sworn their lives as members, not wanting to be pained by the hyperfast changes occurring within the church. I have deep compassion for the aging members of the church, many of whom I hope have picked up this book.

I hear and see the pain that many go through, and I deeply wish that we could have more consistency in this rapidly changing world. Many of the technological changes that the church has made are things that were forced upon it by the COVID-19 pandemic. Churches have developed further their websites. They have commuted worship service to be online to better be able to connect with people who worship from home. Churches moved from collecting tithes and offerings in a brass plate, passed from pew to pew, to be able to accept money online.

The church has moved to adopt and adapt to technological possibilities, oftentimes as a way to reach the financial bottom line, as a way to profit, as a way to survive in a world where survival means money (remember the conversation on fiscal trauma?). I do not want to say that these decisions were wrong, and, indeed, I have played part in many of them. I realize that, as the pastor of small, rural churches, I have not made these changes as adeptly as many others in larger churches with multiple staff and more technological prowess—able to reach and connect with vast members via streaming platforms and curated digital experiences. I cannot have videos of myself in the third person with the words of the Scripture simultaneously running across the screen like some others.

Even while the church has begun to make some changes for technology, they are all, it would seem, connected with capitalism. Again, this is not innately problematic, it just is. I have seen many technological changes intended to strengthen the church as a business in need of a financially contributing congregation. But because we are beholden to this model, do we use the same technology to try to touch the pain of the world around us? I'm going to move from talking about computerized technology to what the dictionary calls, "the sum of the ways in which social groups provide themselves with the material objects of their civilization."[8] And I might start to preach a little.

The problem arises when our limited resources are stretched thin, forcing churches to compete for dwindling support. With most people in our country no longer attending church, many congregations rely heavily on tithes and offerings from an aging population. As a result, churches often find themselves vying for the same shrinking group of people, a cycle that will inevitably end as that group passes away. I think this was behind the schism that the United Methodist Church has been going through during my writing of this book.

If we need to have the money conversation around technology, maybe we can talk about different ways that technology can help us get money. And I'm not just talking about turning our churches into Amazon wholesale warehouses where we skim 10 percent off of the top or trying to find ways of chipping into megacorporations. When we follow the revenue streams, we find that connecting with multinational corporations has immense problems like the hyper-use of plastics, the continual use of fossil fuels to traffic goods over thousands of miles instead of using local resources, and the further enslavement and exploitation of impoverished labor in countries that we will never see.

I have thought of some powerful ways that the church can have revenue locally, things like microlivestock: growing edible crickets and mealworms

---

8. "Technology," Dictionary.com.

for fat free, high fiber protein alternatives that are not destructive to the environment. There are things like roasting coffee purchased from all-women farms or run by people who have been rehabilitated from life in gangs—responsible networking and connection across the country and world. We could connect with contractors who have resources to donate as tax write-offs and have them build affordable housing for low wage workers.

In order to make some of those things work we need to be part of a larger ecosystem that is willing to pay more for ethically sourced goods. With our current addiction to technology we never stop to ask how it is possible for us to still buy cheeseburgers for less than two dollars, or how can we buy a pound of bananas for fifty cents when the fruit itself comes from three thousand miles away. (By the way, the answer is essentially that we are complicit with enslavement.) But even beyond the things we consume, there are ways that the church can rethink business.

Churches are immersed in social ecosystems that are developing new technologies and changing. And even though those technologies are not reliant on circuit boards, they are very rapidly developing. When churches inevitably die, their bodies are objectified by so-called developers who say, "This building has good bones." With this statement, somebody else is asking, "Can these bones live again?" Looking to church buildings, people are wondering how they can be used in new social technologies.

Can church buildings be used to house homeless people? Can they be used in some way with the housing crisis? Would it be possible for somebody from the church to put their money where their mouth is, to be like the rich ruler that Jesus told, "Sell all that you own and distribute the money to the poor" (Luke 18:22 NRSV). Could our rapidly declining rural congregations and rural towns be like Sodom and Gomorrah, which God promised to save if just ten righteous people could be found (Gen 18:32). Is there just one righteous person who is willing to open their home up to somebody without a house? Is it possible for somebody to start an epidemic of sharing, in which we learn to radically connect with others? What would it look like if the church started to be the centerpiece of a new social technology in which everyone on the street did not need a lawn mower because they all shared one, where everyone shared appliances? What would it look like for church people to live in common with those around them, to truly practice the power of Pentecost that penetrates into our protected lives? In a world of quickly reducing resources, some people may find it hard to hold on to the age-old fears of communism that emerge when talking about sharing or the fear of getting to intimately know their neighbors. People may find themselves becoming more and more brave to reimagine what community looks like, and they may do it from the center of a church that is getting recentered at the margins.

Technologies of all types are springing up. We can look to different examples like what Bruce Katz and Jeremy Nowak talk about in their book *The New Localism* in which people rely more on those around them than on those far off. I think that most communities will continue doing the old thing as long as and even after it is viable. Churches adapting new technology, whether that technology benefits themselves or others, have one thing in common: they do it because it has become necessary. They do it because the former way of doing it has died.

The only way for us to come to new ways of beginning to learn about possible technologies is to grieve the old technologies that have died, to have a funeral for them, move their technological remains, and make way for new technologies. Sometimes things may be recycled. In a church where old video equipment has been collecting dust in a closet for a decade, it may literally be recycled. Sometimes it can be recycled and used by children. Many wealthy churches getting new computerized technology will give the old to a less well-endowed church with the same paternalistic and loving attitude.

But sometimes the carcass of what has been needs to be directly buried in the ground. Sometimes things just need to be returned to the earth (unless there are batteries; then they and any other remnants of modern technology definitely need to be recycled). What I mean is that sometimes it's OK just to give something back and be grateful for it. When we see remnants of the way things used to be, and we realize that they have become part of our legacy, we should name them. We should lament what has gone and died. We should have a funeral service for it, so that we can move on to what is next, to the future. When things die, and when they are properly buried, it creates space for what is living, for what is next.

And what is next needs to be radically centered on helping us to be connected to the presence of God in the world. Jesus rarely said, "Believe in me," and most often said, "Follow me." He rarely talked about heaven as eternity but always talked about the kingdom/reign of eternity breaking into this world with divine love and peaceful persistence. I believe that many people will not even consider joining a church in the future if they do not see the needs of the world around them radically touched in the church. I doubt the church needs to have all current technology embodied, but I believe the church needs to, at the very least, be doing the best that it can. People have a way of sensing if Christians, like the institutions we so often make up, are only out for ourselves.

Are we aware of the greater needs of the world around us? Does our use of informational technology and social technology show that? Somehow, the squabbles that we have over who has full membership in the church (the reason for the United Methodist Church sawing itself in half) seem small in comparison to the fact that our world is verifiably going through a sixth major extinction on par with the extinction of the dinosaurs. When our children are looking at animals that have disappeared in our lifetime the way that I used to look at pictures of the Tasmanian tiger, we realize that what God created on this world is being killed at an exceptional rate. When we realize that those at sea level are projected to be in a floodplain in less than twenty years, somehow the question of "how good is our live streaming service?" seems to be put in a different perspective. When we think about the global rise of fascism and the violence that can be done by autocracies, the question of online giving becomes a little bit more manageable.

Speaking for the church, I will say that most of the bigger questions are beyond our grasp, beyond our comprehension, and beyond our desire to talk about, because they are beyond our comfort zone. May our comfort zone go back to hell from whence it came! When we allow our comfort zone to die and find our faithfulness in response to the pressing needs of the world around us, we find that God continues to work through the unmistakable presence of the imperfect church made up of discordant people who somehow stick together as a family. The technology of the Holy Spirit is the original *e pluribus unum* making one out of many. We should be a witness of people who can look into the face of the most grim possibilities of death that are threatening not only us but the world around us, and we should say that God still calls us into those spaces. We may not know how we will make it, but an acknowledgment of God with us is enough to get started. We find our truest belief in the possibility of resurrection when we go into these places where we are unequipped and unprepared, constitutionally like sheep among wolves. May the Lamb of God lead us.

3.

Silent Symptoms in the Shadows
Signs of Decline

Obsessed, oppressed, suppressed, depressed:
Unconfessed, unaddressed... unrest
Yearning for the best, burning in the chest
Making di-stress a mistress, causing sickness;
Coronary leaks and creaks on top of coughs;
Staring at the droopy-eyed ogle, as if to lift it up;
The Lord's Prayer as Healthcare for those on welfare—
A better hope for those already but not yet:
Broken and whole
Surviving dread's
Emotional toll,
Alive and dead.

Symptom of Death: Being Sick in the Body

Having a stomach virus is not the same as having a head cold, which is not the same as having cancer. Sometimes you don't realize you're sick, but something at work inside you is killing you. Sometimes when you're sick, your body is strangled, but your mind is clear. I imagine there are some sicknesses which are just the opposite, like the way that depression stifles your mind, even while your body is technically unhindered.

The same is true for the church. Different types of sickness exist within, and some sicknesses feel much different than others. The sickness of polarization reminds me of the mental illness of severe anxiety. Every small molehill becomes an insurmountable mountain, causing outrage and inability to pass. The lethargy of death slowly creeping into the church reminds me of depression within my own experience. The body of Christ, in the institution today, ceases to have much if any feeling. It's not that they are really sad or really angry. Rather, the collective body seems to have an absence of the possibility of feeling at all.

After years of smoking the grass of our own self-absorbed excellence, we are left with the respiratory illnesses that cause us to be unable to experience the movement of the Spirit, or at least its permeation through our intravenous experience. Rather than singing out our favorite songs, we find ourselves spewing and spurting their words out, like a person with a thirty-year-smoker's cough, hooked up to oxygen.

All sicknesses do not feel the same, but, unfortunately, when the immune system is compromised, we are vulnerable to several illnesses all at once. And having layer upon layer of illness makes it difficult to distinguish between them, to find the root causes, to treat the symptoms, and to know if there is any healing other than death and resurrection.

Symptom of Death: Clergy Stress

We've all felt our hearts strangely warmed—with the temperature gauge on the warming being turned up to fuming. We've all had a message shut up in our bones, burning to get out, causing inflammation because the burn lasted so long. And when I say "we've all," it's almost statistically verifiable through the depth of work accomplished by the Clergy Health Initiative, through Duke Divinity School, which found out that United Methodist pastors have the worst heart health of any professional demographic in the United States of America.[1]

A simmering pot cooks the food just right, so that it's appetizing for the people to eat. Indeed, without some amount of heat applied, the ingredients served are raw and less apt to be digested. But that which is on our plates right now has been overcooked, and we've been overlooked, leaving

---

1. Duke Clergy Health Initiative, *Clergy Health Trends*.

the message burnt and the messenger burned-out. When I say "we," of course I mean pastors, but it's so much more true for young, new, or racial minority pastors, including many female pastors.

As a pressure cooker, the church of our socio-historical moment is vulnerable to putting extra pressure on everyone, not just pastors. And yet, like a pot left on the back burner, when the chef is too busy to notice, many of us have been seared by injustice. If justice is "just as it should be," then the injustice isn't as a result of malice on the part of the higher up leadership but of a twofold lack of ability to act justly and lack of courage or vision to recognize and admit this deficiency. We don't push back as much on the recipes used to attempt to "bring us on to perfection" as against a half-baked attempt to serve us up before we are ripe for serving.

We realize that it is part of the Christian tradition to thrust servants into the world "like sheep among wolves"; it isn't this part of the ministerial occupation and vocation against which we push. We realize that many of our predecessors, mentors, and leaders have grown to their current levels of clout precisely because this has worked for them. What we resist is a broken system in which the faces of the system don't recognize the extent to which it and they need reform. What we resist is a method of cooking up pastors in which the method burns out the pastors and then blames them for being charred. And then, when the pastor is burned-out, they are moved to a different pot and the leadership therein seeks to expel them—immediately recognizing the burnt taste—bringing shame to the injured pastor, doing nothing for what at first injured them.

Here are a few problems with the recipe that we're not confronting:

- The future of the church seems to be one in which we will either need alternate methods of revenue or pastors will need to be bivocational. And yet this antiquated focus on funding does nothing to dream a new paradigm.

- Countercultural pastors bring the best perspectives for growing our capacity, but they're held with the greatest fear, as if they are the ones causing the threat.

- When associate pastors or any of the aforementioned minority pastors confront people of power in our systems, they are often dismissed quietly, being irreparably struck down, and this is being done under the guise of an ecclesiology of grace.

- We are held accountable, en masse, to language of the eighteenth century without ways of reckoning with current trends shown to be factual—like that many male pastors have caused irreparable damage through sexual misconduct with parishioners, and many female pastors have been victims of sexual harassment. In our annual meeting of clergy, we say that all clergy are "without blame" in their general conduct and administration.[2]

Clergy stress has become so rampant in the system as to have redefined the system itself. Being stressed out is a badge of honor pinned on by consumeristic congregants. Overwork is the new work.

Symptom of Death: A Worthiness Contest

In some places "overwork" is accidentally required. My testimony is that for new, young, or minoritized people serving the church a certain amount of hustle is needed to come closer to the center of the method of church. For example, people who want to become pastors need to answer questions that were, in some cases, written ages ago and for heterosexual, white men who were raised in only one method of church. The further people are from those markers, the more difficult it is for them to fit in.

Even though the people who hold the positions of power want to fling open the doors for diversity, we still have many aged rubrics for measuring people who would come in. Every institution has these. I am not saying we should get rid of them. But I will lament how they often come across as a worthiness contest. In the ordination process for clergy, which is similar to tenure in the United Methodist Church, candidates who are better able to answer the questions are allowed through more easily and have historically received better treatment after ordination. As I have struggled in this process, I have written much.[3] In what follows are a few of those comments:

---

2. This means that they are not currently under investigation for a complaint. But it really misses the mark when the body either know of people who have been under investigation and have left or cases where damage has not been dealt with yet we are intentionally saying that everyone is "without blame." I love the original idea of wanting to be open and honest with the whole group, but this antiquated language can have the opposite effect of appearing that way.

3. I mention ordination a handful of times in this book. I began writing this in earnest in 2019 amid my season of several delays in that process. As I have reread and edited this book, it does at times feel like I am complaining or speaking from an open wound. I leave these remarks here for a couple reasons. As I mention elsewhere, most of the great minds of my generation of pastors have already left the church. Most young pastors do not last five years in full-time ministry. From what I see, most of them do not get a platform to share their frustrations. The pain that I have written has been shared by many others. And so I leave these words in here to dignify those who are not longer with us in the church.

I'm sitting here, thinking of all the people who've been delayed and whose young careers have decayed and who have been dismayed. I'm remembering the moments of pain for several friends, their faces moving in front of mine like the faces of children on a merry-go-round that won't stop. I'm trying to fixate on one of them, but I can't. Their scared and scarred countenances are emblazoned on my soul and in my memory. What happened to each of them? What was their individual story, for the ride to go from joy to horror, before they got off?

Older United Methodists have jokingly called us "snowflakes."[4] We are fragile, yes. But so were they, once, before power became assurance and the responsibility to arbitrate our futures made them sure they were on the right side of the church legal codes. So many of these I didn't even know—until I transgressed them. While so sick that I could barely see the screen I was typing on, I said a snarky comment, an ode to one of my favorite works of music, "Are my answers to the System's satisfaction?" In no time, the watchdog was barking at me, taunting me to step out of line. It felt like when white people will say racist stuff about Mexicans, seeing what I'll do, whether they can keep me or need to oust me. I'm such a snowflake.

It's cold. Not just because my body aches with a virus, but it's cold in the atmosphere of the church, and the body of Christ aches. People fight over the rainbow flags in the church. And we flit and flutter about like butterflies—indirect and fragile in our flight. It only takes one night of frost to wipe out an entire generation of butterflies during their migration. In this minimal migration to the future of the church, I'm seeing the best minds of

---

4. I wrote this poem during my time with the ordination process.
"Snowflakes Thaw"
The ones made new are falling down
griping of puddles that could drown.
The old ice looks and says, "you freak."
Ignoring crystals feel unique.

After all snowflakes did thaw
the age-Old glaciers finally saw
the fragile things which they did jeer
were not so subtle nor so mere.

Spread around, the flakes annoyed,
but then their absence left a void.
They were ignored for all their swarming,
but in the end there came the warming.

What we only see as fragile
in another way is agile.
Time for us all to pay the price;
in the end we're made of ice.

my generation freeze to death. Looking through research, this is at least a twenty-year trend.

We are at a moment of revelation in the church. The fact that so many older clergy have literal heart failure and so many young ones have heartbreak is telling. It's revealing. It's shaming. We do not do a good job of protecting our hearts, because our boundaries are shot to hell.

I pity the ones so close to the UMC that they unknowingly do harm and miss the mark. I pity the bullies, doing the church's bidding, because bullies are by definition responsible for getting you to shut up and get in line, and they rarely if ever see the full consequences of those actions, the ones they've hurt having learned it's not acceptable to be vulnerable.

At this moment, my mind is in so many places, but my heart is in Jesus. I wonder what his credit score would have been with his long absences from gainful employment. I wonder if we would have heard his "point of order" under Robert's Rules, because he would have been wearing a lanyard identifying him as laity.[5] I wonder if I will become more like a Pharisee as I go through the ordination process of this church that I love. And I wonder how I'll be punished for wondering.

But it's not my wondering or my emotion that keeps me coming back. It's an action—a fulfillment of my faith. The action of hope—*la esperanza del Espíritu Santo*. I practice the action of hope today hoping that the people who drive the ship will advocate for grace for us in this process, us who feel as if Wesley's offspring have forgotten grace. *Ayúdanos, Señor*.

Symptom of Death: Dislocation

There is a disconnect now, within the church, and I don't know if the disjointed parts will ever be able to come back together again. Many people will say that it is the polarization between the right and the left, the partisan political parts pulling against one another, but that's not it. People will say that it is the conservatives versus the liberals, the people who think that homosexuality is a sin and those who do not, but like every partisan issue, this is just a symptom.

There is a disconnect, and the pain it causes is so excruciating that the individual parts which are separated are almost inconsequential. I just want the parts to come together, to make the hurting stop. When I was a high

---

5. At our annual meeting, the different levels of ordained and not ordained clergy and then laity all wear different colored lanyards. Some people would say that the ordained voices, recognized by the color of their lanyards, carry more weight in the large group conversations governed by Robert's Rules of Order.

school student lifting weights to get strong for football, I lay on my back on the weight bench, extending a small barbell from my chest, across my face, down past the crown of my head, attempting to strengthen my shoulders. What was meant to make me stronger injured me, because my form was impoverished. For a short time I dislocated my shoulder and separated two bones in my shoulder during that injury. I watched as if in slow motion while my arms were pulled out of my view by the weight of the barbell, and I heard what resembled the crackling of bamboo twigs as my shoulder was injured.

At that moment all of my nerve endings except for those in my shoulder went silent, and my entire self focused on the excruciating pain, not knowing whether the distance was a millimeter or a mile, craving for what was separated to be rejoined. It was only a small distance, but any distance between the members that were designed to join one another felt like a chasm, and all that I wanted was for what was separated to be reconnected. During my senior year, in that football season in 2005, I played with a separated shoulder. We won the state championship, but the separation still plagues me today. Sometimes, whenever the weather is getting colder and the pain comes back to haunt me, I remember how I failed to let myself heal immediately. I remain grateful that I at least still have my arm, that it did eventually heal.

But that's just my body. The body of the United Methodist Church has opted for amputation, cutting off members that have been dislocated. In some ways I wonder if the amputation happened long ago. Sure, we are encountering schism as the church does from time to time. But the real-est, deepest schism happens in a way that is not so easily viewed.

Without wanting to we have created a schism between the parts of ourselves, like Lord Voldemort in the Harry Potter series splitting his soul more than a handful of times. Mari, one of my mentors, used to say, "The church is not the headlights of society, as it should be; it is the tail lights." Following the faux lights of US culture, blindingly shining and afraid of the dark, the church is too often just along for the ride.

Even as I originally wrote these words, I asked myself, "How can you say this? Have you not read our social principles? Have you not been a part of the board of church in society conversations, led the immigration ministry task force, participated in vital conversations from the general commission on race relations, and have you not helped lead conversations about our mission of making disciples of Jesus Christ? Have you not preached at revivals and participated in evangelism workshops? Have you not been out on the mission field?" I ask myself all of these questions knowing how hard

I have worked, and how hard the rest of the church has worked. But our endless work does not undo the end result of a suicidal act.

The end result, from what I have experienced, is that the body of Christ has all of the resources, theology, and history of the everlasting Savior of the world being at work within us, around us, and in spite of us . . . and yet the "hands and feet of Christ" are still so often immobilized and unable to move, like dislocated appendages held together only by strained ligaments and stretched skin. The end result is that I have so often found myself writhing in pain, almost unable to name the obvious dislocation, just wishing that the parts could come back together again, wishing that we could move.

I've felt God calling me to preach since I was seventeen years old. I've lived more than half my life feeling called to serve as a pastor. I have served in eight churches since then, four of them as a full-time pastor, and preached at more churches than I can remember—in Methodist, Baptist, nondenominational, Pentecostal, English and Spanish speaking, Black, white, and Latinx spaces. More often than not, I have felt the tension of dislocation.

Part of our problem is that the US church has made its home in the dominant and popular society being married to the temporal powers, and now we are experiencing a divorce. We are experiencing a different type of dislocation, from being in power to being disempowered, and nothing could be more beautiful for the possibility of a return to our gospel roots. Even while I am glad that we must return to what it means to be Christians as a minority, I realize that this constitutes a very real dislocation in the ideology that we have created for ourselves.

For myself and other leaders, this moment is especially difficult. The US church over time has moved from Christian leadership being centered in small groups (as it was in bands and classes in the first Methodist revival) to being elitist and centered in divinity school-trained professionals, complete with our own pension system. As the pendulum swings again, we will find that the strength of Christian leadership is moving back to small groups, and that the church will be unwilling or unable to support pastoral compensation packages of eighty thousand a year.

I find that myself and every leader is in the midst of another great awakening, a worldwide Christian reformation. Something great is about to happen, and is already happening, yet for some reason I feel only the pains of dislocation and death.

This is the current work of pastors and church leaders. We experience the pain of dislocation, and we only want what has been separated to come back together. It is quite possible that the body which held the members together may not ever be able to bring the discordant parts together as one.

Something must die or, better yet, we must name what has already been dead. Then and only then will we be able to celebrate resurrection.

I have been connected to so many living and vibrant parts of the United Methodist Church and the global church, and yet in many of the churches where I have worshiped I have met a spirit of hostility toward the lived practice of what we should believe. It has often been a hostility of people being painfully dislocated from each other and wanting to be amputated from each other.

The Pain of Dislocation

Every June since 2011, you could find me huffing and puffing on a Spartan race track, an annual obstacle-racing pilgrimage I started as a balm for my soul. As the years cascaded by, I noticed that it's not as easy to stay prepared in your midthirties as in your midtwenties. Each race was sprinkled with familiar obstacles that morphed subtly in my eyes, not because they had changed but because I had. Among these perennial hurdles the monkey bars and related exercises held a certain notoriety, testing my grip, shoulder flexibility, and upper body strength—and often making their appearance after the two- or three-hour mark when exhaustion had already set in.

In the race of 2021, the monkey bars claimed more than my energy. As I swung from bar to bar, my shoulder popped out of its socket. The pain was as profound as it was immediate, but as I released my grip and plopped on the ground it instinctively popped back in place. The initial surge of pain might have subsided, but the incident served as a stark reminder of the need for strengthening my surrounding muscles and shedding some excess weight to ease my journey from one obstacle to the next. Into my thirties, it also brought my mind back to the pain of injuring the same shoulder playing football as a high schooler. When we suffer the pain of dislocation once, it makes it easier to do so later. We have to be more intentional as time goes on.

When you think about dislocation, it's usually in the physical sense—a joint displaced, an unbearable pain, a body in distress. We don't hesitate to rush to the aid of someone suffering a physical dislocation. Yet when dislocation seeps into other facets of our lives its grip is no less painful, but its visibility is often overlooked.

This other kind of dislocation refers to a sense of disconnection from our fellow humans despite existing within the fabric of a larger society. It's a disorientation fueled by shifting work paradigms, the transformation of shopping habits, and the ever-expanding web of technology—elements that promised to simplify our lives but have instead cast us adrift on islands of isolation.

Consider the deindustrialization of the United States. Sure, industrialization had its fair share of issues, but it also gave workers a sense of purpose, a sense of belonging. As industries faded and jobs vanished from the coal-ridden Appalachian towns, a cloud of despair and dislocation settled over their inhabitants. Similarly, the advent of online retail behemoths forced local businesses to shutter, scattering more seeds of economic and communal dislocation. I have felt this unique pain in each of the rural communities I have served.

As technology continues its relentless march forward, it perpetuates our dislocation. While sitting in cars, our interaction with the world beyond our windshields is limited to exchanges with pixelated faces on cellphone screens. Artificial intelligence gets us to ask computers for questions instead of our friends or elders. This technological isolation has cleaved us from a fundamental aspect of our humanity—the need for genuine, face-to-face connections.

Empathy comes easily when we see someone physically hurt, but societal dislocation, though no less painful, often slips beneath our radar. Instead of confronting this techno-dislocation, we take refuge in the very mechanisms that bred it—globalism, technology, individualism, consumerism—deepening the divide between us.

In this landscape of fractured connections, I see the church as a lighthouse, a beacon of hope. I've seen people step away from the church, often to escape the friction of human interaction. But this departure only leads them onto the barren path of dislocation, a path that bears striking resemblance to smoking fifteen cigarettes a day. Being isolated literally erodes the blood vessels of the body. Isolation is a fertile ground for decay, and humans, by our very nature, are social beings.

The church isn't immune to disagreements or resentments. But isolation is not the answer. It's within the heart of the church that we can counter dislocation, cultivating unity, compassion, and mutual understanding, and breathing life into our shared humanity. In the next chapter, we will talk more about dislocation by way of conversation about loneliness, grief, and mourning.

4.

Lonely, Grieving, Leaving
The Emotional Toll

The edifice that cradled our aspirations stands now, as bare as cupboards ravaged by war, as empty as the soldier's side of the bed. It echoes with silence, the ghost of laughter and whispered secrets lingering in its corners. It is a white-washed sepulcher, a monument to past living, scrubbed clean but holding only the echoes of life, only the echoes of what was once vibrant, once cherished now perished.

The hush within these walls is punctuated by the weight of what was and the glimmer of what might yet be. A pale promise protrudes—a potential Glory that dances like a solitary dust mite in the beam of morning light, daring to say it exists and wants company.

Our eyes smolder with embers in the ashes of lost dreams. They burn like the inquisitor's fire, a scorching intensity from tears held captive. The flood is near, the damn near to breaking, yet we fear the drowning, the deluge from our despair.

We've seen them depart, the ones we loved, watched their backs fading into the horizon, leaving nothing but the echo of their names in our mouths. It has left us grieving, left us clinging to the tethers of memories woven into the very fabric of this house, this church building.

Yet I remain. Anchored not to the past nor to the present, but to the potential of what was once held within these walls and the promise of what they might yet herald. I stay because this house, in its silent testimony, whispers of hope amid the wreckage and abandonment.

I will yet light a beacon for those lost in the night, for those engulfed by the burning darkness. I will ignite a fire of hope, of steadfast belief, even if it means shattering the steeple to create a perch for the lighthouse's light. This house, this potential symbol of God's gracious love, will bear the beacon, a testament to resilience, to the unyielding Spirit that causes hope amid the lonely, the grieving, the leaving.

The Lonely Building

The profound realm of loneliness, grief, and mourning in the church culture I have experienced may be a foreign place to you, but I want you to see it—whether by images of the church building, like in the poem I just shared, or personal testimony. Grief, as defined by the Mayo Clinic from a scientific perspective, is a potent and occasionally all-consuming emotion.[1] It doesn't merely emerge in the face of the death of a loved one but can also be triggered by a terminal diagnosis.

Dr. Vivek Murthy is the nineteenth and twenty-first surgeon general of the United States, and in 2016, at the end of the Obama presidency, he issued an advisory about loneliness as a major health concern. In May of 2023 he again issued an advisory about what is described as the epidemic of loneliness, how it causes premature death, and how social connection can be an antidote to it.[2] Even with public debate about it, we as Christians in the US sometimes struggle to name our loneliness.

In order to more deeply understand our personal grief, I want to start with an alternative lens through which to view it: considering the building as a body that encapsulates grief. This perspective may seem unconventional, yet it offers a poignant metaphor for our collective sorrow.

As I share my perspective on grief in the church and town I will remind the reader that I am, in practice, a rural pastor. And so a lot of the frustrations deeply connected to rural space resonate with what sociologist Robert Wuthnow talks about in his book *The Left Behind: Decline and Rage in Rural America*—that rural residents are not so much concerned about economic

1. Mayo Clinic, "Complicated Grief."
2. Office of the Surgeon General, *Epidemic of Loneliness*.

issues as they are about losing their way of life, their community values, and their moral compass in an increasingly urbanized and globalized world.

As a solo pastor, I have spent countless hours alone on rural church campuses and have endless familiarity with somber feelings. I feel much of the grief of loss and abandonment that Wuthnow talks about. If I were to give voice to the thoughts and emotions of the building itself, I imagine it would echo the following sentiments:

The building, gazing upon historic Church Street, becomes acutely aware of the death of its companions as it registers their lifeless structures. Its corridors and hallways, hushed as a crypt, echo with an eerie silence, mirroring its loneliness. As I meander through these deserted spaces, the portraits of yesteryears invoke a sense of nostalgia—black and white Sunday school portraits of fifty smiling men sweating on the front steps of the church—a yearning for what used to be, a sentiment I'm sure the church building shares.

Yet there are moments when the building seems to spring back to life, as if stirred from a deep slumber. I recall one such instance when we hosted a group from the local rural hospital. I believe it was a gathering for breast cancer awareness, underscored by vibrant hues of pink and purple. A throng of women filled the space, their energy palpable. In that moment, the church felt vibrantly alive, pulsating with a sense of purpose and community.

However, following the conclusion of that event, the building reverted to its usual state of emptiness. It felt hollow once again, the walls echoing with the ghostly absence of laughter and conversation. It seemed to grieve the loss of its vibrant past, and the quiet corridors resonated with this sense of sorrow. The sadness of the building resonates with the sadness of struggling rural spaces elsewhere.

The Grief of Lonely Towns

Driving up to the historic downtown section of Emporia, Virginia, I saw a beautifully displayed sign, surrounded by immaculate seasonal flowers. The sign's colors burst with 1950s vibrancy, reminding me of other painted signs I'd seen, so old as to be suspicious of lead paint. I wondered to myself, "Who is this sign designed to attract?" As I drove into the historical section, looking for the café advertised on the internet, I drove past repurposed buildings, old shops trying to reinvent themselves for customers, and the majority of the storefronts I saw, and even second-story businesses, were covered with plywood, the signs of what used to be there also being covered to avoid experiencing the shame of what did not last.

As I drove by a second time, looking for a café that ended up being closed down, everybody standing in the same spot looked at me with what felt like wonder and suspicion, their shoes marking their favorite spot on the pavement the same way that my church folk have shoes marking the ground in front of their favorite pew. I imagine that looking beyond my dented-up, ten-year-old Chevrolet Equinox, looking past my bushy hair that had escaped my man bun, and looking past my squinting eyes, some of the onlookers probably hoped I would bring business to the dying downtown.

As I finally left downtown, begrudgingly going to Cracker Barrel to enjoy my coffee and write the wedding sermon for the next day, I once again saw that nicely kept sign alerting everybody to the historic downtown area. It reminded me of the sign in front of each of the two congregations I served at the time.

The signs in downtowns, as well as in front of our churches, meant many things in the past, and currently I think they are there as much for our own obstinate optimism and lingering hope as they are for new people and onlookers. As much as we want to make the signs for new people we cannot ignore the fact that they are monuments to a way of life that has disappeared—and we are not sure if they can be reborn in the same place, advertising the same thing, resurrected for a new day, with new meaning, inviting new people.

Having left that downtown area, the feeling in the pit of my stomach caused me to wonder how many people, longing for the bread of heaven, had driven by the church campuses where I serve, hunger in their souls, thinking that the signs out front were intended only for the people who already knew what they meant. I wondered what it would mean for our signs to take on a new meaning. Like many rural towns that have intentionally changed to become a biome of remote work for digital commuters who cannot afford city life, I wondered what it would be like for the church to rethink how we present our mission to speak to a people who dare not to darken a church doorway but want some transcendent light to brighten their lives.

In my questions and curiosity is both a longing for what once was and a dream that the future might somehow grow to be different yet the same. In the memory of deceased ways and methods of life is the grief that much has died without remembering to plant seeds for what may come next. My life has crossed paths with so many who grieve these deaths, who do so without knowing how to talk about them. Living with dwindling connections to the past or future, without deep relationships to other humans, creates this creeping, unnamed, and often unknown melancholy that surrounds individuals like ivy surrounds the trunk, eventually choking the life from the tree.

Lonely Grief Among Church Folk

Before the wedding I was going to officiate, I was able to hang out with young people my age, something I don't get to do often. I felt so insecure around them because each of them had found a way to make a living doing hard work with their bodies. My dad's voice rang in my ears, "You should probably have a tent ministry, something to fall back on if you serve a church that is unable to pay you." My feelings of inadequacy were more about not being able to work as hard or contribute, or build things like they did, but I noticed a standoffish atmosphere even when I got there.

Most of them treated me the way I had seen millennials treat old pastors, and I wondered if they had ever met a pastor their age. Hushed tones came over them whenever I was around, and again I got my feelings hurt. One of the few things I heard somebody say was, "You can't say that with a preacher around."

"Why the hell not?" I wanted to say back to them. In my mind I ran through a litany of other responses. I could paraphrase the priest in *The Count of Monte Cristo*: "I'm a pastor, not a saint."[3] Or perhaps I could throw in some other jokes and hope to connect through humor.

"We as pastors are another species entirely," the words of my former senior pastor came back to mind, and even though I had resented him for it, I thank him for at least helping me understand how the culture views me. I rail against the idea that I am somehow a different species, but that's how the current church culture views pastors.

A few weeks after the wedding I had a different experience with working-class folk at Bible study in one of the two churches I was serving. The majority of them were retired, though some were still working well into their sixties as teachers. I had said, "My inner circle is mostly pastors, because I need people who I can cuss around." Each of them breathed a sigh of relief, saying that they "cuss a damn lot."

Having parishioners who give you permission to curse, to let your hair down, and still respect that you serve a leadership position in the church is an exception to the current rule. It's not that I want to be able to cuss around people, only that I long for this position, through which I have pledged my life to God, to be taken off the pedestal.

Whenever the current mode of being church finds its demise, I hope that what emerges on the other side is something whereby I can feel like a member of the human species around other humans—that the church might allow the ground again to be level at the foot of the cross.

---

3. Reynolds, *Count of Monte Cristo*, at 52:50.

But until that time, I grieve the inability to sit with others. And on some level I see the grief of church members, each of whom sits and hears me preach on Sundays, as my mentor Mari says, "in a puddle of their own tears," and often unnamed tears at that.

The grief of not being able to experience our full humanity together is also the grief of not being able to be vulnerable together. Because the church has sometimes amputated parts of the full human experience, or taken things God created and called good and renamed them as bad, the church I have experienced has not often lamented an inability to experience the fullness of being human. And we have not even realized a lack of mutual vulnerability, as the Epistle of James says, confessing our sins, one to another (5:16), as a problem. An overemphasis on a gospel that hyperindividualizes a personal relationship with Jesus Christ, to the exclusion of a communal relationship with Jesus Christ, is a recipe for pain and silent grief.

Lonely Behind Masks

As a United Methodist pastor mostly serving the rural church in eastern North Carolina, having held hopes and hazards through pandemics with both sacred and secular people, I can point to my grief as part of a larger grief. I lament and mourn feelings of disconnection, longing to be connected in kinship. The peculiar grief that clergy feel is part of a larger problem: that we are placed on pedestals and removed from the lives of others. While I see the merits of holding faith leaders to a higher standard, it is also tied in with our hypocrisy on a deeper level. The Greek word *hypokrites* literally means "an interpreter from underneath" or "an actor." It's not just pastors who are disconnected from the congregation. The longer church folk have been in church in the United States, the more likely they are to have been taught that "children ought to be seen and not heard" in church, they need to come looking their Sunday best, and need to make sure they don't cuss or let anyone know about their intimate lives.

So much of our mask-wearing comes from the Holiness movement of the nineteenth century and even the Puritans before that. Christians were told to look and act certain ways, under danger of hell, and when they could not, they put on masks to fake it. Ideas of purity and holiness were not only connected to personal behavior.

On a white church culture level, purity and holiness were juxtaposed over against Native/Indigenous and Black bodies who were seen by the church as impure and practicing unholy and pagan religion. The practice of using whiteness as a tool originally disconnected white people from non-white people, but it has morphed to a place of disconnecting so many people from their neighbors and even themselves. The mask wearer may forget who they are behind it.

The mask of whiteness is an idea that made people give up their cultural heritage of being, for example, British or Spanish or French or Portuguese in order to dominate others. We'll talk more about white supremacy in a later chapter. For now, let us grieve the mask of whiteness over the face of the church, this facade which we now recognize separates people from one another and the individual from their truest self. How could we not be lonely wearing this mask?

Whenever we get too used to the masks we wear, we start to create fights about who our false selves are and not about who we are underneath them. Consider the final two verses of 1 Cor 13, a chapter well known to be about the godly love that a Christian community should share. "For now we see in a mirror dimly, but then face to face. Now I know in part; then I shall know fully, even as I have been fully known. So faith, hope, love abide, these three; but the greatest of these is love" (ESV).

For now, we see each other imperfectly, whether through a foggy mirror or from behind hypocritical masks. Now we see only part of each other. But we should hold on to our virtues, knowing that the greatest of them is a selfless love. If we really took that to heart, I doubt we as the church would be compounding our grief at a time when we are already dying. And yet we in the United Methodist Church have just undergone a schism, one in which most of my mentors have left.

The Struggle over Positions and Possessions

At the root of the schism that United Methodists will have gone through is a theological justification by some pastors as to why they should be able to have something of value that some other people should not be able to have. In this case, that thing is ordination, being invested in by the church as a leader. It boils down to a piece of paper bearing the seal of a man-made church talking about either pastoral authority on the one hand or marriage on the other hand.

The stated reason for why churches are leaving the United Methodist Church is that they disagree on matters of conscience surrounding human sexuality. They are not disagreeing with what the United Methodist *Book of Discipline* says about "homosexuality" but upset that those who have given marriage certificates or pastoral license certificates to the LGBTQ+ community have not been punished.

Even if no schism were to happen, and even if we all believed the same thing one way or another about human sexuality, we would still have this type of problem. Our church is steeped in theological justifications as to why the people inside of the church should have what they do in comparison to people outside the church who do not. Historically, the white church in the US has talked about the so-called "dominion mandate" at the beginning of the book of Genesis in which God gives Adam and Eve what different translations call "dominion," "mastery," "rule," and "power" over the earth. Creation care activists say this should be seen as stewardship and care of the earth. Bastardized and taken out of context, this idea has been applied to the "Doctrine of Discovery": the European church said that God gave white Europeans dominion over the indigenous populations of the Americas to subdue them and also the land. This idea still gets used as a justification for why people on the inside are blessed and gifted with things that people on the outside are not.

As the church, we have not recognized a God who blesses and gifts the world with resources enough to share and gives the gift of grace that is too big for the church to subdue and subjugate, but through which we are graciously subdued and enveloped by God's love. Rather than a posture of humility at how God moves in this immense world, we take a posture of pride that puts us at the center of it. Rather than appreciate God's work in many histories across a plurality of religious expressions through an ever-expanding cosmos, we look at ourselves as the center of it all, much like the church did before the Copernican revolution.

I still believe that "this is my story and this is my song."[4] I still believe in and claim Christianity and situate myself through this particular action of God, doing so in a way that does not erase God's action outside of myself. Yes, I believe that God speaks in particulars. And that is why I believe in what we call "means of grace," specific avenues through which I encounter the unmerited favor of God as an individual and as a member of a larger community: things like prayer, fasting, reading the Bible, holy communion, and fellowship with other people who are part of the Christian community.

As Christians, we get so caught up in our own beliefs about our particulars that we forget that it is God who has asked us to follow. Instead we ask the Holy Spirit to follow us. Looking at the Bible, we see an untamed and wild God. We see a God who acts within a religious community bound by strict rules and regulations, many of which carried capital punishment for transgression. And in the midst of this community, we see God, time and again, choosing to call people who have no business leading such a

---

4. Lyrics from "Blessed Assurance" by Fanny J. Crosby (1873).

righteous and orthodox group. God calls people who are prostitutes and drunkards. God bypasses people who can speak well to choose stutterers and murderers.

Pastor Fatimah first told me of seminary professor Willie Jennings saying that when we ask bad questions, we get bad theology. In his book *After Whiteness: An Education in Belonging*, Jennings talks about the importance of challenging places where institutions default to only loving or accepting and including people from a certain space. From this wisdom, I challenge the logic of our schism. The question behind the schism in my church is, "Who shall be called by God?"

We have taken that question out of the hands of God and placed it in our own hands, essentially saying that God does not call Queer people as such to serve as pastors. I understand the objection and the assertion by those leaving the church that they have drawn a line around sin. I understand them saying that they have been entrusted by God to make sure that people living in sin unrepentantly are not placed in power. It reminds me of where Jennings, in the aforementioned book, talks about taking the side of the academic institution instead of taking the side of concerned students. He says, "I was completely right in what I was saying but completely wrong in saying it."[5] The context is different because he is talking about race and not sexuality, but I think the sentiment is the same. One does not have to take the side of the powerful when the disempowered are hanging in the balance.

The calling of Jesus in the Bible is broad and expansive, naming and claiming people who are left out: disabled, disgraced, disregarded, and disliked. On the contrary, the story of the church in the US has become constrictive instead of constructive and reductionist instead of relational. Our calling is bigger than all of this.

The underlying question of who shall be called is at fault in the Great Divorce[6] which has hastened our death. And as the question unfolds, and as I look at the historic disunity among pastors, I realize that this is just a reiteration, with a slightly different tone, of the same question from generations past. Will God call women to positions of power and authority in the Methodist

---

5. Jennings, *After Whiteness*, 62.

6. Here I use the term *Great Divorce* for two reasons, both of which are related, and perhaps the reader can see why. Firstly, the term stands prominently in my memory as the schism experienced by the United Methodist Church, the pinnacle of which was 2022. A simple web search for "UMC disaffiliation" will give the reader unending readings from both sides. Secondly, I also think of C. S. Lewis's book by the same name, which I read in college. It talked about the nature of hell being a reality in which people move away from their neighbors, into isolation. See Lewis, *Great Divorce*.

church? Will God call Black people to serve as pastors with power and authority over white people? Will God call people who have been divorced?

Our underlying question gets to the heart of this problem, the problem of where the grace of God is given, to whom, and through what channels. Without realizing it, we have yet again turned to make justifications as to why physical resources are given by God to one group of people and not to another. I may be most hurt by the leaders of the Global Methodist Church who orchestrated the schism, but I challenge all historically white churches—that we are recipients of vast resources because of this same logic that stripped resources from some for the benefits of others. At the root of it is the question, "Who is worthy?" I weep just thinking about it.

"Woe to me! . . . I am a man of unclean lips, and I live among a people of unclean lips," I cry like Isaiah (Isa 6:5). Like this prophet, I have seen the Lord trying to break into this church, and I see how I am part of the problem. The white Christian church in the United States is the rich young ruler that claims to have kept the orthodoxy, who is told by Jesus, "You lack one thing; go, sell what you own, and give the money to the poor" (Mark 10:21b NRSV).

The very least that we could do is learn wisdom from Marie Kondo who in her book says to give away everything that does not bring us joy. We should give up what does not give to us the presence of God. Maybe "nothing" gives us the presence of God. Not to say that we can never experience it, but maybe the act of holding on to *nothing* is where we experience joy. Maybe when we stop holding so tightly to the things that we claim God has given to us, when all we can do is hold on to God, in those moments we will find joy.

Being a child of the Great Divorce, having spiritual parents on both sides, I see just how badly we have missed the mark and asked the wrong questions. The more I long to give the church of God to those who are outside of its walls the more I see the persistent nature of hope and also the deeply embedded nature of our addiction to self—our impulsivity to believe that God has given the things that we possess to us, the reality that these things end up possessing us.

This reminds me of how demon possession shows up in the Gospel accounts. Possession makes people act with impulsivity that does not reflect the root of who they are. That radical self shows up when they have a brush with Jesus, an encounter that lifts the demonic weight off of them, that pries away the heavy weight that has been possessing them.

The things that consume us in the United States are so often related to consumerism. When we think about our fights with each other in the church being related to material (whether that is church buildings, endowments, or certificates bearing the church's stamp of approval), I hope we can see that it is idolatry rooted in resources, an idolatry that prevents us from living in and giving God's grace. As in the Old Testament, false gods and idols today demand that we make sacrifices to them also. As a child of the Great Divorce, I see the sacrifice being people who are deemed not worthy to share of the great resources.

Ironically, we have used up so many resources fighting about our theological justifications for why we should have certain material things, that there are less resources for us to use in the actual ministry to which we have been called.

I used to think that our resources were something that served us. But now that I see that there is a spiritual dimension of both the dollar and tangible things. I see that we have been consumed by our resources, forgetting that Jesus said, "You cannot serve God and wealth" (Matt 6:24 NRSV).

It is a sign that we have begun serving our stuff when a need for that stuff becomes so great that the idol calls us to die by suicide by cutting ourselves in half. I believe this truth would be the same for all historically white churches in the United States, whether or not they had gone through schisms. How many of the great divorces in the Baptist churches, the Presbyterian, the Lutheran, and the Episcopalian/Anglican churches have also been tied to the fight over material resources, whether the benefits conferred by pieces of paper with stamps of approval or other stockpiles?

In the same way that I hear the question, "If you are so disgruntled with America, why don't you leave it?" I imagine the question, "If you are so disgruntled with church consumerism, why don't you just leave it?" I feel inescapably bound up in this system that has eaten the church I love, that has consumed me also. How can I even understand it?

As someone who receives a paycheck from the church; as someone who is in the leadership of youth and young people across our church; as someone who wants to lead those who can hear me in order to invite in those who are trapped outside, I have been very saddened. I want to have a salary that frees me up to challenge the church that both I individually and we as a denomination would all share what we have instead of finding reasons to keep it to ourselves. But, also, I realize that a necessary change in this church culture may mean a change for many pastors.

I want to continue serving the church, and I want to continue providing for my family through this place. But I do not want to do it in the name of excluding anyone else. I am so grateful that one of the main focuses of my church is race equity and justice, which is dismantling racism and seeking more diversity.

I hope that we can have the conversation about how our history is tied up in the desire to justify why we should have what we have instead of other people having it. When we can honestly name our past and how it affects our present, we can do better in the future. When we acknowledge the terrible questions that have torn us into pieces, we can find ways of letting God mend those pieces.

Whether people are leaving the United Methodist Church to join the Global Methodist Church, or whether we are staying in the UMC, we will be in a church that has used its theological voice to justify having resources while those on the margins do not. I do not know what it looks like in my own life to respond to the voice of Jesus saying, "Sell everything you have and give to the poor." (Luke 18:22). And it looks much different with three young children under the age of ten than it would if I had remained single. But even as a single person, I would probably have a house and be supporting my familiar ones. It's a complex question, but I do think that God gives us an answer. Share!

The direction of our attention is so important. If we spend our attention making fault lines, that is where our resources and energy will go. If we spend our resources and energy holding on to our stacks of unsigned certificates, deciding who is worthy enough to have their names written on them, that is where our energy and resources will go. (I declared to my church, both my local congregation and the District Committee on Ordained Ministry, that I felt called to be an ordained pastor in 2006 and it was not until 2021 that I was ordained. So I know that the struggle of ordination being a worthiness contest is an issue for more people than those who are LGBTQ+.)

When my wife was ordained into the Cooperative Baptist Church, she was ordained by a group of people in the local church who had grown to know her and appreciate her. Even while I appreciate the connectional nature of the United Methodist Church, and while I have surveyed many different denominations and think this is the best one to give me a framework for being faithful to the Lord Jesus Christ, I do think that the Baptists have something better than we do in their practice of ordination.

Scientific epistemology says that we can know the truth of something by being somewhat disconnected from it. By keeping it at arm's length we can entertain the scientific method, observing and deciding what is true and what is false. The church has, in a manner of speaking, employed this tactic. A lot of churches have rules and regulations about who can become an insider, and the people who ultimately make the decision are not intimately connected with the lives of those about whom they are making decisions.

It is really easy to judge someone that we are not intimately close with. It is very difficult to reject people from up close. When our spirit gets close enough to that of another person that we can smell the goodness of God wafting off of their heart and mind, we are more likely to have a mystical experience. Sure, it gets really difficult for us to make the decisions about who is in and who is out, but, at least, if we must make those decisions one way or another, we can do so from a place of intimacy instead of disconnection.

If the old structures of the church must die, I hope that the worthiness contest will also die. I hope that the embedded structures that we use to justify that insiders should have things and our opponents should not have things . . . I hope that also dies. In a secular world, I do not know what the sacred canopy of religion or denomination will look like, but I hope that we will be able to systematize ways of cherishing the sacredness of "the other"—whether they are sexually, racially, or culturally othered—instead of killing ourselves to create false dichotomies about what happens to them.

We struggle over positions and possessions. And yet, there in the middle of the chaos, the Spirit of God hovers.

In the midst of trying to figure out where the rest of the energy in our dying church will go, I bless us to have eyes to see how God has given us more than we can hold, and how God's most enduring mystical gift is something that we cannot arbitrate. May we find hope for coming together, and may this hope be godly enough to even include the people who we wish it did not.

Leaving as Grieving

I have talked about the schism and those who have left. But now I will talk about young people leaving the church. One of my closest friends from childhood talked about being post-church, and he talked about the horror of realizing that he was a statistic—that so many young people have left the church. In a part-time job I have with the youth ministry movement TENx10 I learned from research that in the US an average of one million young people are leaving church each year.

Why are young people leaving the church? As I talked about earlier, I think secularity has a lot to do with it. But, also, I think young people suffer grief by the way the church is acting, and I see many people leaving due to that grief. It looks different in different Christian expressions.

For example, consider the so-called Evangelical churches. I have heard popular Evangelical voices on Fox News claiming to be the only Christian political possibility while also supporting grievous policies that would allow anyone to carry assault weapons that could kill scores of people. I've heard Christians support policies that literally put children in cages under mandatory family separation of migrants at the US border (and, at the time of me writing this, over one thousand children have never been reunited with their parents six years later, prompting me to think how things may yet get worse).[7] I've seen Christians help move the United States of America toward being a plutocracy, in which less than 1 percent of people control most of the money and power.[8]

Hypocrisy like this is why many young people leave the church. Young people do not leave the church because they don't know Jesus. Young people don't leave the church because their parents failed to get them to read Jesus. Many young people have actually had an encounter with Jesus, and this has spurred their decision. On some level, many young people are leaving the church because they realize that Jesus cannot be found within it.

Christian supremacy has paralleled white supremacy in the United States. And so the temptation of the church has been like the temptation of Jesus Christ in the desert. Satan three times tempted Jesus, each of the three times enticing Jesus with ideas of having an abundance of power. It is precisely the superabundance of power-grabbing, this oldest temptation in the New Testament, from which young people are fleeing with their exodus from the church. Leaving a theological home is an expression of grief.

In 2019 I wrote a poem in rap form about young people leaving the church. It is called "None and Done."

> Trying to grasp at truth with a handful of thumbs
> Having left a religion that seemed half dead,
> You came to the cupboard and found only crumbs,
> Trying to find the gift of life which is Heaven's bread.
> Remembering what you used to call the "Dumbday drool,"
> You cringe at the thought of another moralistic lesson.
> Somehow all the kids peaced out of Sunday school,
> As the strength of institutions began to lessen.
> Now as young adults touting self-centered brilliance,
> We find a generation who barely knew the church.
> Now in sloughs of turmoil showing lack of resilience,
> We see it's hard to stand alone upon a postmodern perch.
> I thought the older generation who don't like it loud
> Couldn't hear my new voice so rife with ambition.
> It's hard not to turn to the wisdom of the crowd
> When being outside of the box feels like sedition to tradition.
>
> Young folks these days need validation and fun—
> Post-church people with Afros and man buns.
> You ask about religion and they say they got none;
> What they're really saying though is, "We are done!"

7. Human Rights Watch, "Lasting Harm from Family Separation."
8. Bruce-Lockhart, "Who Are the 1%?"

Wesley warned about conversion free of holy teaching;
It can make one a Christian with a lack of self-worth.
Watch out for religion that can't be far reaching;
It might be "born again," but it's still a stillbirth.
We think we learned a lot, the lessons made us moral
"Do you like this or else you get a prick, like from a cactus."
Trading rule books for a story that first lived as oral;
Church formation sometimes comes to be a malpractice.
We are trying to find the whole, starting out with shards;
Playing through this game has turned into a hiccup.
You're playing through the game while missing some cards.
Then the rules turn out to be for 52 Pickup.
We suffer from a world that has a fleeting bookshelf.
It tells us we are known, because we write our own story.
How nearsighted to think that life is all about the self.
We are nearly blind now, 'cause our eyes do not see history.

Young folks these days need education, Heaven-spun,
Post-church people who really like to shun.
You ask about religion and they say they got none;
What they're really saying though is, "We are done!"

They may be out now, but they started out as different:
Optimistic, rich, and hopeful, like one who found a pearl.
Even if we are mad, please let's not be ignorant—
Many leave the church, 'cause they wanna change the world!
When the worship house fails to be a sanctuary,
We look at Dreamers, and we begin to stall.
The place then turns to be a pre-mortuary.
"We love you a lot, stained glass and brick wall."
"We really want to branch out, but we've tried that once."
Now there's still scars for some when they see the church station.
If you wanna be prophetic, you might feel like a dunce;
It's hard to think anew in space of disimagination!
We can't blame the old saints who been like this for years,
But still we got to move from the mistakes of the past.
It's hard to shift a church that's interwoven with fears;
It's the one thing that conserves in a world that's too fast.

Young folks these days need dedication to come from.
All the church people trying to march to God's drum.
You ask about religion and they say they got none;
What they're really saying though is, "We are done!"

Not all young people leave the church because they have become atheists, but many because they have become a religious category of not having any formalized religion. They are spiritual but not religious. James Emery White, in *Rise of the Nones: Understanding and Reaching the Religiously Unaffiliated*, discusses how churches need to rethink their methods, highlighting that doing things the way they've always been done will probably not yield different results.[9]

A 2013 study by the Barna Group found that a significant number of millennials perceive the church as overprotective and not supportive of their desire to positively impact society. The study highlights that many young Christians feel disconnected from church involvement because they desire to help the world in a way that aligns with their passions and abilities, but do not see the church facilitating such engagement.[10] We came to see the church as the taillights of society and not the headlights, as something that accommodates society and doesn't challenge it, something that goes with the flow instead of pricks the conscience of the people. But why is that?

There are so many reasons, I am learning. Subliminally, we are grieving the problems of a church that showed us a God that it did not follow as we followed the false gods of capitalism and individualism. We grieve and leave because that same church did not teach us how to lament brokenness well. As I write this, so many other young pastors have left ministry and left the church because of our inability to tell the truth and lament. Their grief sometimes overflows to nonbelief, first of all, because our religious fragility is unbelievable.

In my experience, a lot of my generation's frustration with the church goes back to capitalism and individualism. In the South this connects back to the idea of slaveholding religion. Four hundred years ago, when the church was growing up on this continent, it had to find a way of controlling people while also claiming to have ultimate authority. In order to subjugate enslaved people and native populations, it had to twist the Bible to fit itself. As Shane Claiborne says (quoting George Bernard Shaw) in *The Irresistible Revolution*, "God made us in [God's] image, and we returned the favor."[11] The root of the heresy of white supremacy and racism is capitalism. Before there were "white people," there were Europeans who needed a reason to be able to exploit the labor of Black people. Inventing the idea that they were superior, given the burden of controlling the world, and that God allowed them to dominate people who they did not see as people—all of these were the sounding ideas of white supremacy, which now exists in policies that over-police impoverished communities, that erode communities of color,

---

9. White, *Rise of the Nones*.
10. Barna Group, "Three Spiritual Journeys."
11. Claiborne, *Irresistible Revolution*, 94.

and that have never attempted to systematically repair the damage that was done for hundreds of years.

I think young people are able to see this obvious hypocrisy from the church. For people who have been in the church for so long, it is hard to see. But it takes young people no time at all to take a step back, to realize some of these glaring injustices. A lot of church folk will rail against the idea of being "woke." And some church folk will rage against critical race theory. But, at its root, this is just being honest about how the church's roots in the Americas were planted with sinful weeds that need to be surgically removed. Grieving the inability to have these conversations, many young people leave the church.

Woven in the fabric of Western society is the doctrine of individualism, an idea we can trace back to historical movements like the Enlightenment or more recent trends such as neoliberalism. This pervasive idea of self first has also seeped into the church, shifting the focus away from community and centering it on individual experience. When we recenter the church away from community, the threads that bind us begin to unravel; we become less invested in each other's journey.

Under the guise of individualism, faith often morphs into a personal transaction—our unique relationship with Jesus Christ. Yes, a personal bond with God is a critical aspect of our faith, but when we look to Jesus as our model, we find that he did not interact with people as isolated individuals. His actions were not singular but woven into a broader tapestry of community.

Consider Jesus's first sermon documented in the Gospel according to Matthew where he unrolls the scroll of Isaiah. In that moment, he speaks not of individual salvation, but of societal redemption—proclaiming liberty for the captives, sight for the blind, and announcing the year of God's favor, a time of repair and reconciliation for those burdened by financial indebtedness. His message was not about solitary salvation, but communal liberation.

The absence of this profound sense of interconnectedness can often lead people to walk away from the church. When faith becomes a solitary pursuit, we lose sight of the collective responsibility and solidarity that Jesus himself embodied. The church should not be a collection of individuals, but a communion of souls journeying together, bearing each other's burdens, and participating in the shared work of redemption.

Part of that individuality is the disconnection naming how God is connected to the earth. Christianity became this movement that was about emotion and about getting out of hell. Christianity forgot that you do not have to die to experience the pain of hell. And individual Christians, in many places, have begun to live this disconnected reality that allows them to hoard resources in expensive church buildings while their neighbors die in the streets. That shit needs to die. Grieving this reality makes a lot of people who love God and neighbor leave the church.

In *Christianity's Surprise: A Sure and Certain Hope*, C. Kavin Rowe discusses the early Christians' development of institutions to care for the sick and the poor, highlighting their innovative approach in the Roman world. He notes that while the Roman society was aware of individuals who were poor or sick, it had not previously recognized these groups as distinct classes requiring societal response. Rowe states, "The Roman world knew of poor people and sick people, of course, but it had never seen the 'poor' as a distinct group of vulnerable people that required response, and it did not know what it was to care for the sick during a plague in spite of the risk to oneself."[12] This perspective underscores the early Christians' role in establishing institutions like hospitals specifically aimed at serving the poor and sick, marking a significant shift in societal attitudes toward these groups. While the concept of *the poor* existed in earlier texts, including the Old and New Testaments, Rowe emphasizes that the early Christians' organized and institutionalized care for these groups was unprecedented in the Roman context. We did this because we believe that, to God, matter matters. Many young people have left the church because they see us as being more concerned with what happens after life than in this life.

If you look at the way Jesus talks about the kingdom of God, especially in the Gospels of Matthew, Mark, and Luke, you can see that the kingdom of God, or the kingdom of heaven as it is sometimes called, is just as much about a way to live on this planet as it is in the afterlife. The word in Greek that gets translated as *kingdom* can also be translated as *the reign of God*, making us remember that heaven starts now, and that the reign of God has already begun in this world. We grieve that many churches look like wealth and individual power reign.

The Christians who think that heaven is entirely an otherworldly reality have not read the book of Revelation, which talks about God's plan of fulfillment for the world. It says that there will be a "new heaven and a new earth," and that God will come down to earth and make God's home with God's people (Rev 21:1–3). Basically, what we do here matters, and God cares about this place so much that Jesus is coming back to hang out here. To ignore the future is also to ignore the ways that it is directly connected with healing our grief through hope.

---

12. Rowe, *Christianity's Surprise*, loc. 94 of 1691, Kindle.

Right now I remain in the church, but not because the church is doing well. I grieve what is going on in the church and what is not going on. Most Christian denominations in the US are dying, and in some ways that is a good thing, because the shifting sand on which we have built our foundation has eroded and the structures are falling in on themselves. However, after the erosion of the base of white supremacy, capitalism, individualism, and ignorance of God's love for humanity in this world, I believe that God will be doing a new thing.

We in the church have only begun to experience the pain of the church dying. Church scholar Lovett Weems has long talked about something called "the death tsunami" in which the greatest generation and baby boomers, who have with profound finances supported the work of the church, will die out, and Generation X, millennials, Generation Z, and Generation Alpha, will be less loyal to these institutions.[13] So unless the business model of the church changes, it will die.

I believe that in some way, the work of the United Methodist Church and others like it will continue, but it will be in a different form. God has called me to this work, and this place, but I know that we will experience many funerals, both for people, and for the ways that we have done things. As we explore in this book, our service to God is currently "a funeral for outdated methods." Funerals are a time to grieve.

If we do not leave, we will be able to lament and grieve and mourn together, for all of the things that have died. Many of them were good and great and wonderful. It is like the parable of the wheat and the weeds. The good stuff and the weeds grow together until the harvest. We are experiencing a disaster that is wiping out much of it. In this Service of Death and Resurrection, our experience will bring us through the pain of Good Friday, that time in which we feel like Jesus in our midst has been killed. Then we will experience the suffering of Holy Saturday, that moment when we don't know if death can be redeemed. Many racial minority communities live in the space of Holy Saturday for a long time, as we hear about in the writings of some of the Latin American liberation theologians. But if we stay with the space of Holy Saturday for long enough, we will eventually come to Easter Sunday in which the presence of Jesus Christ will be resurrected with us, still bearing the scars of white supremacy, individualism, and a disembodied/disemboweled Christianity. But Jesus will be resurrected nonetheless. I hope that we can find ourselves together in the challenging space of Christian community, not to rush through the grief, but to wait and see what Jesus does.

---

13. Weems, "Coming Death Tsunami."

5.

Attitudes in Ashes
What Must Change

"The Death of Death-Bearing Attitudes"

Institutions, vast and cold,
Turn the young, the fierce to old,
Some leave the church, stories untold.
In a Methodized rhythm, I am enrolled.
Shields of defensiveness we wear,
A weighted armor of our fear.
Erecting walls, we forget to care,
In echo chambers, listening's rare.
Perfectionism, a hungry flame,
In its pursuit, we lose our name;
An endless cycle—shame and blame,
Where target and archer are the same.
The laws allowed, with practiced might,
Cancel the weak, extinguish light,
Drowning voices who dare to fight.
No grasp, just gasps, justice takes flight.
In comfort zones, we lay our stake,

Ignoring the fringes in our wake.
Exclusion is what we should forsake;
In un-easy variety humanity awakes.
So let these death-bearers die.
May compassionate love multiply.
In the face of unity, fear can't lie,
In God's Reign, we'll reach the sky.

In this chapter, I will discuss attitudes that need to die. I will mention "the death" of certain things, referring both to the harm caused by these attitudes and the necessity for their transformation. We start with defensiveness.

The Death of Our Defensiveness

One of the biggest challenges that I faced in the institutional church was that the clergy, who would proclaim that they are inclusive, were the ones who were more exclusive, micro-aggressive, and micro-managing. I was caught off guard by clergy, who would criticize the people in power, [but] were not able to receive constructive criticism without getting personal or defensive.

—Rev. James Kim

But sanctify the Lord God in your hearts: and be ready always to give an answer to every man that asketh you a reason of the hope that is in you with meekness and fear.

—1 Pet 3:15 KJV

Put on the full armor of God.

—Eph 6:11

Human nature makes us want to look to people for both advice and examples. In times of great stress and turmoil, we want to find the person blazing a trail through the forest so we can follow them. We want to find that first good book written about a perilous situation, hoping to find its paradigm. This is especially true in the church. When we are able to name a crisis, whether it is dying of old age or racism or coronavirus, we look for people who have prototypes that can be replicated, and try to build on their success.

I do this with pastoral and prophetic voices, people who speak wisdom in difficult situations. A young clergy friend of mine, James, had been such a voice in my life for years. We both went through divinity school in the same fellowship scholarship designed to strengthen rural United Methodist churches in North Carolina. He was the person I recommended to take my place as a youth pastor in a small church, just north of Durham, when I graduated before him from divinity school. Even though he came after me, he was ordained very quickly and before me and did this while also speaking eloquently and truthfully about the institutional racism of our denomination, catching flak from several different places.

And at the end of June, 2020, he stepped down from pastoral ministry.

James is one tragic example among many of how minority clergy come to bear an undue weight for tackling and confronting the sin of white supremacy as it lives in the roots of our beloved church. But even more than that, he is the victim of a culture of defensiveness, a culture that *at best* is unable to hear criticism of itself, being busy coming up with a defense, and *at worst* comes to wholesale ignore certain voices, institutionalizing a preemptive defense against them. In a farewell essay of sorts, James said,

> One of the biggest challenges that I faced in the institutional church was that the clergy, who would proclaim that they are inclusive, were the ones who were more exclusive, micro-aggressive, and micro-managing. I was caught off guard by clergy, who would criticize the people in power, [but] were not able to receive constructive criticism without getting personal or defensive.[1]

I'm not an expert, but I will speak from my observations on the matter. I will speak from the same perspective of the rest of my work right now, from the perspective of a Service of Death and Resurrection.

---

1. Kim, "Trauma and Church." I know him as James, because through divinity school, he went by his English name. This article is published under his Korean name, Young (or YoungHan) Kim. It was published just after he left the pastorate.

The Death of Institutionalization

We clergy have been institutionalized. Indeed, sometimes it is difficult to trace our own psyche and know where the church ends and our own self begins. To a certain extent this may be healthy. We believe in the church as the body of Christ, and we challenge people in our ecclesiology and theology to see ourselves as interwoven, like a tapestry, like bones and ligaments membered together. We believe that "there is no me without you." And yet when sinfulness lives in the man-made organization of the mystical body of Christ, this becomes sticky, very quickly.

It becomes sticky, not only in the messy sense of the word but also in the sense that the ideologies stick to us, like cat hair to a wool coat. Only a thorough search and a really good piece of masking tape enable us to separate the two. Without awareness and intentionality, the stickiness of our brokenness abides with us, apparent to all who are allergic to it.

In the same way that it is easier for us to see the speck of dust in our neighbor's eye than the log in our own, it is easy for us to tell when others have been institutionalized, to lament and decry that, and to seek to fix other people. We do this with prison reform for example. Methodists, as a whole, are very loving to the formerly incarcerated, writing resolutions and prayers to support them, offering them food from pantries and education. We know the extent to which incarceration and the prison industrial complex malforms men and women. But we cannot see the ways in which *we* have been institutionalized.

I know that I have been formed and reformed by the church, and in many ways I celebrate my institutionalized formation. I am happy to live in a space that celebrates grace, that calls us to make disciples of Jesus Christ for the transformation of the world. We see all of the good that comes from our method of serving God, and for us that legitimates the entirety of our Christian expression. Put another way, we see what works, and we forget that there are parts that do not work. As a rule, we cannot spontaneously see what is wrong with ourselves. That must be pointed out.

Defensiveness is a sin that simultaneously lives in the discipline and order we have created, and also in the individual lives that manage it. How difficult it is to point that out, because we must first get past the wall of personal defensiveness before we can take on the systemic defensiveness.

The United Methodist Church was modeled after the United States government, and many call it the most "American" church. We have three branches of government, directly modeled after the executive, legislative, and judiciary branches of the US government. In order to change our church law, we must go through an extremely long process, as seen in the fight around human sexuality, which is almost as old as the denomination itself. The method of United Methodism was built with defensiveness in mind as seen in its checks and balances. The defenses have helped the UMC to propagate itself and not easily be torn down.

The United States was born with a rebellious spirit, and in many ways this has served us well. However, when we entrench ourselves in ideological bunkers and sounding chambers that prop up our own long-held beliefs, we become more self-righteous and defensive, hearing why our side is *right* and the other side is *wrong*. That good ole spirit of defensiveness is great when you are a persecuted minority, fighting against a behemoth imperial power. But when you are members of a well-endowed historic institution, complete with tall steeples and deep roots, this same spirit of rebellious defensiveness will produce the same results as did the tower of Babel.

We made our church in the image of our country, and in some ways the church remade our imagination in its likeness. Many times this is a gift, but when it comes to defensiveness, we all lose as we retreat further into our ideological bunkers. Our system of church was designed around many eighteenth-century understandings of human society, but it is breaking down in the twenty-first century and what will be left afterward may be a population so small that any posture of defensiveness is simply nonsensical. The church of the future may look across the center sanctuary aisle and find it empty, as if to say to ourselves, "There's nobody from whom to defend ourselves."

The United Methodist Church has just gone through a schism in which many people disaffiliated and created a new denomination under the pretense of disagreement about human sexuality. Indeed, in this moment, the church is finding that there are not many people on the inside left to fight against. I do not want to merely disagree with people, and, like most faith leaders, I am weary of conflict. As I'll mention later, one possible way to shift our method of communicating is to grow toward "calling in" instead of "calling out."

And at the same time, our church institution needs to change. In *Who Will Be a Witness?* Drew Hart reminds us how allergic institutions are to change.[2] The Bible is always against the imperial forces of the world that concentrate power and wealth in the hands of a few while systematically exploiting people who are marginalized. In an examination of the Gospel according to Mark, Hart talks about the event that catalyzed the religious establishment and made them want to kill Jesus. It was when he went to the beating heart and confronted the way that money intravenously flowed through the temple. The money changers would profit from people coming

---

2. Hart, *Who Will Be a Witness?*, chap. 2.

to worship God, even as the religious establishment would. As soon as Jesus threatens the system, it lashes out at him through its strongest members.

Social institutions are not alive, like humans are, but they do have feelings, and when they are hurt, they lash out at whatever causes the threat, like a robot whose defense system has been activated. Social institutions think they will live forever, and when they are caused to rethink their priorities, they may have an allergic reaction to whatever body has caused them to be upset. Pioneers of social transformation, like the Old Testament prophets advocating for systemic repentance, often bear the brunt of pain associated with initial changes. Yet there remains hope that the church, along with other institutions, will eventually embrace necessary changes. My former mentor Pastor Marty used to say about people and the church, that it will continue to do the same thing until the pain of staying the same is greater than the pain of change.

As you read about other things that caused death and other places where the church experiences death, imagine and reflect on what your job might be.

The Death of Legalism and Cancel Culture

As challenging as it is to be in the pastoral profession, some other professions have their own version of deep challenges and stress. A doctor in my extended family, who never committed malpractice, left the field because malpractice insurance skyrocketed in cost over the years. I have spoken with lawyer friends, both in church and the community in which I live, and they have told me how complex certain laws are becoming, especially when certain precedents are set. Across the board, professionals are living in more complex situations, responsible for more, with the consequences being even greater.

Yet this complexity, in many respects, facilitates a fairer society. Often, the intricacies within professional jobs come from the struggles of marginalized groups pushing for recognition and fundamental rights in a society dominated by the privileged. The surge of lawsuits in the medical field and the proliferation of advertisements by vengeful attorneys are just the extreme manifestations of a cultural shift that is enabling victims to pursue justice.

The same is true in the church. A couple of years into my pastoral ministry, every pastor under appointment was required to undergo online sexual ethics training. To my horror, I learned that as many as 10 percent of adult women in the church, at some point in their lives, have been the victims of inappropriate sexual comments or conduct by their male pastors. These wounds do not heal until they demand justice.

Living and serving at a time when the church is being reformed is a tremendous joy, but with it comes a tremendous burden. Many of the historic failures of pastors are coming to be common knowledge, and with this is a profound sensitivity among the rest of us. We understand the value of vulnerability, and we want to, as the apostle Paul says, "boast all the more gladly of [our] weaknesses, so that the power of Christ may dwell in [us]" (2 Cor 12:19 NRSV). And yet we realize that our weakness and failure could have us recategorized as pariah and anathema.

Add to this the proliferation of what many call "cancel culture." When it was first introduced to me in 2020, I did not know what the term meant, but when it was explained, it deeply resonated with much of my social frustrations. Cancel culture was described to me as the phenomenon that makes us want to disconnect from anybody who crosses one of our nonnegotiable ideological lines.

For example, if my nonnegotiable is racism, then when somebody starts acting out what Robin DiAngelo, in her book *White Fragility*, calls "colorblind racism,"[3] I will end up rejecting them. After the deaths of George Floyd, Breonna Taylor, and Ahmaud Arbery, I saw cancel culture run rampant on Facebook as I read post after post of people celebrating how many people they had evicted from their list of friends, culling and cleaning. Even while I realize this can be an important and necessary self-protection mechanism, especially for people of color who have trauma and PTSD from racism, I also realize it further disconnects us from people who can either learn from us, or, heaven forbid, from whom we can learn something.

The Death of Church Cancel Culture

The church created a cancel culture—not the version in the headlines but a different version. The way it works in today's culture is to cancel out powerful people who have abused that power. But in many ways, the church has practiced canceling out people who stood beyond its exclusive claims. I partially appreciate this, because it preserved so much of the beauty of truth that I hold dear. But, also, the church has oftentimes canceled out weaker and fringed voices.

I have heard church people railing against cancel culture for lacking grace, and in some ways I appreciate the critique. In *The Persuaders*, Anand Giridharadas makes the argument that we should move from a "call out"

---

3. DiAngelo, *White Fragility*, chap. 3.

culture to a "call in" culture, inviting people toward amends, to find common ground.[4] I appreciate that as a corrective to cancel culture.

Church cancel culture operates differently from its pop culture counterpart, primarily due to our historical tendency to sidestep conflict. The key distinction, as I see it, lies in the approach: Church communities tend to echo the behavior of Joseph, Jesus Christ's stepfather, who upon discovering Mary's pregnancy, sought a discreet divorce under the cover of darkness, and probably accompanied by a well-meaning "bless your heart." Our efforts to appear kind often extend to our decisions of disconnection. Sometimes our conflict avoidance is so profound that we'd rather weather a schism, effectively canceling half the church, than confront our differences head-on.

In my ten years and four rural church appointments as a United Methodist pastor, I have often made mistakes and angered people. By nature, I am extremely conflict-averse, and I engage in conflict because it is the only way to survive. The world is in chaos, and ignoring this fact is a good way to end up in an early grave.

Through the necessary moments of conflict, usually talking about some form of a needed change, I have seen a pattern repeat itself. The person in conflict just disappears. The work of ministry is enough to keep me grounded and in the present moment, and so I rarely notice. I wish I did, but I don't. When in conflict, people often just ghost, canceling out the one with whom they are conflicted. It is like the selfish, safe version of what Central American Christians have experienced when members of the church were "disappeared" by death squads. Except instead of armed executioners taking people away to be killed because they challenged the status quo, they took themselves away to protect their emotions—because they wanted to live the status quo.[5]

At its best, what happens is that someone will come to me and say some version of the same thing: "Hey, have you talked with John Doe recently? I have not seen him in some time." If somebody is really loving or has a good relationship with me, they will say something like, "I heard that John Doe was upset with you and ended up leaving and going to the Southern Baptist Church some time ago."

Let me share a specific experience. In my first year serving in Murfreesboro, I began helping a local nonprofit organization called the Cultivator at their English as Second Language (ESL) class. In this experience, I met so many beautiful people, most of whom were Mexicans working at a local

---

4. Giridharadas, *Persuaders*, chap. 6.

5. Just search the internet for the term "*desaparecidos*" and read up about this phenomenon in Latin America if you are not familiar with it.

hog farm through a multiyear "TN" visa. One such family, of Alejandra and Paco, began attending our local church. Whenever they would show up in worship, I would at least offer a prayer in Spanish or do my best to interpret the "prayers of the people."

Within this same year of 2017, the US began a policy at its southern border to separate families who crossed together, many of them wanting to legally seek asylum or refugee status. I started praying about this in church. Four different families ended up leaving the church, and one of the ringleaders, a reverend doctor and retired Anglican priest, wrote me a letter explaining that I had on four occasions, whether in Sunday prayers or the newsletter, mentioned the immigrants, and because I had brought in partisan politics, these families left.

This type of cancel culture makes one walk on eggshells, always afraid that others are going to leave. The fragility reminds me of the plantation economy—that, racially speaking, certain lines were never to be transgressed. And if those lines were transgressed, the retribution would be swift and without warning, costing relationships. The difference between then and now is that now we do not have a violent warden to enforce the rules. People just leave as enforcement.

Coming through multiple pandemics in these subsequent years has not helped our ability to relate to each other. COVID-19 is not the only one. Racial disparity, economic disaster, and global ecological meltdown are pandemics that separate us from one another and cause us to operate with a sense of scarcity.

This is similar to what I mentioned in chapter 2, talking about dislocation. As we hope to end this attitude, I invite us back to the love ethic. May we remember the words of Jesus Christ who called us to "Love our enemies." As the biblical Epistle 1 John says, "Those who say, 'I love God,' and hate their brothers or sisters, are liars; for those who do not love a brother or sister whom they have seen, cannot love God whom they have not seen" (1 John 4:20 NRSV). And I would add, How can we love even our enemies unless we are in relationship with them? Before you proceed, pray for an ideological enemy close enough to contact, close enough to try to love.

The Death of Perfectionism

Let us begin this conversation using the early modern language of the early Methodists, a linguistic lineage that persists in the ordination process. Among the questions posed to pastors during ordination are these: Are you going on to perfection? Do you expect to be made perfect in love in this life? The expected answer is "yes," a response that often sets our twenty-first-century nerves on edge, cultivating more anxiety than grace, more graveness than wholeness.[6]

Young and new clergy, who cannot assume authority as swiftly as their older, more established counterparts, often find themselves under the heavier hand of the "Discipline." In public, we hear the language of "blamelessness," while in private, we are subtly taught that we must be at fault if we're unable to achieve this so-called perfection. We're bound to eighteenth-century words that beget shame when perfection remains elusive, creating a space for perfectionists to unknowingly burden others with shame. "Going on to perfection" becomes "Going on to Perfectionism."

When conflict arises within the church, it is often hushed, concealed under the weight of this perfectionism. A sincere pursuit of "truth and reconciliation" would necessitate wrestling with our perspectives on blamelessness and perfection. For instance, during the annual conference, district superintendents declare in the closed clergy session that all pastors are blameless in their work and administration. If we could candidly address the conflicts we encounter, it would engender a deeper respect for pastors, humanizing them and removing them from idolatrous pedestals, thus fostering a stronger connection with laity. It seems that the original intention of using the language of blamelessness and perfection was to help the church confront conflicts, not suppress them.

This imposed perfectionism presents a substantial hurdle for young people striving for change. The mission statement of the North Carolina Conference of the United Methodist Church (where my membership resides) is, "Healthy Congregations and Effective Leaders in Every Place Making Disciples of Jesus Christ for the Transformation of the World."[7] Whenever I have challenged leadership or methods of the church, the perfectionistic impulse is to ask, "Can you do it better?"

It puts immense pressure on would-be revolutionaries to articulate a better way. My former mentor Marty, God rest his soul, said to me, "Do not tear down what you are not willing to help rebuild." I appreciate that. However, we do not need to have an answer for everything. We can voice our thoughts on issues we are familiar with, and it's acceptable to remain silent on others. To refer to Esth 4:14, I believe many young people have been chosen "for such a time as this." Like Esther, we are voices of challenge

---

6. It was not until 2023 that I heard a bishop give needed commentary to this, saying that we don't expect to never sin again; that it is an expectation of coming to the place where we are so obedient to God that our desires are perfectly wanting to be faithful. Like being on a mountaintop, it is not a permanent state.

7. North Carolina Conference of the UMC, "Vision Statement."

and uplift in our faith community. If she had chosen to remain silent, the consequences would have been dire. The same is true for faith leaders confronting perfectionism with imperfect ideas.

Our denomination and its constituents strive to achieve perfection of obedience to God, embodying a blend of "sinner and saint," as Martin Luther put it. We can observe a graceful balance between tradition and innovation across various general commissions and agencies, conference committees, offices, and boards. However, if we continue to succumb to our perfectionist tendencies, we risk burning out young, energetic individuals by placing them in contexts that are too demanding.

How can we address this issue? We need to explore how the early modern language of Methodism can be reframed into modern language that dignifies our experiences, recognizing the harsh reality that perfectionism is a threat to the well-being of young clergy. For instance, the question "Do you expect to be made perfect in this life?" was originally intended to kindle hope for entire sanctification, a state where we are wholly healed and capable of following Jesus. John Wesley equated Christian perfection with holiness and a perfect desire to love.

This question can become an impediment rather than an invitation. A possible revision could be to replace "expect" with "expectantly hope" and "be made perfect in this life" with "have a perfect desire to live love." Even as I read my suggestion, I realize that we in the church usually change certain words in our source text for our own comfort. The result is something wordy that we insiders appreciate, but which is hard to fathom for a newcomer who has not seen the revision history.

In Matt 19, Jesus said to a rich young ruler that if he wanted to be perfect, he needed to sell everything he had and give the money to the poor, and then he could follow Jesus. In this logic, I think that if we want to be perfected in love, we could at least start to let go of some of the things that make us so comfortable, in order to follow Jesus. Comfort is our next category for conversation.

The Death of Comfort

For a life oriented to leisure is in the end a life oriented to death—the greatest leisure of all.

—Kenneth Lamott, as quoted by Anne Lamott in *Bird by Bird*

In this final section of attitudes that need to die, I talk about comfort, first from the church perspective and then I will relay a personal story before sharing one more thought about comfort in the church.

As I learned long ago, we can distinguish between the social institution of the church and the mystical body of Christ, that great cloud of witnesses which will continue into eternity. Even within the United Methodist Church, despite the discussions of death within our method of church, I can identify numerous locations where life is thriving, like a cilantro plant in July. To some, my words may seem outrageous. How can I talk about death when so many have worked tirelessly to make room for the new life that God is bringing?

Before I discuss where I see this in the wider church, let me present both sides of the paradox from my own life. On one hand, I have been a pastor to several local congregations or in a director role within our regional conference. On the other hand, I am a minister, carrying the same calling as every baptized member of the church.

As a pastor, I have always grappled with discomfort. Being a multiracial Latino man with white-passing privilege, my upbringing in a charismatic, non-denominational church, and my formative years in college influenced by Southern Black worship traditions have all created a beautiful contrast—sometimes even conflict—with my United Methodist identity.

My discomfort stems not only from being a "messy, mestizo, mosaic," as I refer to myself in my blog, but also from the vast complexity of being a pastor. I will delve deeper into this topic in a subsequent section on mission, but suffice it to say that leadership in United Methodism does not fail due to a lack of options. Rather, we are often paralyzed by the abundance of them.

Throughout eastern North Carolina, where I serve, I have witnessed examples of clergy and laity coming together with clear ideas of mission and being the church. However, I've also seen many contrary examples, leading me to believe that a disconnect between clergy and laity is endemic to the US church experience.

Pastors often have strong ideas on leading the church, usually favoring what they are most comfortable with. Growing alongside these pastoral ideas is a crop of notions from the congregation. With time, these two can cross-pollinate, but this process is slow. It was after research suggested that a pastor's most productive years were half a decade into an appointment that the United Methodist Church ended the centuries-long practice of moving pastors every four years. This change is to our credit as a church, but the struggle of bridging an increasingly diverse pool of pastors and congregations persists.

In my first two appointments, I often heard an adage from the laity, which resonates with the experiences of other young and new clergy: "You are really good; you won't be here long." This sentiment fosters disconnect between clergy and laity, increasing the likelihood that each will operate within their comfort zones. The fields of thought are planted parallel to each other, but they rarely intersect, or so it is assumed.

From a clergy perspective, it is easy to say, "We clergy live in a state of discomfort, while the laity strive for comfort." It's easy to become defensive about the uncomfortable space between us right now. But the truth is almost everyone within the United Methodist fold has lived in relative comfort compared to our neighbors. When I entered pastoral ministry, I realized that the total annual investment in my life—including travel allowance, continuing education, housing, utilities, pension, health insurance, and salary—was about twice as much as the salary of an average full-time pastor in North Carolina where I reside. It appears that the discomfort we are experiencing as a church merely invites us to taste a reality that a majority of our neighbors have long been familiar with.

We can identify numerous realities that make it difficult for us, as different members and ministers of the church, to empathize with each other's discomfort. But first, let's acknowledge that our Service of Death and Resurrection invariably moves us all toward discomfort. It may be more challenging for the affluent to embrace this, and so we should listen all the more to those who have been forced to live in discomfort for an extended period. My own testimony of moving out of my comfort zone involved doing just that.

My Own Experience of Discomfort

In the year 2017, I found myself being reborn as a Latino. When Ismael Ruiz-Millan, my conference's first-ever Latino district superintendent, declared me to be "*un orgullo de la comunidad Hispano/Latino*"—"a pride of the Hispanic/Latino community"—I was deeply moved. I was then invited to join the Hispanic/Latino committee for our conference, a door-opening opportunity that led me to head the immigration ministry task force in 2017 during a period when the immigrant community was under severe distress. This, in turn, allowed me to also join the refugee and immigration committee.

In retrospect, I discern how God was gently nurturing me, akin to a fetus in its mother's womb, enveloped in love and nourishment, fed almost intravenously to my soul. One day, I found myself reborn into this community, inwardly crying out like a newborn, stumbling with Spanish, and leaning on the hospitality and nurture of others to teach me how to savor the mother's milk of the many nationalities condensed into the term "Hispanic/Latinx."

While growing in my identity, I was serving two predominantly white churches, which extended their hospitality and welcome to our Spanish-speaking neighbors, many of whom were Mexican nationals here on temporary work visas. We launched an ESL class, which led to diverse families attending worship. We secured grant money for monthly translation services on Sunday mornings, hired one of the ladies as a part-time lay minister, and began hosting monthly bilingual dinners—then the pandemic struck.

As we adjusted to the new normal, we collaborated with more partners to initiate food distributions within the local Spanish-speaking migrant and immigrant communities. Around the same time, I was challenged by Alejandra, Murfreesboro UMC's first Spanish-speaking member, to start a worship service in Spanish. Later, in the chapter on Holy Saturday, I will explain more about this story. Suffice it to say, she and the Holy Spirit were convincing. So, despite my limited Spanish, I dove into the deep waters of initiating a worship service in a language I barely spoke.

I share this account within the context of a section on comfort to assert this: It is only by stepping out of our comfort zones, venturing into territories where we feel ill-equipped, that we truly come to rely on the movement of the Holy Spirit.

We embarked on these ministries because God opened the doors of relationship, because they were needed, and because we were willing. We did not possess the necessary resources, financial or experiential. Thus, we began learning from others who had made ministries work despite scarce resources. Other United Methodist pastors serving Hispanic Latino congregations across Central and South America showed me ways to minister without the resources we typically think we need.

For me, entering the realm of Hispanic Latino ministry was akin to a rebirth. After spending twenty of my thirty-five years preaching to the United Methodist Church, it bestowed upon me the invaluable gift of a beginner's mind. Familiarity can make us overestimate our competence. Continuing to follow the mission of Jesus Christ to go to the margins—outside of our comfort zones to the people who have been canceled by the powerful, those who have been abused by legalism and selfishness. In so doing, we will learn to love justice and walk humbly with our God.

Disaster Insurance and the Quest for Comfort

On January 1, 2018, I watched a series of videos on Facebook that chronicled an unthinkable event for one church congregation. The Rose Hill United Methodist Church building was on fire. As the warmth of the sun began to rise over the horizon, a destructive heat was simultaneously building within the church's electrical system—a speculation the authorities would later confirm.

At the moment of disaster, a virtual community gathered to witness the unfolding tragedy, most locals being primarily connected online via Facebook. The *Duplin Times*, a local newspaper servicing Rose Hill and several other small towns, swiftly captured the architectural carnage in a few pictures, posting them under the caption "CHURCH FIRE—A fire destroyed much of Rose Hill United Methodist Church this morning. More information as we get it."[8]

Across the Facebook universe, the depth of unspeakable pain was evident as people chose to share the words of others when they found themselves unable to express their grief. On that morning, there were few posts written by members of the RHUMC congregation, but many shared the newspaper's post, later adding their own heartfelt words—reminiscences of baptisms, weddings, and departed saints who were primarily remembered through the building itself.

Five years earlier, within that same building, I had squatted at the front of the sanctuary, clad in my black, flowing Geneva gown as the pastor of that congregation. With my hands, I had crudely mimicked the structure of the church as I recited the familiar nursery rhyme during the children's moment, "Here is the church, here is the steeple; open the doors, see all the people." I then explained to the children that while we refer to the building as "the church," it is actually the congregation that constitutes the church.

During my brief tenure as their pastor, my first appointment out of divinity school, I often lamented after trustee meetings, pleading to God, "Why can't we just get rid of these buildings? They consume so much energy and hinder us from doing your work!" This heartfelt prayer, which had echoed in every church building I'd served, surfaced in my mind as I watched the blaze. "This is going to be a profound pain and a profound opportunity for them all," I pondered, foreseeing the potential and the ensuing discussions.

In the ensuing couple of years, they engaged in heated discussions followed by a legal battle with a large mutual insurance company that caters to

---

8. *Duplin Times*, "CHURCH FIRE."

churches. The company was reluctant to pay unless the building was reconstructed exactly as it was before the fire. I recognized this as an institutional tendency. Much like humans, systems crave to restore things to their former state.

While serving as a pastor in Murfreesboro, I had a similar experience when hail damaged our roofs in May of 2019. After years of battling with the same insurance company, we finally reached a settlement, albeit with a clause that prevented me from discussing the case details. However, suffice it to say, I have witnessed in many ways our instinctual desire to revert to a prior state of comfort.

This brings to mind similar occurrences on a governmental scale in the US such as corporate bailouts from the CARES Act and, earlier, the motor company bailouts. The powerful often receive some sort of bailout, shielding them from the harsh reality that everything, even the comfortable way we wish to live our lives, has a lifespan.

As far as the church is concerned, I pray that we can bear the pain of death and the discomfort of doing things differently, of involving new people, rather than exploiting our power to extract resources from elsewhere, just to maintain our comfort.

Superstructures, in a sense, will always fight tooth and nail to preserve themselves. This is why we need prophets. Are you willing to endure the discomfort, an experience that feels like death to many, so we can step out of our comfort zone and see what God has planned next? Or are you content to remain on life support?

For a significant part of my life, I was ensnared in my own comfort zone. In some places—my house, my screens, my car—I still am. But I am gradually finding comfort in discomfort, and I am becoming more at ease with the knowledge that speaking honestly can unsettle others. As the old church saying goes, "Jesus came to comfort the afflicted and afflict the comfortable." My sense of anticipation and excitement now outweighs my sense of dread and anxiety. Unfortunately, for many others, it's the reverse. As a result, many who are entrenched in their comfort zones might struggle to grasp what I am discussing without substantial effort and pain.

I encourage you to experience the taste of suffering and discomfort. One of my mentors, Mari Wiles, was reimagining the concept of the short-term mission trip years before it became a trend across the US. When I was in college, she taught us that it's not about the mission we envision. Instead we are the mission, and it's akin to a pilgrimage. We step out of our comfort zone expecting to discover that the Holy Spirit has already been active there and that this Divine presence will transform us in a potent way.

In this quest, we must understand that discomfort isn't a mere inconvenience; it's an opportunity for growth and transformation. Embrace it, not just for our individual spiritual journeys but also for the growth of our church.

6.

Prophetic Whispers
Embracing Mystical Visions

Among the ruins of another ignored sermon,
A prophet stands, voice like a somber violin,
In the little wooden church building of my memory.

My hands are two birds, trying to fly in prayer,
Lifting toward Mother God, who holds me
Like a hen hugs her chicks.
And yet I am a ship alone in the chaos,
Adrift on the waves of tomorrow's hopes.

In the sanctuary, I speak of death
In order to call for resurrection,
my words stinging like salty sea made of tears.
In the wounds of a church world, sewn shut in silence,
I speak of change, an echo in the wilderness,
A hailstorm against fortresses of comfort,
Inside which people say,
"How sweet sounds precipitation on tin!"

In the stillness, I kneel and listen and speak
My heart a burning bush in the desert of despair,

Barefoot on the sacred ground of "I'm with you,"
A seer and seeker, listening and speaking,
Of the ending and the becoming.

The "Prophetic" in My Eyes

When I was growing up, the word *prophetic* meant an accurate description and prediction of what was going to happen in the future. As a good evangelical family in Colorado Springs, we grew up with *The Left Behind* book series in the 1990s. I'm sure that in the previous decade my church enjoyed Hal Lindsey's *The Late Great Planet Earth* and Edgar Whisenant's *88 Reasons Why the Rapture Will Be in 1988*. But as I grew older, I came to see prophecy as something different.

As an undergraduate student in Chowan University's religion department, I learned from Dr. Brabban, in a class called Apocalypticism, about the church's historic fixation with the future. He said several times, "The way to discern whether or not a futuristic prophecy is going to happen is just to wait."

After graduating from Chowan, I went to Duke Divinity School in 2010 and many of my classmates and professors taught me a new way of thinking about prophecy. Multiple people told me that, "instead of foretelling, we should consider it as forth-telling." In other words, my definition changed from the prophetic being "the ability to accurately describe and predict what is going to happen in the future" to being "the ability to accurately describe what is going on in the present." Growing up in a "full gospel" type of Pentecostal church, this resonated with the "words of knowledge" or "words of wisdom" that I had heard spoken.

At the root of the prophetic is a mystical encounter with the Divine. As a divinity school student, I went with an undergraduate charismatic campus ministry to a prophetic conference in which they said that the basis for all Christian prophecy is these ingredients: "Stop. Look. Listen. Stop." Stop what you are doing. Look and listen for what the Spirit might be saying or showing. And then stop again to process how God might be directing you with these things.

As I have grown to think more about what the prophetic means, I have grown further away from wanting to label myself as prophetic. Old Testament prophets and even Jesus Christ spoke "truth to power." It usually put them in conflict with the powers, and the powers usually ended up winning in those conflicts. I see the challenge to be obedient to God in this way. The

Latin root of the word *obedience* is the verb *oboedire* which means "to listen to, pay attention to, or to obey." In order to obey God, one must first listen. The voices of those who listened to God's heart in order to speak echo loudly throughout history.

Dr. King once said, "We must speak with all the humility that is appropriate to our limited vision, but we must speak."[1] This was the prophet who, while he was still being threatened for speaking against white terrorist groups and Jim Crow segregation laws across the US, continued on to speak against the intersectional triplets of racism, militarism, and materialism.

I do not often want to speak up and challenge the church, but, when necessary, it becomes, as Jeremiah said, like a fire burning in my bones, unable to be contained. My body listens and must respond by obeying. Prophecy is tied up in visions and dreams, because the future toward which God calls us is both already and not yet a reality for us. Unlike "frameworks" that are so popular with organizations and institutions, visions may be hard to follow but they touch us in profound ways that change us. Sometimes we make visions clear and plain, as with the vision statements of companies and organizations. In this way, I am going to think about the prophetic in conversation about "generalists." And then, after some specific vision statements, I am going to share some visions that I have had.

All of my thoughts about visions of the prophetic are rooted in this Service of Death and Resurrection. My witness of death and life within these pages is one part of a much larger conversation. This book is a conversation both about and with the church, telling the church that its historic "method" has died. Institutions, like people, oftentimes do not like to admit to death, even when it is apparent.

The act of bearing witness to the things causing death and that have died in the church is a prophetic one. And we must together live into that conversation. The prophetic conversation usually exists at the margins of any institution, but if enough of us can share in the challenging conversations at the margins they move to the center. It is my hope that we as a whole church will continue to take ideas of liberation and God's justice and bring them closer to the center of who we are, even as certain sinful things which have displaced them die and are removed.

Keeping Ahead of the Flames

In David Epstein's book *Range: Why Generalists Triumph in a Specialized World*, he provides an insightful analysis of a tragic event involving

---

1. King, "Beyond Vietnam."

firefighters in Montana.[2] The Mann Gulch wildfire of 1949 led to the death of thirteen smokejumpers, elite firefighters who parachute into remote areas to combat wildfires.

The fire, initially considered manageable, rapidly grew out of control due to high winds, trapping the firefighters. The crew foreman, Wag Dodge, realized the imminent danger and took a counterintuitive action: he lit a fire in the grass in front of him, creating a safety zone or "escape fire." He tried to convince the others to drop their tools and join him in the already-burned area where the approaching wildfire wouldn't reach.

Unfortunately, the smokejumpers couldn't grasp Dodge's innovative solution in the heat of the moment and continued their attempt to outrun the fire while carrying their heavy tools. Epstein argues that the firefighters were so conditioned to their usual procedures and tools that they couldn't adapt to Dodge's unconventional strategy, even though it was their best chance of survival.

Epstein uses this tragic incident as a metaphor to underline the importance of adaptability and breadth of thinking. He suggests that an overreliance on routine and specialization can hinder our ability to see novel solutions and adapt in rapidly changing circumstances. In the broader context of his book, this story illustrates how generalists, who can adapt and think across traditional boundaries, often have an advantage over specialists who are deeply ingrained in their specific fields. Wag Dodge, who "dodged" the flames, is similar to those we call prophets in our Christian tradition.

Many in the church regard those who adopt a prophetic stance as individuals somehow more enlightened, closer to God. Setting aside the question of divine proximity, it is essential to understand that prophets are individuals who perceive an impending calamity and feel compelled to warn others. Let's take a moment to examine a few prophetic voices:

- In the Old Testament, we find major prophets such as Isaiah and Jeremiah who attempted to caution their people about impending crises. They sensed the oncoming disaster and dislocation and employed innovative strategies to communicate the imminent danger. Just as Wag Dodge's escape from the fire was a desperate, creative response to an unprecedented crisis, so too were the words of Isaiah and Jeremiah innovative warnings in times of dire circumstances, whether preaching or embodying their messages. They implored their people to abandon their metaphorical tools of routine and narrow thinking, urging them to embrace actions like uplifting the widow and orphan, working for God's justice, and practicing *shalom*.

2. See Epstein, *Range*, chap. 11.

- In the early days of the United States, prophetic voices like Sojourner Truth[3] emerged, challenging the societal norms of the time. Born into slavery as Isabella Baumfree, Truth became a passionate advocate for abolition, women's rights, and prison reform. Her iconic "Ain't I a Woman?" speech was a testament to her adaptability and wide-ranging understanding of the societal injustices of her time. Her prophetic life resonates with Epstein's central argument in *Range* about the value of generalists—having a broad perspective allowed her to become an influential voice for change across several social fronts.

- Similarly, Frederick Douglass[4] emerged from the inhumane conditions of chattel enslavement in the US to become a leading abolitionist, author, and speaker. His speeches and writings exposed the brutalities of slavery and made a compelling case for abolition, transcending his own personal experiences and drawing a broader picture of societal wrongs. His prophetic style embodies what Epstein calls the power of breadth over depth, in terms of having a wide-ranging perspective that can create meaningful change. The prophet is called to see both the forest and the trees.

- In contemporary times, voices like Rev. Dr. William J. Barber II[5] echo this prophetic call for broader thinking and action, rooted in the morality of the Bible and God's liberation. As a Protestant minister and social activist, Rev. Barber has become a leading voice for social justice in the United States today. His wide-ranging advocacy aligns with Epstein's theory, demonstrating that the ability to think across traditional boundaries and apply a broad perspective can lead to significant social progress.

- Sister Simone Campbell[6] offers us another witness of a prophetic stance. As a Roman Catholic nun, attorney, and poet, Sister Simone

---

3. National Park Service, "Sojourner Truth." "Ain't I a Woman?" was delivered in 1851 at the Women's Rights Convention in Akron, Ohio. In this speech, she challenged prevailing notions of racial and gender inferiority by sharing her personal experiences and questioning societal norms.

4. Douglass, *Narrative of the Life*. His first autobiography, published as *Narrative of the Life of Frederick Douglass, an American Slave* in 1845, garnered significant attention in its day and has been awe-inspiring to me each time I've read it.

5. You can learn more Rev. Barber in his book *The Third Reconstruction: How a Moral Movement Is Overcoming the Politics of Division and Fear* or by searching his name online in reference to the North Carolina NAACP or the Moral Monday movement.

6. NETWORK, "Sister Simone Campbell." Sister Simone is the executive director of NETWORK Lobby for Catholic Social Justice; she has been instrumental in promoting healthcare reform, immigration reform, and economic justice.

has shown a wide range of understanding and advocacy across healthcare reform, immigration reform, and economic justice. She stands as a testament to the power of broad thinking and adaptability in addressing and acting upon various societal injustices.

- Rev. Alexia Salvatierra,[7] a Lutheran pastor of Guatemalan heritage, is a prophetic presence who has been instrumental in faith-rooted organizing for justice, particularly within Latino communities. Her initiatives address immigration reform, poverty, and global peace, and she is committed in empowering and fostering faith-rooted organizing. Her broad understanding of the interconnectedness of various social issues and her ability to apply her knowledge and skills across different contexts show how a broad range of skills and connections helps in "*la lucha*." Rather than focusing on one specific area, Rev. Salvatierra has leveraged her range of experiences and knowledge to effect change across multiple fronts.[8]

I have been connected by text message chains, email threads, or Zoom meetings with Bishop Barber, Sister Simone, and Rev. Dr. Salvatierra. I have worshiped in person and online with them, sharing Bible study, prophetic lament and hope, and cries for repentance. I can see how they simultaneously encourage people to build deep relationships, a wide range of understanding, and calls to action.

Being a prophetic voice, at its core, means perceiving a coming or present crisis and urging people to abandon the burdens that could hinder their journey toward safety. This is for me embodied in testimony and witness. Most prophetic voices are simply individuals who have recognized the danger on the horizon and feel an overwhelming urge to guide others to safety. They are the ones holding out the torch, illuminating the path of resilience and survival, or in the case of Wag Dodge, the ones trying to prevent the torch from burning down everything we hold dear. They are the ones calling us all to leave our comfort zones and step into a new, more compassionate and equitable reality, because the comfort zone is becoming the death zone. I was thirty-one when I started this project, and as I type this I am thirty-five, about to age out of what is considered in my church "young clergy." And so, in this next space, I am issuing an invitation and call to young people in the church, especially young clergy.

---

7. You can find more about Dr. Salvatierra's work on her personal website: http://www.alexiasalvatierra.com/media.html.

8. See Salvatierra and Heltzel, *Faith-Rooted Organizing*; Salvatierra and Wrencher, *Buried Seeds*.

An Invitation to Young Leaders

James Baldwin, in his powerful epistolary essay "The Fire Next Time" writes to his nephew James, "I'm not at all sure . . . that I want to be integrated into a burning house."[9] I feel likewise as so many other young clergy do intuitively, like I have been ordained to climb a corporate ladder that is on fire. If brought into the proverbial house of grace that John Wesley talked about, I think, as though I can't even get through the front door, that this house also is on fire. We have been, in one way or another, talking about this fire for a long time. Like Wag Dodge, we are trying to get people to drop what encumbers them and leave the fire.

The year that I was licensed as a pastor, having just graduated from divinity school, in 2013, I remember hearing Lovette Weems talk about the forthcoming "death tsunami" in the United Methodist Church. Ten years ago, he talked about how the average worshiper was in their seventies, with the average member being in their sixties. The average person is knocking on death's doorstep, and, with them, so much of our way of life—whether we like it or not.

In response to this, here's a statement and a question: We must recognize the death; now what?

Many of us recognize that this country in which we live is in free fall. The various groups with whom we have aligned ourselves cast the blame from one to another, and, on some level, we probably cannot help but be caught up in this zeitgeist. And yet if we look beyond the issues that make us think we are more different than we really are, we see troubles that affect us as humans. There is a reason why everything Jesus said went back to *love God and love people.* There's a reason why John Wesley's words begin and end with *grace.*

Behind all the layers of complexity we think exist, it's a simple thing to love the person next to us. We think we cannot love them without loving the systems to which they are wedded. But our task right now is to name how many of those systems are defunct and dying precisely so that we can come to a place of new life.

There's a reason why the prophets were disempowered young folk. The people with the biggest and best pedigrees and the well-seasoned warriors had too much to lose to speak *truth to power.* I'm reminded of the words Paul spoke to his little band at Corinth saying, "Consider your own call, brothers and sisters: not many of you were wise by human standards, not many were powerful, not many were of noble birth" (1 Cor 1:26 NRSV).

---

9. Baldwin, "Fire Next Time," 273.

Likewise, most of the prophets were unknown and many would have been known as laity to our professionalized understandings of church.

Many of us have more clout and positions of authority than the biblical prophets would have; relatively, we are empowered. We see at the beginning of Jeremiah's call story that he was young. Likewise, we assume that Isaiah was young when he realized, "I am a person of unclean lips, living among people of unclean lips" (see Isa 6:5). Mother Mary was more than a child, just barely, when she proclaimed the world-shaking words of the Magnificat, "[God] has brought down the powerful from their thrones, and lifted up the lowly" (Luke 1:52 NRSV). I believe that we young clergy have been created for such a time as this. We intuitively know that the world around us is crumbling, but we also know that we serve one who speaks of a *"new heaven and new earth"* at the end, as a completion to all things. We know that the world around us is dying, and even the world underneath us groans. In some ways, yes, these are birth pains, but we also believe that resurrection comes from death.

We are not people who have caused the death, although some people who have chosen to remain asleep to the death will accuse us when we speak openly about it. But speak openly we must, because our very future depends upon it. I ask you to join me in a service not too dissimilar from our funeral service. I ask you to join me in a service in which we realize that our service to God and neighbor at this time *is* a Service of Death and Resurrection.

May we remain servants of the Lord but also may we do so as servants of death and resurrection, people who speak powerfully, truthfully, telling forth about how the church should live in this moment. I invite you to join me on a journey in which we name what is dead and dream about what may yet come. The ways we can think about telling this story are myriad. When we reflect on the vast corpus of lamentation, angry prayers, and calls for divine intervention present throughout the Bible, we find good company, even if it is company that was not included in the Revised Common Lectionary. May we speak about what is dead in order to be enlivened. As we do so, let us be reminded that it was those who were present with Jesus at his crucifixion, who weathered Good Friday and Holy Saturday, who were first at the empty tomb. Amen.

A Dream About Church and Bondage

I awoke from a dream about bondage and the church.

On the one hand, I saw the oppression of a young Latina lady with a couple children, someone I knew in real life. Her children were the same age as mine. *What must my subconscious have been assuming about her from this image of her being oppressed?*

In the dream, she was running to the church, looking for the sanctuary. It felt like Sanctuary in the political sense, like she was running to a place of refuge. I saw a glimpse into the pain she must have felt to leave abuse, whether from a person or a country or otherwise. The sides of her mouth were turned down as she heaved deep breaths, like the tears and air were fighting for space in her nose and throat as she bellowed and ran, hanging on to her young children.

My surroundings reminded me of medieval basilicas I'd been in, and I was a priest. The bishop told me that I could not house her in the church, because of all the artifacts that she might steal. I looked around the sanctuary and saw stained glass and silver. Calm and cozy cushions, each with the name of a saint, but none of them in Spanish or with her name.

I was one priest of a few in that space, but none of the other priests listened to her cries either. Her words pled through the audible cracks that come with exhausted vocal chords, as if the words themselves were trying to find a frequency that could break through the walls of our charity. All of the priests listened to the sound of the church, like a cruise ship saying, "I do not have room for anyone else." I ran to the wall and ripped the artifacts off, tearing them to pieces as much as I could. Then I ran into the sanctuary where parishioners had started to arrive, waiting for another priest to start service. And I threw the pieces on the ground, yelling at the top of my lungs, "I WOULD RATHER BE DEAD THAN SERVE A CHURCH THAT CHOOSES ARTIFACTS OVER PEOPLE!" And I looked through the open door that this woman was running to. And she was nowhere to be seen, devoured by the chaos of the world around the church. Like the steward of the bread running on a treadmill to feed people dying of starvation in the wilderness, I was exhausted, moving nowhere, and I was too late.

I was driven into exile after that, both like Jesus being led by the Spirit into the wilderness for forty days and also like Legion being tormented by a thousand demons—both held by God's own hand and abused by the reality that I could not be the welcoming hands of Jesus to a woman who was sinking and reaching toward the place that called itself the House of God.

And that was the end of the dream.

Continuing Honestly as Servants of the Church

We live in a culture that likes its prophets dead. This idea was encapsulated in a sermon delivered by a classmate of mine at Duke Chapel during our time at Duke Divinity School. She was referring to the Rev. Dr. Martin Luther King Jr. who was widely detested by the white church during his lifetime. However, following his death, the very same people seemed eager to honor him by naming freeways after him, feigning alignment with his message, or at least pretending to have eventually come around. With our prophets gone, we can manipulate their voices, shaping their words to align with the outermost boundaries of our comfort zones without making any genuine systemic changes.

Once you perceive it, you'll understand the necessity of adaptation and flexibility. What is *it*? For us in the church, it is the impending crash. The so-called "death tsunami" has been a popular topic for quite some time, and I'm aware that I'm far from being its sole herald, yet at times it feels like I am. The influential voices in our society have subtly addressed our contemporary issues, but these discussions are often embedded within a larger narrative that perpetuates the status quo.

So how do we challenge the status quo? It links back to our earlier discussion on comfort. While I am currently in a good financial state and my family is well-fed, this won't always be the case. We must anticipate discomfort as we consider the possibility of being unsettled by the Holy Spirit.

Today's professional clergy bears resemblance to the Levites of ancient Israel. Others labored and harvested and then provided for the Levites allowing them to offer spiritual guidance, lead worship, and manage the temporal affairs of the temple. We've structured our lives in a similar way, but we need to prepare to shift toward the apostle Paul's model—working as a tentmaker and not relying on the congregations he served for financial support.

The primary issue is that many clergy have only been trained to be clergy, and we will likely struggle to maintain our livelihoods the way we're accustomed to rather than embracing a situation where we may not be able to uphold our current standard of living. This problem is already causing widespread pain.

I don't yearn for the reality of the church to change, but I sense the necessity to articulate that we'll soon enter a phase where ordained pastors will need to be at least bivocational. Most non-ordained pastors are already bivocational. Critics might accuse me of sabotaging the system by discussing its flaws. Part of me wonders if clinging to this illusion and investing all my energy into it could somehow revive its viability.

Still, countless metaphors inundate my mind signaling the impending end of this way of operating.

Observing our system is like inspecting your garden after the first frost, realizing that what were healthy plants only the day before now bear wilting leaves. The subsequent frost will kill a few plants; the next will wipe out the remainder. With only a week or two left in the harvesting season, it's clear that drastic changes, which should have been anticipated weeks or even months ago, are essential.

Our system resembles a woodpecker venturing into an urban jungle that was once its habitat. Buildings clad in faux wood paneling, as hollow as they appear, deceive the woodpecker into starvation as it pecks at numerous surfaces, finding not a single worm to satisfy its hunger.

Our instincts guide us to repeat the practices of countless generations. It's not that our instincts are flawed but our inability to recognize and adapt to the changing world around us that becomes our downfall.

There are days when after the Service of Word and Table (a tradition handed down from the Church of England and the Roman Catholic Church before them) I'm enveloped by despair. I feel like a lone polar bear drifting on a thinning ice sheet, a mile from land, having witnessed my loved ones disappear beneath the frigid water and wondering when my turn will come. We persist in our usual ways until, at last, the end is upon us. The world around us has altered, the atmosphere has warmed, and we failed to adapt in time.

A Humble Dream

At the dawn of the year 2022 I had a dream and a vision of myself as a leader in our annual conference, and I wrote about it in my journal. Perhaps it was because I had led the Youth Ministry Task Force for the conference. Maybe it was some other reason. When I awoke, I wrote in my journal about several things.

I said that I should not want to be liked. My fear is that I'll be misunderstood. Like, I don't want people to judge me without getting to know me. As I write this, Brené Brown's words come to mind quoting Teddy Roosevelt's "the man in the arena" speech about "daring greatly" and ignoring the critics in the cheap seats as we are the ones in the arena.[10] We shouldn't pay attention to people who are in the seats making criticism if they aren't with us contributing. If they are with us, their voices matter more.

I had a vision about wanting to be humble, and the more I want to be humble, the more people lift me up, and the more I want to not be lifted up, the harder it gets to be humble. I remember screaming and crying as a sixteen-year-old at a youth event when I was touched by the Holy Spirit, "I DON'T WANT TO BE GREAT!" I am feeling my desire to return to my

---

10. Brown, *Daring Greatly*, introduction.

Pentecostal roots. I need someone to guide me. I will always need someone to guide me. I want to chase a sustaining encounter with the Spirit—primary and not secondary. Like manna in the wilderness, the Bread and not the crumbs, where it is, not where it's been.

These words live in a chapter about the prophetic to name the struggle in my heart and mind. My heart longs to remain humble and unseen, and yet people need as many voices as possible urging them to "speak truth to power." During this wrestling, some wisdom from the Alcoholics Anonymous tradition has offered help. A drag queen in recovery, whose name evades me, talked about the folly of publicly naming themself as a member of the AA community.

Fans would come up to this queen who had given up their anonymity and say, "You have been such an inspiration to me for getting yourself sober!" And sometimes they had "fallen off the wagon" and relapsed, even while being praised for sobriety. When we get public notoriety for something we know is fragile, we run the risk of falling hard from a pedestal we never should have been on.

As a Christian, I would say any effort at being prophetic is an effort to follow the Word of God, the wisdom of God made known in Jesus Christ at work through the Holy Spirit in this world. If we create our own image or celebrity of what this looks like, it automatically undermines what we are supposed to be doing precisely because our task is always to point beyond ourselves. In that space, sometimes God speaks. I had this dream where I had a conversation with the Mothering Holy Spirit. I won't claim that it was a theophany, but it felt that way to me when I woke up. I'll let you listen to my words and you decide if there's anything that rings true for yourself.

An Encounter with the Holy, Mothering Spirit

I woke up from a dream where She was lamenting about the church continuing to divide for the wrong reason. "Homosexuality is so silly a thing to tear yourselves in half over," She said.

I said, "But it's not a sin, right?"

She responded—more like retorted, "Loving who you love is not a sin. And whatever you think that means, it doesn't mean y'all get to do whatever you want either! You are a chosen people, a royal priesthood."

"Is that where holiness comes from?" I asked.

"Holiness is in the pressing, the pursuing, the praying." As She said it, my heart felt like my middle school self, wanting to crawl inside her bosom for affection—the type primarily driven by first-time hormonal and animalistic need.

"I see," I could barely say.

"You're cute . . . I could say, 'That dog is smiling,' and you'd feel so accomplished, my child, noticing the same thing." And with that She laughed, but not a condescending laugh—one of invitation, the invitation to see and remain humble.

"What don't I see?" I asked, trying to find out what I needed to say, feeling insecure.

"Come here and close your eyes. Give me a hug," She said, opening her arms in embrace.

As I walked over, as we hugged and I closed my eyes, I saw the faces of the people on the other side of the church schism. I saw how much I loved them. I saw their yearning to follow the heart of God—the same feeling from a different direction that I'd gotten from the people whom I thought were now on my "side."

I cried.

"Y'all are sooo smart, aren't you—still wanting to look at what's in your neighbor's eye, when your own is itching too hard to see. But do not lose heart. Hasn't the next generation always been able to get a better vision for reconciliation about the things their parents accidentally 'rent asunder'?"

"But the church?! It's falling apart overnight," I protested, feeling like I needed to tell Her the obvious.

"Things are indeed falling apart." She looked me in the eyes. "These things do hurt me. But it's not what you think that hurts me. You guard and guide systems, the thing that protects the way you think you see the Divine—all you Masters of Divinity. It's the way you just stopped talking to each other and built fences around yourselves—that's what hurts the most. Not the building crumbling. With perspective, no structure is as beautiful as it's said to be . . . except maybe Notre Dame and this ancient brick church in Addis Ababa."

My confusion must have shown.

She responded to my facial expression.

"I was joking, maybe playing favorites a little. But as you know, no building of any human-made institution lasts forever. And in a thousand years, most of the buildings' names will be lost to human memory."

"Nothing lasts forever," I said, getting into my melancholy energy.

"This is what I like about you—how you can brood like a recluse spider, sitting and watching from the shadows and appreciating their ever-changing artistic rendering on the walls. But don't let your emotions make you forget what you have been told—that the gates of hell won't prevail against the church."

"Soooo," I started to ask, "don't get sad about the church schism?"

"I am sad about it," She said, as if not wanting to refute everything I was saying. "And I invite you to remember that the people from whom you are divorced are still a part of the same body. Sometimes I think the church is still learning to walk, like a toddler. Sometimes it's like a twelve-year-old, hating certain parts because they embarrass each other and can't work together. But the joke is on you—you're still going to heaven together."

"Is there anything I can do to feel a little bit of that here on earth?" I asked.

"It depends, always, on what kind of Passion you walk—not for its own sake. You know whose sake it's for. That's the thing about splits in the church. They start with the right Passion in mind and then devolve into the self-righteous worthiness contests they are trying not to be."

"So, how do we get away from that—the self-righteous thing?" I asked, but somehow said with hurting anger in my voice.

With a slight smile, a squinched-up nose, and squinted eyes that were looking into my soul, She said, "Maybe, my learned young lawyer, you should have asked instead, 'And who is my neighbor?'"

I sat with that question of "Who is my neighbor?" I remembered the sermon of Martin Luther King Jr., "On Being a Good Neighbor," about the parable of the good Samaritan. He talked about how the Samaritan had every reason to despise the Jewish man because of matters of ethnicity, but he saw the humanity of him and therefore helped him.[11] At the root of a prophetic response lives humility. For those who attend historically white churches, this means an ethic of ethnic/racial and cultural humility. In the next chapter I will focus heavily on this, but I will end this chapter with a conversation about paying attention to the reality of being a leader in a historically white church—that important quality of the prophetic.

The Master's House

That vision was steeped in the reality of the divisions in the church. In my experience, those divisions, in the United States, are profoundly connected with the idea of white supremacy. I've reflected on what Robert Jones

---

11. King, "On Being a Good Neighbor," 19.

defines as "White Christian America"[12] (a term that inherently raises questions: why "Christian America"?) and the implications of serving a church descended from this history, a church still grappling with the possibilities of true diversity. What does the future hold? Venturing into that territory can be a daunting task. As a turning point in this chapter on the prophetic and as a preparation for the next chapter, I will share some thoughts[13] about the nature of being prophetic and confronting whiteness.

There's a bitter irony to how contorted white theology, or, more precisely, evangelical theology, has become. When it gained power, it fostered an individualistic, relationship-centered, anti-structural perspective that encouraged people to connect with those already congruent to themselves. It rendered Christianity a domain of spiritual progress, where overt problems were thought to be confined to an individual's sinful heart. This perspective absolved Christians from the responsibility for the systems they inhabited. It lent them the illusion of power and offered a convenient tool for justifying enslavement and racial domination—an uncritical reading of the Bible. This interpretation also allowed them to ignore the call of Martin Luther King Jr.

In *White Too Long*, Robert Jones recounts how a young Jerry Falwell dismissed Martin Luther King Jr., criticizing his use of biblical prophets and insisting that the preacher's role wasn't political. Yet a decade after the assassination of Martin Luther King Jr., when Bob Jones University lost its tax-exempt status due to discriminatory practices, an incensed Jerry Falwell took a political turn helping to found the "Moral Majority" movement and Liberty University.[14]

Surveying both the historical and contemporary landscape of the United Methodist Church, despite its ongoing decline, I discern tremendous potential in our theological commitment to both personal and social holiness. This is at the core of what it means for us to live out the mission

---

12. See Jones, *End of White Christian America*.

13. In my thoughts, I've dwelt on how the "Lost Cause" theology has spawned unsanctioned, unofficial groups—bristling with firearms, intent on protecting their way of life. Trevor Noah astutely pointed out on *The Daily Show* years ago that when similar gatherings occur among non-white men, they are often branded as "gangs." Noah, *Daily Show*. These groups lack the firepower, the capacity for intimidation, and often live under far graver conditions than white militias. The frustrations voiced by these white militias seem trivial when juxtaposed with inner city gangs, groups navigating systemic poverty and police brutality, seeking support as their social fabric frays. The anger of the white militias appears rooted more in perceived threats, fear of what might happen. Paralyzed by their own fears they strike terror into others sharing videos of military-style training. Oh the irony that many white people cannot see the danger of white militias attempting a coup but get scared when they hear rumors of the Black Panthers organizing.

14. Jones, *White Too Long*, 103, Kindle.

of Jesus Christ in the world. Even as the toxins of white supremacy have interwoven themselves into our belief and practice, I hold steadfast to the notion that the seed of both individual and collective holiness, once sown, can yield a harvest sufficient to sustain us as one and many. However, the challenge lies in bridging that gap. Glancing at the local church libraries, once bustling hubs when Sunday school classes brimmed with students, I see a surplus of personal holiness literature.

I suspect this is the church's current understanding of its relationship with social holiness: the church aims to generate personal investment achieved through an emphasis on self and personal holiness. It operates on the premise that a certain percentage of converts equals financial contributions, and that increased funding fuels pastoral efforts nudging the institution toward a commitment to social holiness. When the church appears to be "doing the work," each member can feel connected, albeit nominally.

Consider this: if the church participated in the food bank (an act of social holiness rather than personal holiness) and if the funds gathered on Sunday mornings bolstered that ministry, each individual could claim association with it having fulfilled their duty. But how do we stir the apathetic souls who have withdrawn to their front porches, shielded by complacency, oblivious to the stumbling addict, their neighbor, on the street? How can we reestablish the vital connection between our individual actions and the wider world, the systems we inhabit? How can we nurture a deeper understanding of the ecology we're part of?

We often retreat from these questions into a desire for control—wanting, desiring to be masters of our fate. As a newcomer in many of the spaces where I serve, I often find myself sitting in someone else's chair, dwelling in someone else's space. It's not necessarily a specific person's presence that lingers but rather the evil essence of a master—a spirit fueled by insecurity and a desperate need for swift answers, a sense of certainty. I find myself in the master's house.

Poem: "The Master's House"

I'm living in the Master's House, playing second fiddle like the pastor's spouse, but not because of marriage but a miscarriage of justice that left just us non-white people begging for scraps, trying to mitigate the resource lack with maps, clamoring for resources like mice being the second one to the traps.

I'm serving in the Master's House, but serving sounds nice if you've got stability, like a white man with false humility. In the wake of the way it's always been, like a cascade, falls duplicity. I thought I could make it through with a false ethnicity, because whiteness has a gravity, whether you go fighting or willingly.

I'm struggling in the Master's House, because I see the so-called wall of diversity, and I'm appalled. The picture of the young, woman pastor before me, who broke the glass ceiling broke the trend of old white guys' pictures dominating like proof-texted "inerrant" scriptures, sitting like inherent fixtures—"open hearts and open minds." And now I'm the first non-white pastor here.

I'm complicit with the Master's House, because no matter how I want to escape the rabbit's snare, behind the pulpit is the Master's Chair, used for smashing what's labeled as vermin, not knowing you but controlling them to stay a virgin, preaching from the Implicit Biased Version, ignorant of its own perversion while proselytizing and preaching conversion. But they say, "Just preach a sermon." It's an impossible burden.

I'm encumbered in the Master's House, by a weight that I can't wait to cast off or cast out like Jesus speaking a verb and kicking demons to the curb. I've got the weight of bygone Evangelists of whiteness, leading from blindness, killing justice with politeness, feigning scriptural rightness, under the guise of Southern niceness.

I'm sick of the Master's House, because people in need come to me and think I'm the Master, because I represent it . . . I resent it. I am the pastor in over my head and I can't swim. It's a charity game rife with an unseen propensity to a dehumanizing obscenity. The disempowered, on her knees, becomes an actor and begs the pastor, treating him to his favorite flavor, so he'll share money and be the "savior."

I'm wheezing in the Master's House, because it's rotten and slowly what used to be holy has turned moldy and grody. But on the outside the Church house still looks like a plantation, and the descendants of the formerly enslaved don't know of its damnation, and I don't know how to take a breath to speak the translation.

I'm a steward of the Master's House, somehow given the task of giving it back to Jesus, who should have been the original master. But instead of a literal shattering, members want a digital remastering. We all see the death, and the future of resurrection is a Divine Call. I'm exhausted, and want to know: "Who's answering?"

In this master's house the challenge becomes how do we sow the seeds of both individual and collective holiness? How do we stimulate growth in the shadow of towering structures built during more prosperous times? The answers aren't straightforward but the journey is essential—journeying from the master's house of perceived control to the master's house of Christ, a space of inclusive love, humility, and service. It's a transition, a call for adaptation and growth.

The master's house is a metaphor, a symbol of power structures long-ingrained in our societies, and yet the Divine Master's house is an invitation: to reexamine our beliefs; to nurture the compassion of a masterful God that does not demand domination and destruction; to commit ourselves to a theology that celebrates both personal and social holiness, a theology ready to adapt and thrive amid diversity. That is the house I strive to inhabit, and that is the future I envision for the church.

Moving from Mastery to Uncertainty

Contemplating the church's ties to the plantation system, I find it increasingly challenging to use the term "master" within the context of faith. Growing up, I learned of Jesus Christ as our master, but as I've become aware of the term's other uses within the church's history it's been stripped of its magic. Instead of summoning mystical images, it now evokes concrete ones: white bodies exerting control over non-white bodies, all under the same religious roof.

Mastery, at its core, is about control, and religion has too often been entangled with a need for control, especially of bodies. For the church to endure this pattern needs disruption. Although older generations of Christians may comfortably continue thinking of Jesus as master, I believe that younger or more antiracist people can more clearly see why this language is challenging and complex.

Peeling back the layers, we can recognize that the quest for mastery runs deep within us.

Throughout my time in divinity school, first getting a master of divinity and my decade-long journey through the ordination process, I've observed many church leaders mentally crippled by the pursuit of mastery. A subtle message often emerges: "Jesus is the master. To serve him, we must master what we do, and do it excellently." While there's truth in striving for excellence, when paired with a history of dominance and the notion that those who aren't masters are inferior it breeds a damaging spirit.

How many "master lists" have we constructed, striving for comprehensiveness, only to end up depleted when we realize we've omitted something? Using the term *master*, even for our lists, prevents inclusivity and stifles our ability to acknowledge what's omitted.

Perhaps most daunting is the idea of the "master plan." Within Eurocentric spaces, like the church I serve, there's a prevalent trend: when we invest money, especially when we engage consultants and formulate plans for the future, we trick ourselves into believing we've achieved mastery over our situation. Five-year plans, anyone? These would not be bad ideas if the world was not shifting impossibly fast; we must admit that we are not masters of the situation. Being prophetic means being flexible and calling the church toward greater flexibility.

Fortunately, in the geographic area where I serve, fewer people are claiming mastery over their areas of study or work despite their knowledge having grown significantly over the past five years. The COVID-19 pandemic underscored how little we know when faced with unexpected challenges. The divisions we endure, including the schism within my own church, teach us mountains of lessons. I began this chapter discussing the value of broad-ranging experience in enhancing our honest, truthful stance as church leaders. I will conclude by suggesting that a piece of prophetic leadership cultivates a stance of uncertainty even as we live out our expertise.

A Posture for Seeing Death: Uncertainty Specialist

In light of this conversation about mastery and the role of the church, we might borrow a term from Dr. Sunita Puri, a palliative care physician: the *uncertainty specialist*. I first heard this phrase when Kate Bowler interviewed her on her *Everything Happens* podcast.[15] As in medicine, this phrase brilliantly encapsulates the role prophetic leadership should adopt within the church.

The prophetic leader, like Dr. Puri, should be an uncertainty specialist. They help the church, their communities, and even their colleagues grapple with the uncertainty of our faith journey. In the religious landscape, as in medicine, we often desire absolutes. Yet part of prophetic leadership is learning to navigate uncertainty. It's a prophetic posture that acknowledges the present state of affairs and calls the church toward the uncertain path in our Service of Death and Resurrection. Below I will name a few postures

---

15. Bowler, "Sunita Puri: The Uncertainty Specialist."

that Dr. Puri mentions,[16] as ways that we can grow in prophetic leadership in this moment:

- The Role of Silence: Silence holds immense power in conversations. I talked about the need to "stop, look, and listen." This way of encountering the Spirit's guidance occurs in silence. For more on the idea of silence, I highly recommend Erling Kagge's *Silence: In the Age of Noise*. I think this is where we start. Silence precedes communication, because it is a method of communication with God. Consider the Bible story of Elijah in 1 Kgs 19 hearing God in a whisper, or, perhaps, the sound of silence.

- Communication: A prophetic leader underscores the importance of clear, compassionate, and concise communication about the state of our church and what we aspire to for its future. This involves unlearning certain communication habits that no longer serve our communities effectively and adopting new ones that foster understanding and growth.

- Palliative Care: In the spiritual sense, the prophetic leader's role mirrors that of a palliative care doctor—to alleviate suffering, particularly for those facing advanced spiritual distress. This could be existential crisis, doubt, or the pain caused by disconnection caused by schism. I strongly argue that this is separate from devolving into being a chaplain for a dying institution. We must be, as Jesus said, "Wise as serpents and innocent as doves" (Matt 10:16 NRSV), knowing when to employ comfort to those who are dying and challenge to those who still have life to live.

- The Borderlands: Prophetic leadership involves working in the "borderlands" between life and death, faith and doubt, certainty and uncertainty. The prophetic leader is akin to a guide or Sherpa, helping communities navigate this challenging terrain. I recommend Gloria Anzaldúa's book *Borderlands/La Frontera*, which from a Queer Latina perspective talks about borders not only being physical but also cultural and related to identity, stating that we need to move past binary thinking and dualistic cultural limitations.

- Honesty and Gentleness: The prophetic leader must champion honesty when communicating with their communities about their present state and future visions. However, this needs to be balanced with

---

16. Bowler, "Sunita Puri: The Uncertainty Specialist." The transcript is available at https://katebowler.com/podcasts/the-uncertainty-specialist.

gentleness. The approach to conversation involves self-introduction, explanation of their role, assessment of the community's awareness of their situation, and discussion of their hopes and what's important to them in the context of their faith. As we seek to be honest in our personal work, I recommend the work of Archbishop Desmond Tutu (especially his work with his daughter Mpho in *The Book of Forgiving*) that talks in part about his healing journey with South Africa as part of the Truth and Reconciliation Commission after apartheid.

As uncertainty specialists, prophetic leaders aid the church in traversing the complex and often uncertain journey of faith. Their care extends beyond the spiritual to address emotional, communal, and existential distress. In this uncertain era, the church needs prophetic leaders who are not masters but guides—those who lead with the humility of knowing they do not control the journey but can provide comfort and clarity along the way. This is our call to prophetic leadership: a call to inhabit the master's house with the wisdom to know that mastery is not our true role but stewardship and service are.

Conclusion: Not Taking Things Personally, but Personally Communing

As we navigate this uncertain path, embracing our role as uncertainty specialists and prophetic leaders in the church, one invaluable lesson stands out: the importance of not taking things personally. I've arrived at this wisdom through a lengthy journey of repeatedly taking things personally and have recognized the profound influence it has on my ability to lead and serve effectively.

The structures we operate within often cultivate a culture of personalization. We are taught to internalize criticism and setbacks. This leads to an environment where hurt and disappointment can provoke retaliatory actions designed to soothe our egos, sometimes leading to toxic behaviors. It's an insidious pattern, one that's been historically prevalent in pastoral conduct, manifesting as defensiveness, arrogance, or even abuse of power.

There's profound wisdom to be gleaned from Don Miguel Ruiz's book *The Four Agreements*, particularly the agreement about not taking anything personally. When we understand and truly internalize that people's actions and words are often more about them and their struggles than about us, we begin to shed the chains of personalization. This is not about absolving ourselves of responsibility or ignoring constructive criticism but rather about maintaining a clear boundary between what we can control—our actions, reactions, and decisions—and what we cannot—others' opinions and behaviors.

One of the best practices for not taking things personally is in the sacrament of holy communion. Even while trying to speak challenging truths to the church, holy communion allows us to connect with each other in a way that says, "The ground is level at the feet of Jesus. All are invited to the table of God's grace to feast together." We are prevented from falling into self-righteousness when we come to the table to be treated as equals.

For the most part, the words of holy communion are historic and traditioned. Therefore, the people receiving communion may believe that they do not need to take personally anything that the one serving the meal has said or done. Likewise, the one serving can expect that God will do great things through the bringing together of people at the table, and they can simply accept God's grace poured out equally. It is an exchange in which people come to God together, in a physical way, and it is not *about* anyone. It is a free gift, a time to be reconciled. At the table, people are brought back together and able to refrain from taking other things personally that people have done. More broadly, in light of God's grace and gift, we may learn to say, "I can take God's grace personally, but the trifling comment of my brother can go on somewhere."

Embracing this perspective liberates us. It shields us from unnecessary hurt, enables clearer judgment, and allows us to navigate our roles with a calm objectivity that's integral to effective leadership. As prophetic leaders and uncertainty specialists, our resilience and wisdom will be measured not by how infallible we are but by our ability to learn, grow, and serve with humility and compassion in the face of uncertainty. The work ahead is daunting, but the promise of resurrection—of new life—fuels our commitment to navigate the uncertainty. Showing up in uncertainty and agreeing not to take things personally is important for the work outlined in the next chapter.

7.

White Supremacy's Demise
A Necessary Death

In the house of faith we say love reigns,
But there God stands—with whitewashed stains:
In the pews, the pulpit, and even in prayer,
A ghastly presence, a chilling air

God's folk, rise up, come from the dead
Christ casts out Legions, with Daily Bread.
In the name of Jesus, let liberation ring
In the bells of Heaven, "race" has no sting.

Born Again a Person of Color

Around 2013, as I became a full-time pastor, my identity shifted as I began to see myself through the lens of my indigenous and Latino identity. In a sense I was born again as I grew to appreciate these parts of myself. The idea of whiteness tries to erode anything not willing to assimilate. When I began to stand with my Mexican-American colleagues and grow into my Mexican heritage, I realized the forces at work against those wanting to remain distinct. It showed me a small piece of the struggle that Black US citizens have felt in their attempt to remain distinct.

I was born with "passing privilege" meaning that I can pass as white most of the time. That is part of the so-called American dream—to be able to assimilate into colorlessness enough so that you are not ostracized for your ethnicity and culture, to become colorless and cultureless, we might say.

According to the rules of whiteness (and yes, the United States has had many of these throughout the years—just google "the one drop rule" to see one of the most infamous), I am not white. I wish that nobody was white. How beautiful it would be if my white family had seen themselves as Scottish and Irish by descendancy. How beautiful if my brown family had hung on to their Chichimeca or French or Jewish ancestry. How beautiful it would have been if the people who wanted to profit from stealing Black bodies and land from indigenous people would not have created the idea of whiteness . . .

Amid the reality we have, waking up as a person of color had a profound impact on my psyche. As this seed began to sprout, I began to see the problems of white supremacy in the world and the church world that surrounds me. This realization did not come to me in a single, defining moment. There was no sudden awakening, no dramatic revelation. Instead, it was a slow dawning, a gradual coming into consciousness that stretched across the years of my life. It was a journey of self-discovery that involved people asking me, "Where are you really from?" and involved me realizing why people at church would give my Latino dad the side-eye and my white mother a hug of Southern hospitality.

In a romantic relationship, the opportunity for growth gets stymied and stamped out by the posture of defensiveness that comes out, refusing to yield ground or concede ideas, needing to protect and hold steady. This is where I am going to move, talking about my encounter with white supremacy, because defensiveness—that telltale sign of fragility—oftentimes comes out first.

Defensive Roots

Defensiveness, in its essence, is a survival strategy. It is a root, deeply embedded in the soil of our psyche, feeding and supporting the towering tree of our beliefs and attitudes. It is not inherently negative; in fact, it can be a healthy response when our faith or values are under attack. However, when defensiveness morphs from a rarely used survival tactic into a way of life, it becomes a problem. It becomes even more problematic when it is weaponized by an empowered majority to subjugate others.

This weaponized defensiveness is starkly evident in the cultural collaborative of white supremacy, particularly in defense of "The Lost Cause." This term refers to a concerted and concentrated literary and cultural campaign that sought to reconcile Southern white culture with the defeat of the "Confederate States of America" in the Civil War.[1]

"The Civil War didn't end in 1865; that's an objective fact," my friend whom I'll call Jones, a self-avowed "member of the Southern White Race" and "a Confederate who lives as an eighteenth-century man," often reminds me. He argues that the Civil War didn't truly end until the 1960s with the Second Reconstruction.

Indeed, the South may have lost the Civil War, but it won the culture war well into the twentieth century. The ideas of white supremacy grew in the US North and the West, spreading through literature, music, and fear-based propaganda that followed the Great Migration of Black people out of Southern cities during the lynching era.[2] White supremacy has always been present throughout the country, and wherever Black folk have gone, their mere existence has triggered a white backlash.

At the heart of this spread of white supremacist culture was defensiveness. Fear of Black men becoming sexually active with white women, defense of "states' rights" and the right to be self-sufficient, and anti-Jewish sentiment fueled by the belief that Jews and Bolsheviks were corrupting the South and America, all stemmed from a defensive posture.

The United Methodist Church in the Southern United States, too, has been deeply affected by this culture of defensiveness. Our church was once a slaveholding denomination. The theological heresy of white supremacy, the belief that God ordained the white race to be stewards over people of color and the rest of the world, not only found a home in the church but it was largely born in the church.

In *The Cross and the Lynching Tree*, Dr. James Cone cites white supremacist Methodist bishop Atticus G. Haygood who said in 1893, "Now-a-days, it seems the killing of Negroes is not so extraordinary an occurrence as to need explanation."[3] Methodists were not only aware of white supremacy, we normalized it by our apologetics and defense of it.

As my divinity school professor Stanley Hauerwas often said of chattel slavery, "What do you do about something that is so wrong that the damage

---

1. For more about "The Lost Cause," read *Baptized in Blood: The Religion of the Lost Cause, 1865-1920* by Charles Reagan Wilson.

2. For a primary source on this time period, see NAACP, *Thirty Years of Lynching*. For a more general history on the topic, see Manfred, *Popular Justice* (which refers to this time period as the lynching era).

3. Cone, *Cross and the Lynching Tree*, 6, Kindle.

from it can never be undone?" One of the things to do is to remember it and always reckon with what it has done to you.

Jonathan Wilson-Hartgrove, in his book *Reconstructing the Gospel*, talks about "Shriveled heart syndrome," (originally coined by Dr. David W. Stowe) which is the effect that hundreds of years of slavery and the defense of white supremacy has had on white people.[4] In order to dehumanize a brother or sister, we have to destroy parts of our own heart and soul. Before we can come to the work of reconstructing the gospel and struggling for reformation, we have to reckon with our own complicity and the effects that shriveled heart syndrome has had on us.

We cannot simply decide to stop being defensive. We have to acknowledge the historical, hidden forces at work on us that have led us to resist each other through a lifestyle of defensiveness. This lifestyle not only keeps out things which would hurt us but also keeps other people out of our hearts and lives.

The United Methodist Church, like many other institutions, has been deeply influenced by the culture of defensiveness and white supremacy. This influence is not just a historical artifact; it is a living, breathing part of our church today. It is a part of our theology, our liturgy, our community, and our individual hearts and minds.

But acknowledging white supremacy is only the first step. The next steps are to confront it, to challenge it, to dismantle it. This is not an easy task. It requires courage, humility, and a willingness to face uncomfortable truths. But it is a necessary task for the health of our church and for the integrity of our faith.

As we embark on this journey of reckoning and reformation, we are not alone. We are part of a community of believers, a body of Christ, that is bigger than any one of us. We are part of a tradition of faith that has always been about love, justice, and reconciliation. And we are part of a God who is always working to bring healing, wholeness, and redemption to a broken world.

The roots of white supremacy run deep in the United Methodist Church, but they do not define us. We are defined by our commitment to the gospel of Jesus Christ, our dedication to the work of justice, and our love for all of God's children. And with God's help we can overcome the legacy of white supremacy and build a church that truly reflects the kingdom of God.

White supremacy started out with the prideful beliefs of Manifest Destiny which quickly manifested as anti-Black and anti-indigenous beliefs and violence. It grew from there in opposition to other non-white people and

---

4. Wilson-Hartgrove, *Reconstructing the Gospel*, 161–63.

cultures. As I have grown as a Latino pastor, I have seen this more and more. This testimony is where I turn next.

An Example: White Supremacy and Immigration

The intersection of white supremacy and immigration is a complex and often contentious one. It is a conversation that is fraught with misconceptions, fear, and prejudice. It is a conversation that is deeply influenced by the narratives of white supremacy that pervade our society and our institutions. And it is a conversation that is desperately in need of understanding, empathy, and compassion.

This conversation came into sharp focus for me during a dialogue with a fellow United Methodist pastor. He was a white pastor eager to start a Spanish-speaking ministry in his church, but he was also deeply concerned about the legal status of the Hispanic population in his area. His question, posed with sincere curiosity and a hint of fear, took me aback. It was a question that revealed a deep-seated fear of the "Other," a fear that is all too common in our society.

I responded by challenging his notion of the "right way" to immigrate. I spoke about the complexities of visa types, the labyrinthine immigration system, and the near impossibility of securing a long-term stay in the United States. I spoke about the realities of immigration, realities that are often obscured by fear and prejudice.

The pastor's concerns were not entirely unfounded. He was worried about the perceived criminality of undocumented immigrants, a common misconception that I was quick to challenge. I explained that overstaying a visa is a civil offense, not a criminal one. I also challenged his belief in the American dream, the idea that anyone can succeed with enough effort. I questioned whether this dream was truly accessible to all, including immigrants.

This conversation led me to reflect on my own experiences and thoughts about immigration and white supremacy. I poured these reflections into the following poem, which does not reflect all immigrants' stories but does reflect some of the harsh realities:

"Seeing the X in the Latinx"

I invite you to think of the Latinos and Latinas, the Latin "X"-es, because *X* marks the spot of where you learn the piece of the identity you didn't know before, where you sit and explore, the ones you didn't know you ignore . . .

I want to talk about the Latinx folk,

the ones you don't know if you should call *Hispanics*, who had to perform travel gymnastics to cross borders to get here and face US antics, the ones who are victims of secret police tactics, who church folk see and assume are all Catholics.

"But we don't have any Latinx y or z's in my town," someone might say . . . because they don't know where "they" stay. *Escúchame—*

There are trailer parks in the woods, houses built by discarded goods carried plank by plank on the backs of the people who carry the economy.

How would you get your shoes shined and unscuffed at the hotel before going to sleep on that pre-fluffed, over-stuffed pillow, looking out through your windexed window at the maids who are moving on to mow the blades of grass . . . and how could you eat that fast food with dime a dozen tomatoes, without the Latinx *campesinos* who toil the soil, so you could eat what they provide, what they can't afford to buy? How would we live our lives if we really had to think of seeking unity with the Latinx neighbors we don't know exist?

Let me tell you why they came here to reap the harvest. In a sense, the *gente* Latinx ARE the harvest of the Empire that hurt their homes.

The United States has had more than fifty armed interventions in Latin-America over the years, everything from the CIA destabilizing governments that seemed too Red to protecting the right of the deceptively named Chiquita to take the bananas and make them travel thousands of miles to sell them to you for fifty cents. Do you ever wonder why we can buy bananas from thousands of miles away for less than fifty cents a pound? It's because we raped and murdered the people and stole the land and so much more.

At the Border they have a saying, "We didn't cross the Border, the Border crossed us," because one day they awoke to find that they had been moved from Mexico to the USA. Why do you think US citizens are called Gringos? Green—Go. as in, "hey green uniforms. go."

It's all a game of thrones, a game of hidden mass graves with no names and broken bones, a thing that's played with high altitude surveillance drones, with tapped phones, language as bad as sticks and stones, immigrants living on land they'll never own, people unknown, who feel alone, afraid to let it all escape through unspeakable groans.

But Immigrants know God, because God was an immigrant whose name was *Jesús*.

God is in the wilderness that they sometimes cross.

God is dead, sitting bloated as vulture food in the wilderness in South Texas, in the real Death Valley, where immigrants die of thirst, knowing the risk and thinking it's better than what they left behind. God is resurrected in the hopes of those who cross with the prayers that they won't be abandoned by *El Espíritu Santo* in a godless place. God has third degree burns from being cramped next to an engine and almost being cooked alive, trying to creep into a country that told him his asylum claim wasn't good enough, even though he was already maimed.

God is inside of an unwed peasant girl named *Maria*, who is pregnant through no fault of her own but still risks shame for the child she bears, whom she will birth across a border in a foreign place, hoping that this baby will have or bring more hope than she had.

God is in an undocumented immigrant youth who dreams of college, who hums a melody born from hope and defiance. The tune grows louder, carrying the rhythm of feet that marched before him, feet that crossed borders, feet that built nations, feet that carried the weight of a thousand prayers. He lifts his voice, singing not a song of the past, but an anthem of what could be: a world without fear, without division, where strangers become neighbors, and neighbors become kin.

He sings with fire in his soul and tears on his cheeks,
his voice rising like a phoenix above walls and wire,
calling out, "Imagine with me a place where we all belong.
Can you see it? Can you feel it?
The day will come when this dream is no longer mine alone, and we will build it together. Then, the community will be as one."

Reflecting on this conversation and the poem, I was struck by the power of white supremacy to shape our perspectives and our conversations about immigration. I was reminded of the need to challenge these narratives, to seek understanding and empathy, and to work toward a society that truly values and respects all of its members. This is the challenge that lies before us, and it is a challenge that we must meet with courage, compassion, and conviction. To me, meeting this challenge sometimes feels like meeting an anthropomorphized lie.

White Jesus

The concept of "White Jesus" is a deeply entrenched image in the collective consciousness of many Christian communities. This figure, often depicted with "fair" skin—as if non-pale was unfair, blue eyes, and flowing blond or brown hair, is a far cry from the historical Jesus of Nazareth, a Middle Eastern man born in Bethlehem over two thousand years ago. This "White Jesus" is not just a benign misrepresentation of historical facts but a symbol of white supremacy that has been used to justify oppression and discrimination against non-white bodies.

Christena Cleveland, a social psychologist and theologian, refers to this phenomenon as the "whitemalegod" concept.[5] This concept is not just about the physical representation of Jesus, but also about the attributes and values associated with him. The "whitemalegod" is often portrayed as endorsing and upholding the power structures of white, male-dominated societies, thereby reinforcing systemic racism and patriarchy.

The emotional toll of living under the shadow of the "whitemalegod" is immense, especially for non-white bodies. It is a constant reminder of their perceived inferiority and marginalization in societies that uphold white supremacy. It is a daily struggle to reconcile their faith in a God who is supposed to be loving and inclusive with the oppressive structures that this God is portrayed to support. Considering all of this, one day I wrote a letter to "White Jesus," the image that I knew was a bastardized representation of the Christ and Savior of our faith. I invite you into that emotional correspondence.

Dear "White Jesus,"

You can die. You can go on somewhere, because you are not our Savior, although you are the lord of the lives of so many people in the church. You are an imposter, pretending to be the Son of God, pretending to be made in God's image, but having been remade in the image of white supremacy. You are not God, but you are a god. You are not the Holy Spirit, but an evil spirit.

---

5. See Cleveland, *God Is a Black Woman*. Through Dr. Cleveland's many different offerings, I encourage you to go deeper in the liberative work of embracing your sacredness and resisting the social evils that disconnect us. You can stay up to date with her most recent work at her website: https://christenacleveland.com.

You are not the Alpha and the Omega; you are the devil. I cannot deny that you exist in tandem with the real Jesus, and I cannot, in many cases, figure out where you stop and the Son of God starts. That is what makes it so challenging to confront you. I am sick and tired of seeing you steal away souls who otherwise might serve the beautiful, brown-skinned Palestinian Jesus, the One who stands with and appears in the least of these.

Your followers do not have to get their hands dirty, except when they are beating up the followers of Brown Jesus.

It is much preferable for white-passing folk to follow a lord who uplifts a life already lived. "Your best life now," you say through your mouthpieces, ensuring that any crosses to kill us won't come from you—what a brilliant version of Christianity to follow! You appear as an Angel of Light and more. You are the Angel of White—pure light, the one who sends envoys of the white messengers into the world. Your messengers like Tucker Carlson curate your world and make your followers divest themselves from me and the community I inhabit . . . you dis-member them from what we call the body of Christ.

M. had you written all over her face when she came to me and said she wasn't coming back to church. This eighty-five-year-old woman, who's been perched in a pew in that place for decades, decided not to come back, and I bet she doesn't even know why. She stumbled over her words, talking about Black Lives Matter and the state of the world, thinking she'd be better off outside of the Fellowship, unknowingly forcing her five followers to flee with her. I started talking with her, knowing the "hallelujah corner" would bow down to whatever her whim was. But she said she was done. Others are now done. Their grandchildren saw your lie for what it was, and they're done too.

I saw your menacing malicious countenance crouched behind M., like a master moving the marionette. Did she mistake you for the Galilean? Did she even stop to ask if her Christ was the Jesus of Nazareth? Doubtful.

I'm so doubtful because of you. Hiding in plain sight. You tricked these sheep into thinking that your reign was only a pie in the sky by and by, scaring them into thinking they'd end up in a seven-circled, fairy-tale land of fire if they didn't follow you. But like Jesus of Nazareth, your *basileia* is based on terra firma. Your reign reeks and wreaks havoc that paints a picture called "order" based on the chained conscious-less consciences of your greatest "moral" agents that act out codes that you've craftily curated.

White Devil, the greatest trick you ever pulled wasn't even convincing people who think they're white that I'm an agent of the Devil. It was in convincing them that you don't exist. When I talk about racism, they look at me like I might as well be talking about a unicorn—something they've never seen, having willfully blinded themselves by their worship of you.

These old folks living in this rural, Southern county will remember Black men being publicly whipped in the county seat in 1955. They'll remember hearing about Black men being shot by police years ago, or, more often, going to prison . . . but they didn't know you caused it. You convinced them that white supremacy is a myth.

I can't even talk about your lies in church, because the tapestry woven in front of Jesus of Nazareth is a picture of lies. You have convinced so many in the church that the same Jesus who was killed by State violence for being a political, nonviolent revolutionary was somehow not related to politics. You've convinced them that the calling of Christians is to somehow be apolitical. You evil entity, you have pushed so many church members so far toward fascism that they say anything to the left of that is going to have heads chopped off like confetti, as in the French Revolution. You told them that setting up free healthcare clinics like Jesus did will somehow overthrow your way of strife, which has become their way of life. I breathed onto their exposed nerves when I prayed for undocumented families that you tore apart, for the children who became orphans, and several families who think they're white left the church. I don't know if their devotion to you is love for being remade and baptized into your image or if it is a fear of having you exposed for the lie you are.

I pray to Jesus of Nazareth all the time, but it seems that the most frequent answer I get, or at least the loudest, is from you. Not in a still small voice in my heart, but from your guard animals who raise their hackles at me. I believe that the body of Christ, the real Christ, has the potential to cause healing for what you have done. But I haven't experienced that from many of the members. And what's worse, the ones who suffer in following the Galilean are drowned out by you. Most of what I have experienced is your bustling biceps bruising my heart when it beats for the oppressed or your flagrant feet stomping my toes when they step out of line.

There has been a dis-membering of the body of Christ, and I have seen that with people leaving the church. Maybe, with me talking about your rival Jesus, the one who was born in Bethlehem, they came to think that the bodies of the two Christs are incompatible. Maybe they realized they can't be in a space where the One that is not you is worshiped and preached. I will at least applaud them for that. Maybe this is a moment of revelation when your colorless countenance might somehow be seen for what it is.

But you are the ruler of the air, the Lord of this land, and you hold so much of the power. Even if the oppressed people decided to burn down the matchstick homes made by enslaved labor two hundred years ago, your followers bear arms that salute you with their endless supply of ammunition, and we could all die in a Kristallnacht as white as snow if you didn't need the souls of others to suck for energy, their bodies and blood to imbibe for sustenance.

I wish you would go away. I wish you would go to hell. But the more I look around the more I see that maybe your remodeling is doing that work, so you won't have to move. I got nothing except a vague promise from a revelatory Vision some follower of the other Jesus had, that not only the Roman Empire but all empires made in the mark of the beast would burn. All I got is a belief that one day the One, of whom you're the imposter, is gonna come back and make you go on somewhere, to make a place where every tribe, tongue, and nation can be at home. That brings me more joy than the ten thousand curse words I've said to you in my heart. You may be winning this fight, and I have a feeling you'll feast on my flesh before it's all over with. But to the real God, a day is as a thousand years, and I bet you don't have more than a few hours left.

With Disregard,

J

Why It's Hard for the White Church to Grieve

Remember in chapter 3 when I talked about grief? I'm inviting you back into that space. White supremacy both causes death and needs to die. As we move in that direction, it needs to be grieved. Coming to terms with white supremacy is a complex and often painful process. It requires a deep and honest examination of oneself and one's place in the world. For those of us who benefit from white privilege or anti-Black or anti-indigenous supremacy, it requires acknowledging the unearned privileges that come with being in a society that has been shaped by centuries of racial inequality. It requires confronting the fear of losing these privileges and the power structures that uphold them. And it requires overcoming the ignorance and denial that often serve as barriers to this understanding.

One of the most significant challenges in this process is acknowledging privilege. This privilege is often invisible to those who possess it, woven into the fabric of their everyday lives. I've heard that explaining it to someone who benefits from it is like trying to tell a fish that it's wet. Good luck! Color privilege is in the ease of finding a band-aid that matches your skin tone, in the assurance that a routine traffic stop won't escalate into a life-threatening situation, in the freedom to walk through a store without being followed or harassed. Acknowledging this privilege means confronting uncomfortable truths about the systemic nature of racial inequality and the ways in which one has benefited from it. This can be a daunting prospect, but it is a necessary step in the process of grieving white supremacy.

Another significant challenge is the fear of losing power. White supremacy, by its very nature, confers power and privilege upon white people. The prospect of dismantling white supremacy, therefore, can be threatening. This fear can manifest in various ways from outright hostility toward efforts to promote racial equality to more subtle forms of resistance such as defensiveness or denial. But we need to keep in mind that non-white people, as far as I can tell, are not trying to impoverish white people. But rather, it is an attempt to decenter whiteness. Being moved from the center, where you have had all of the power, may feel like a loss of power. But, also, it is a necessary step toward sharing.

Finally, ignorance and denial play a significant role in the difficulty of grieving white supremacy. Many white people are simply unaware of the extent of racial inequality and the ways in which white supremacy perpetuates it. This ignorance is often not malicious but rather the result of living in a society that is designed to shield white people from the realities of racial injustice. Denial, on the other hand, is a more active form of resistance. It involves rejecting or minimizing the realities of white supremacy, often as a way to avoid feelings of guilt or complicity. The Intercultural Development Inventory (or IDI for short) is a great tool to learn how to relate to other cultures,[6] which inevitably leads to learning how you relate to other ethnic and racialized groups.

Grieving practices of white Christians have largely been affected by white supremacy playing out in our experience of human death. In the book *Corpse Care* by Cody Sanders and Mikeal Parsons it becomes evident that white US citizens, particularly white Christians, have inherited a particular set of attitudes toward death. These attitudes have in some ways been influenced by underlying structures of white supremacy and a historically underdeveloped theology of the body (this is in comparison to other ethnicities that have a more embodied relationship with death like is seen in the Black Church).[7]

White supremacy, while typically understood by explicit actions, has subtly invaded the way we deal with death and grieving. The white US tendency toward indifference or apathy to the dead body, as pointed out by Sanders and Parsons, can be interpreted as a reflection of this influence. On

---

6. For more information about the Intercultural Development Inventory, visit https://www.idiinventory.com/.

7. See Parsons and Sanders, *Corpse Care*, especially the introduction.

the one hand, one could argue that this indifference to the dead body has been borne out of a cultural history that privileges the mind and soul over the body, which has roots in Puritanism and other Christian interpretations that emphasize the transcendental and devalue the material. By viewing the body as merely a shell for the soul, this perspective neglects the body's sacredness and potential for meaning-making. But on the other hand, this attitude can be connected with structures of white supremacy that emphasize dominance and control, often through the negation of the body, particularly bodies that are racialized, gendered, or otherwise marked as *other*. Consider the ways that dehumanized Native American bodies were left slaughtered on the ground in the so-called "Indian Wars" or the horrific things that white terrorists often did with lynched Black bodies.

Sanders and Parsons talk about the commodification of deathcare and the move toward more impersonal, commercialized, and industrialized deathcare practices like formaldehyde. This went along with the rise of industrial capitalism—which connected to white supremacy through things like the extensive growth of cotton in the US. The removal of death from the domestic sphere into the hands of professional undertakers and hospital staff has created a detachment from death and dead bodies, impacting the ability of white US citizens to fully engage in the grieving process.

This industrialization and commodification of death, in which bodies are quickly removed from homes and prepared for burial or cremation by strangers, disrupts the opportunity for an intimate, community-based, Christian mourning process. It diminishes the chance to recognize and honor the sacredness of the transition from life to death and prevents the opportunity to sit with the pain, loss, and transformative potential in the grieving process. A lack of embodiment in the Christian faith, especially around death, has made it hard for people who have been socialized by whiteness to grieve. I hope this makes someone sad and pisses someone off enough to want change.

Grieving the harm of white supremacy is a complex and challenging process. It involves acknowledging privilege, confronting fears of losing power, and overcoming ignorance and denial. But it is also a necessary process, one that is crucial for the work of racial justice and reconciliation. It is a process that requires courage, humility, and a willingness to engage in difficult conversations. But most importantly, it is a process that requires a commitment to action, to actively working toward a more just and equitable society.

A Generational Curse

United States culture, across all its geographical diversity, is steeped in tradition, a tapestry woven from generations of shared experiences, values, and beliefs. Yet entwined within this tapestry, as argued in Richard Rothstein's *The Color of Law*, are threads of white supremacy subtly and overtly influencing the sociopolitical fabric of the entire nation, not just the South.[8] The "Doctrine of Discovery" and the idea of "manifest destiny" were both handled by and propagated through the church in the United States, as parts of the demonic presence of white supremacy.

The history of America, with its periods of slavery, segregation, and systemic racism, has provided fertile ground for the growth of white supremacist culture. This culture has permeated through generations, defining aspects of US identity. It manifests in monuments glorifying figures who committed treason against the United States, in narratives that romanticize the antebellum era, and in social norms that perpetuate racial inequality.

Central to shaping this culture is the "Lost Cause" narrative reframing the South as a victim—a noble cause unjustly defeated—and recasting the Confederacy as a defender of states' rights and a way of life, rather than a defender of slavery. This has profoundly influenced the collective American psyche, shaping perspectives on history and identity, fostering a shared sense of victimhood, and breeding deep-seated resentment toward perceived threats to a way of life. Consider that the first movie played in the White House by President Harry Truman was *The Birth of a Nation*, and this same president who coined the term "make the world safe for democracy" after World War I played a hand in uplifting the "Lost Cause," which made the United States unsafe for democracy.[9]

This generational curse has continued to play out, and not only in the political sphere. Racist attitudes are often justified through distorted interpretations of Christian teachings further entrenching white supremacy within the culture.

In his book *The Color of Compromise*, Jemar Tisby illustrates how the church, across all parts of the US, has been complicit in upholding this systemic racism. The theological heresy of white supremacy, the belief that God ordained the white race as stewards over people of color, found not just a home, but fertile soil within the church.[10] As Robert P. Jones quotes from the Public Religion Research Institute findings in *White Too Long*, "The more

---

8. See Rothstein, *Color of Law*.
9. Kendi, *Stamped from the Beginning*, chap. 24.
10. See Tisby, *Color of Compromise*.

racist attitudes a person holds, the more likely he or she is to identify as a white Christian."[11] As the conclusion to this chapter, I turn toward dreaming of what it would be like to be free from the demon of the idea of whiteness.

Exorcism of Whiteness

Ever since James Cone invoked the image of the white devil half a century ago, numerous theologians, regardless of their self-identification as liberationists or not, have described whiteness as a malevolent force. Ibram X. Kendi, in particular, doesn't focus on white people, but rather on "people who think they are white," underscoring the artificial construct of racial whiteness.[12] Perhaps it's more accurate to deem it a destructive distortion of creation. The vibrant uniqueness, the divine image within individuals, is blurred and painted over—whitewashed, one might say—when people are mislabeled as "white." There was a time when Dutch, French, and English immigrants proudly celebrated their diverse cultures. However, in order to justify enslavement, theft, and genocide they felt the need to create an inferior category, a "less-than-human" identity, for others. By fashioning subjugated groups, they erected a superior pedestal for themselves.

When we contemplate transcending whiteness, the idea of exorcism emerges as an essential aspect. But how do we rise above a lexicon permeated with racism? Even antiracists must use the language imposed by the racists' rules, which begins by recognizing our constructed homogeneity under the umbrella of whiteness. How do we embody the apostle Paul's message in Gal 3:28 (NRSV): "There is no longer Jew or Greek, there is no longer slave or free, there is no longer male and female; for all of you are one in Christ Jesus"? How can we encourage the white church to disassociate from whiteness while also remaining steadfastly antiracist? Attempts at such disassociation often unwittingly give birth to subtle forms of racism, like color-blind racism, which, in the process of homogenizing humanity, inadvertently disregard the distinct pain and suffering endured disproportionately by some.

Racism behaves like the mythical Hydra: sever one head and two grow back. It resembles the demon mentioned by Jesus, which upon being exorcised finds its previous dwelling cleaned and empty, returns, and brings along seven more demons.

While contemplating metaphors I envisioned racism as an invasive species entering an environment with no natural defenses. But even that

---

11. Jones, *White Too Long*, 175, Kindle.
12. See Kendi, *How to Be an Antiracist*.

analogy is tainted, as the term *invasive species* has been appropriated by white nationalist rhetoric to stir fears about migrants, immigrants, and refugees entering the United States.

As I envision a post-racial world, I'm drawn to a Scripture passage that many antiracist preachers have expounded upon: the healing of the man possessed by a demon. Sadly, even after two millennia, we often refer to him as "the demoniac" rather than "the man healed of demon possession." We're stuck viewing him through the lens of his past afflictions rather than the liberating possibilities brought forth by Jesus.

Upon being freed from his demonic possession, the man became unrecognizable to those who knew him. His former identity had, in effect, died, and he had been reborn, or, as conveyed in John chapter 3, "born from above." When the things that bind us are shed, we acquire a new identity.

In the transformative process of death and resurrection we should not only mourn the relinquished positions of power but also rejoice in the new, enriching experiences and identities we stand to gain.

8.

Strategies for Survival
Living amid Death

In the swollen swirl of days, heavy and pregnant with tasks
Constipated with undigested work orders
We have a choice of whether to burn our candle at both ends
With waxy weakness puddling amid our desperate dance.

We can choose to keep being burnt out or be called names.
If they will call me incompetent, at least I can choose when.
"Targeted Incompetence" is my new name tag
A cacophonous phrase clinking against capitalist productivity,

That demands to be a gatekeeper to my sanity,
A warden that holds me hostage amid unanswered emails.
Like a rebellious teen singing a song against the cogs of the machine
I call out a chorus for balance in a world of teetering chaos.

My song of time to self is a letter of radical self-love
A quiet revolution written and sung in the presence of others
Who will say yes to love and no to a lusty voracious beast
That thinks it owns us but is angry from owning not even itself.

Secularity and Staying Alive

Remember in chapter 2 when I began the conversation about seeing death by talking about secularity? I want to say a few more words about secularity, drawing again on what I've learned from Andrew Root, particularly about how we can help people to have faith in the midst of a world that is so rooted in unbelief.[1]

At the core of this shift toward secularity is this concept known as "the immanent frame."[2] It's the idea that what's right in front of us is the only thing that's real—leaving less room for belief in something bigger and beyond our immediate experience. The big question is, how do we connect with folks living in this immanent frame and introduce them to the idea of a living God, especially when faith feels fragile and doubt is a constant companion?

Faith is fragile, but this fragility isn't necessarily a bad thing. It can actually create a space where we can meet people right where they are—people who are searching for meaning and purpose in their lives. In a sense, people are replacing religion and the transcendence it offers with behaviors that numb their existential pain. Sociologists would say it's like they've swapped out what Karl Marx said of religion as the "opium of the people" for something else. Or I would say that humanity has forgotten the God of the Old Testament prophets who speaks to the brokenness of the people and heals their collective wounds. Humanity has forgotten the God of the Psalms who heals and binds up the brokenhearted.

A lot of young people in this age of secularity don't think God speaks to them. So, are the days of believing in a God who communicates with us directly over? If so, what's next? In this world, everyone gets to speak their own truth, but the church is implicitly told not to speak its ultimate truth.

But here's the thing. We can rediscover belief through meaningful encounters and stories. In *When God Talks Back*, an anthropologist studies Vineyard and Pentecostal churches. Whether or not you believe God speaks, the book suggests that prayer has a positive impact on people's lives.[3] Whether or not it is prayer for you, I encourage you in this chapter, even with the world around you only believing in what is in front of it, to stretch your faith.

Stretch yourself to believe that God is working through the community around you. Stretch yourself to pray. Stretch yourself to invest in yourself,

---

1. Root, "Why Are They Leaving?"
2. See Taylor, *Secular Age*, especially chaps. 15–17.
3. Luhrmann, *When God Talks Back*, chaps. 5–6.

even when and especially because you don't have time to do it! Let's be on this journey of survival together.

Earlier in this book, I examined a few attitudes that cause death. And before I go on to talk about what "staying alive amid death" looks like, I want to mention a couple of other things that cause death as a way of feeling the urgency of practicing life-giving behaviors.

"The Death of Loneliness"

We are many parts that make up a whole. Even though we are well-connected, we often experience a kind of demise, the death of loneliness. Yet when we cling to the Connection we have to each other and the Communion initiated by God, we may yet experience the death of loneliness We first experience death caused by loneliness, and then thanks be to God, loneliness dies.

Loneliness, like a cancer, silently erodes the body of Christ until congregation by congregation we are put on life support, isolated from our members, stigmatized from larger society. In the same way that several illnesses can affect the human body at once, they affect congregations of people at once. The atrial fibrillation distracts from our underlying spiritual stagnation. The diabetes of ingesting communion but not working out our faith comes with nerve damage, fellowship gone numb. All the while we are lonely.

Isolation cancer is like a blood cancer, simultaneously affecting one member of the body and every member of the body. It travels through the vessels, wearing us down. It's an atmospheric condition, a gas that we breathe in or in the water that we drink. Only with great intentionality are we able to combat this cancer.

We may attempt to trick ourselves, saying that we are not affected by this cancer. After all, we are not hurting as badly as some of the other members. Nearly two millennia ago, a church body heard the words, "As it is, there are many members, yet one body. The eye cannot say to the hand, 'I have no need of you,' nor again the head to the feet, 'I have no need of you.' On the contrary, the members of the body that seem to be weaker are indispensable" (1 Cor 12:20–22 NRSV). When we see one isolated member of the body ailing in loneliness, we ought to attend to that member, because its importance is already underestimated.

The loneliness we experience is in our marrow. It weakens our bones, eroding our skeletal structure. The body stores its nutrients in the skeletal structure so that when we are fasting or when nutrients are less dense we can pull from the bloodstream and also the bones. Therefore, if our day is plentiful, we may not realize the deficiency in the body. However, when the day of need comes, the pain will be systemic: when we call on the different parts of the body for help, realizing that they all have been affected by the same malady.

After recent research was released, we all began to realize that social media is more appropriately "unsocial media," and yet we cannot quit it any more than an alcoholic can simply drop the bottle after having been diagnosed with liver problems. For some the drink of choice is Facebook, and for some it is Instagram, Twitter, or PornHub. Some are more accustomed to pouring themselves out and some prefer to drink in what others have gushed. All of us give more of ourselves than we realize through the screens, like a fortune being spent on booze, five dollars at a time. We need to realize that we are powerless to stop the loneliness that rampantly drains our energy. We need to realize that our lives have become unmanageable. We need to realize that only the higher power of Jesus Christ, into whose body we have been baptized, has the ability to bring reparation to our souls.

We are justified by the love and grace of Jesus, each of us saying, "It's just as if I'd never had a blemish on my life." And yet when we get on social media, seeing well-curated images of biceps and bosoms that are more bustling than ours, we feel like each of our blemishes is a burden, forgetting that God loves us with all of them.

Climbing back into the screen, our minds drink deeply of the intoxicating idea that it can make us feel better, and it does for a moment. But it is a drink that does not satisfy in the long-term, demanding more attention of our minds and souls than we realize until we are hopelessly addicted. The platforms showing us people just outside our reach remind us that we lack so much. We signed on to the screen to feel better, but we ended up seeing someone who seems better than us, and we leave with ideations of our own inadequacy.

"It will make me feel better next time I sign on," our minds tell us, not realizing that we have been studied like ants in a colony, for the sweetness of social media to draw us back to itself. Inside our minds, seeds of loneliness have been planted, genetically engineered as hybrids of loneliness, given to us by the platforms we freely use. But we plant them inside ourselves. The fruit of addiction and longing rapidly grow like an invasive species in our thoughts, crowding out our otherwise disciplined life, drawing us back to the interweb of our social media.

When we get back on, we check to see how many "likes" we have. And even if someone likes or positively comments on an image of our life we wonder why more people did not do it. "What is wrong with me?" we find ourselves asking.

In a desperation to find community, we share something a little bit more personal. We open our lives bare for others to see, drunk on the wine of the world, wishing to see that we have been uplifted. Perhaps we have been brought a little bit closer into the social media fold, wrapped more intricately in its devices. But having shared something too personal, our family is frustrated with us. Our relationships in the real world begin to suffer, because it seems that only through the screen lit dimly can they see the seemingly "real you" illuminated. Our addiction deepens. We are more lonely.

In ages past, humanity did not have the luxury of tricking itself into thinking that things were all right. Our ancestors couldn't post played-up lies on the internet, and they rarely had the luxury of believing these lies. People had to listen with more senses than their ears. Their food, void of USDA expiration dates, told them if it was good to eat. Their friends swiftly approaching the village told them with a facial expression if they were being chased by a bear or if they had found the clean drinking water they sought. Their eyes told them if the clouds spelled rain or a cool, overcast day. They were connected to fewer people and a smaller corner of the world but with greater depth.

Today we are less often called "members" of the society than we are called "consumers" of it. We are still Homo sapiens, created in the image of God, according to God's likeness, but we have been remade into something else, a species that is primarily identified by its spending power and ability to absorb and suck in. This, of course, is a false identity, but it remains true.

We are so programmed to believe that we are consumers of the earth that we forget this is not our original coding. It is a virus implanted into us by the powers and principalities of this age that want us to buy certain products. We are the products, really, and our time and energy are bought and sold, in the form of the data we trade for endless "free" products. We are never told flat out, "This is who you are," but the sum of the parts of the world around us paint a picture that leads us to believe a lie. It tells us that reality only exists in endless consuming of media, of products marketed to us, and of people. We consume things, thinking it will make us whole, but it is a bottomless hole into which we place the things we buy.

Is it any wonder then, that we also place things in all of our bodily orifices? Food porn, engineered to react with chemical dependencies in our brain, calls us to cram calories in our mouths. Emotional music and streaming songs, endlessly similar to each other but demanding our immediate attention, cling to the side of our heads in earphones designed to be barnacles to our brains. Flesh and silicon ask to enter or caress other orifices, hoping to simply stimulate nerve endings, telling our bodies that they are not alone. But loneliness is not about what enters the body or entices the eyes. It is about the heart and soul.

Polarization as we know it in politics is a reality that God did not create. It uncreates. It unmakes what has been made in a way that says, "If you don't want to be robbed, you can only be with people like you." I used to think that tribalism was the issue, but I remember in history when different tribes lived together in peace. God successfully brought twelve tribes together, and even though they fought a lot with other, non-Hebrew tribes God told them that they should live in peace with these. God had them live at peace as long as they maintained their identity and did not worship the gods of the other tribes. Does God support tribalism?

What we call tribalism today is much a different thing than the tribalism of the Bible. Whereas, in effect, God said to the tribes of Israel, "Welcome the immigrant in your midst," we now say, "if you're an immigrant, your body and mind must be assimilated or you don't belong." Whereas God said, "I will bless all nations through you," we now say, "What we have is ours. US first." Whereas God said to the people of ancient Israel, "You will be my witness to the world and a servant nation," our foreign policy now says, "give me your resources."

The table at Thanksgiving dinner used to be a beacon of light in a cold time. But fear of differences has made us shorten the table while *refined* palates have caused us to remove elements of the feast. We question whether partisan politics will be brought up, because we have grown intolerant of what is different. Rather than loving the diversity of opinion, our minds wander and wonder how to deceive people who are different, afraid that someone might deceive us.

Polarization is a symptom of the cancer of loneliness that causes us to eat up our resources. We spend more on our insurance and items which bring the assurance that we don't need each other. Rather than ask to borrow a lawn mower, we will dig into our savings to fix or buy another one when we are in need. Rather than ask for help when our car breaks down, we will call a mechanic to change our tire. We see the struggle in our resegregation on a national scale, too. Rather than work through our differences, our politicians shut down the government. Rather than share resources, we build walls so we don't have to see poor people.

The problem is not that we have a unique cultural identity. Living in a post-Christian country, I am afraid of the disdain for tribalism, because it might be used against Christians. The problem is that we think that our tribes are the only ones that matter, and we have forgotten that we are connected. The body cannot say to one member, "I have no need of you." And likewise, a society of tribes and cultures that have naturally been created cannot say to each other, "I have no need of you." In fact, the group that seems the most despised might actually be the most important. We should be challenged by these words from Hubert H. Humphrey, the thirty-eighth vice president of the United States, "The moral test of government is how that government treats those who are in the dawn of life, the children; the twilight of life, the elderly; and the shadows of life, the sick, the needy, and the handicapped."[4]

We are lonely individuals, members of a lowly nation. Drawing from the writings of Saint Augustine, many later theologians would talk about humans suffering from a condition called *curvatus*, or *homo incurvatus in se*, that "humanity is curved inward on itself," unable to see anything else.[5] Like a hand with a tightened tendon that cannot open up, we cannot open up to our neighbors or to God—unless something happens.

The cancer of loneliness has many symptoms, some of which I recognize. While our addicted selves try to find healing in things that do not heal, we cannot hear the truth about our loneliness. Unfortunately, it is only when we hit the bottom that we can hear the truth. The psalmist writes, "Out of the depths, I cry out to you, oh Lord!" (Ps 130:1). If you are in the depths of loneliness right now, I am speaking to you. If you are not, then I am planting an idea of what you might do when and if you hit that depth.

In the same way that a body with blood cancer may never be healed of it, we may never be healed of loneliness in this life. And even if we are, we are always vulnerable to a relapse. It is the condition of this world and the unhealthy culture around us. But the story does not stop there!

Jesus is the Great Physician, one who can do surgery on our prideful souls. Loneliness is not about social media, political persuasion, or the things we do to our bodies. These are manifestations of our loneliness but not the cause. Loneliness originates in the heart and soul.

We see the life of Jesus—his birth, ministry, passion and death, resurrection, and ascension. Then, of all the crazy things, we are called to be

---

4. Knight, "Quote from Humphrey."
5. For more on this theological idea see the scholarly work Jenson, *Gravity of Sin*.

followers of Jesus. Christianity is not failing because it does not work. It is failing because we are not followers of Jesus. The things that Jesus did, we have not even tried.

The cure for loneliness lies in literally trying to love the hell out of each other. The cure for loneliness lies in allowing God to love us through the changing of our lifestyles. Are we brave enough to try that?

When our bodies are physically devastated by cancer, we must go through a treatment that feels like it is killing us. And truthfully cancer does kill part of our bodies. I know people who walk with a limp, because of cancer treatment, much like Jacob walked with a limp after wrestling with God.

Are we willing to be passionate, to undergo a divine therapy for our loneliness? If we are, part of us may die or be diminished in the process. But when that happens, we will realize that what died during our disciplines was not really us. Like a cancerous tumor being cut away, or like a toxic vine that has grown into the bark of an oak tree being removed, we will feel agony and have scars. But after a time of healing, and through a process of recovering, we will come to see that our loneliness has been replaced with connection and communion.

If we are going to contend with our loneliness, we must first admit that it is a problem, a monumental issue that we are powerless to combat by ourselves. Loneliness is monumental in the way that the copper in the Statue of Liberty is monumental. The Statue is made of copper, but we never really think of the tons of metal standing there. So many aspects of our culture stand like a monument. We say, "Look at the social media, the corporations, and the name we have made for ourselves!" But so much of what we have created is made of loneliness. Until we realize that we have structures built of loneliness, we cannot come to connection and communion.

When we realize that we are powerless to control our tendency toward loneliness, like so many individuals in the Bible, we cry out to the Lord.

When we become willing to make a truthful and honest inventory of the ways in which we are isolated, God then asks us to turn our direction. Jesus said, "Follow me." When we follow, we repent and turn away from the isolating things that keep us from the love and kinship of Jesus.

Something dies. In order for our isolation and loneliness to die, the processes and patterns that created it must also die. But when something necrotic dies, it gives way for new life, for resurrection.

We crave connection, and we were made from it and for it. God's essence is connection—Father, Son, and Holy Spirit—three in one. One of the holiest ways we find connection is through communion. Sometimes this means coming to the table in worship to receive holy communion, and sometimes it means recognizing the holiness of the moment when we are at a physical table with others.

Every change requires a starting point, and this is my invitation to you as you make the journey toward deeper connection. The next time you are at a table with other people, close your eyes and say to God, "Thank you for being here. Thank you for this opportunity to communicate with other humans. Thank you for the beauty of our differences, and thank you for loving us all the same."

It may seem like something so small, trying to fix your own loneliness in a world of lonely people, but it is not. When one member of the body is sick, it can make the others sick. And likewise, when one member of the body begins to be well, it offers wellness to all of the others. Be well.

The Discipleship Problem

Loneliness is more than a trend; it is a way of life. The way loneliness affects us is, however, a trend. As with many trends, our methods of being lonely were exacerbated by the COVID-19 pandemic. Pastors, who previously spent six out of eight hours a day by themselves, preoccupied with the busywork of an over-professionalized occupation, found that they were spending all of their time in isolation. The many Zoom meetings only underscored a painful truth—nobody really saw or heard them. Church members, who once found solace in their staid seat in the pew, realized that without that hour on Sunday morning they were utterly lost—and nobody seemed to miss them. The slightly truncated online worship service did not cleanse this lonesome feeling. Everyone seemed to be without.

Some well-prepared churches were able in the pandemic to bridge the loneliness gap. On the surface of things, this seemed to be magic. Trying to find quick answers, many came to surmise that it was the result of those congregations having more money, and to some extent that might have been partially correct. Underneath the surface, though, a painful reality about our loneliness exists.

Our old method of church is dead and, still hanging on to it, many people are dying of loneliness. The method, in its infancy, was founded and grounded in connection and togetherness—in *discipleship*. When discipleship disappeared, or when it was changed, it ceased to draw people together and began making people lonely. Even if this does not seem to apply to your congregation, you have been affected by it in some way.

The United Methodist Church currently has more resources on discipleship than perhaps any other denomination in the world. One of the best-funded general work areas is the General Board of Discipleship, which cranks out literature, ideas, and plans for discipleship and growth. The United Methodist Church's own mission statement is "to make disciples of Jesus Christ for the transformation of the world."[6] For years, the 95 percent white US church has invested millions of dollars and tens of thousands of words in official documents trying to be multicultural, antiracist, and racially diverse. And yet all of these attempts at growing still leave people feeling lonely.

We hear about all of these ideas and endeavors, but we do not often hear about why our attempts to form disciples often fall flat. New studies and attempts at connection use appreciative inquiry, lifting up the virtue instead of denigrating the vice, and, indeed, this is very helpful in many respects, especially because it moves past the probability of being bogged down in defensiveness. However, without naming the ways in which we have missed the mark, we cannot move closer to each other and further from the loneliness that still sits at the core.

Most members of the church, practitioners of the method, do not know the historic reasons for our loneliness and are unable to articulate the contemporary purveyors of it. Part of the reason that we are lonely is that we bought into a notion of the Christian gospel that was individualistic, which said that the main thing that counted was an individual and their relationship with God. This replaced the Methodist band and class meetings with Sunday school classes, replaced a liturgy in which everybody was an equal participant with a professionalized service in which everybody showed up to be fed by one person.

In the twentieth and twenty-first centuries, US consumerism has further tainted this understanding of the gospel, recreating many church campuses to look more like shopping malls than houses of worship. And even in the small, rural areas that have remained unchanged for one hundred years, the world outside has changed, and the church inside has become frozen. It's a striking paradox: many well-endowed churches, which have grown with broad yet shallow spirituality, have distanced themselves from discipleship methods that cost a lot of the individual. Meanwhile, some quaint churches, echoing the authentic spirit of Methodism that once flourished, often lack the tools and materials to cultivate discipleship.

---

6. United Methodist Church, "Mission Statement."

Dead and Belonging—Community and Communication

Reflecting on the journey from death to the hope of resurrection, I'm drawn to thoughts of company and community. In the same way that we can't be brought into this world alone, we ought not leave this world alone either. Rather we are intricately woven together like different threads by a loom. We may think that we are self-made individuals, but we find our limitations when we get sick and need many more than one team of people from different hospital sectors and during recovery to help us along our way. One of the tragic realities of life is that we forget how much we need each other.

Our tailor-made likes and preferences cause us to become exclusive and we cause pain we do not even realize we are causing. On a micro level, we see exclusion where middle- and upper-class people move toward each other and away from poverty. We may think we are well-connected and interconnected, but that is because we are part of systems that enable us to never see the toll that our lifestyle causes. Consider this: The "United" States has so many church denominations with the word *united* in their title: the United Methodist Church, the United Church of Christ, the United Presbyterian Church, the United Reformed Church, the United Pentecostal Church International, the United Brethren in Christ, and I could go on. Most of these groups only unite the people who were already insiders.

When the term "United States" was coined, the indigenous population was in the process of being erased through genocide and the Black population was not even seen as human. Women were not given full rights. Indeed, when the Declaration of Independence says "all men are created equal" it originally referred to all white, land-owning men. In a similar way, when historically white denominations formed, they did so with an eye to unite like-minded people without an understanding or intention of racial equity and inclusion.

On a trip to Duke Divinity School, where I had diligently working toward both my master of divinity and doctor of ministry over a span of a decade, I was struck by how much the space was made only for some people. I was months away from getting my second degree from that place. Eager to flex my muscles in their state-of-the-art student recreational facilities, I got my necessary digital ID, understanding the protocol for non-residential students like myself.

After confirming online that graduate students had access, I confidently approached the gym only to be told I lacked a membership and my program didn't cover one. Feeling slightly defeated but still hopeful, I returned to the divinity school, my anchor point on campus. To my dismay, even the shower there was locked. As I contemplated my next steps, a friend from the housekeeping staff mentioned that the showers were only for faculty and staff.

Drawing on my alumni status, I remembered the perk of using the exercise facility five times annually. Yet when I tried this approach I faced another rejection because they had discontinued that program. Determined to break a sweat, I decided to sprint on the bleachers of the football stadium. But, alas, even that was locked tight, with passing football players confirming the track's unavailability.

For somebody who was in a different program none of the barriers would appear obvious, but as soon as I stepped one foot outside of the meticulously drawn lines of entry I realized how this place has been designed to keep some people in and everybody else out. The beautiful walls that I had seen as vehicles for vines and flowers I now saw as oppressive structures designed to tell would-be visitors where they *are* and *are not* allowed.

This same thing is true in the church. When newcomers enter they see pews with people's names on them, seat cushions that have been left in specific places because specific people have sat there for decades. They might notice that one place on the pew has wear marks where the wood stain has been rubbed off by somebody having sat there for hundreds of hours, coming and going, with the same six-inch precision. Everything about the space tells a story to newcomers: that they are outsiders who do not understand the way things are or how they got there.

I remember hearing about the so-called worship wars that happened in the 1980s and 1990s, when churches in the United States began having open conflict about the type of music and worship services, whether they would be so-called contemporary or traditional. It is a very similar fight that the church has had before, whether arguing about a simplified, revivalistic, or traditional order of worship. I remember hearing an old timer talking about how the worship leaders and church members who had been at the church for a long time were being asked, in some cases, to change very little. He said something to the effect of, "If you have been at this church for a while, you might be asked to change somewhere between 10 and 20 percent of your overall experience of the church to better accommodate new people."

The idea is that almost all of the things you take for granted about worshiping in the church, the location, the expressed culture, the artistic culture in pictures and stained glass windows, the racial history, and especially the language and assumptions of what it means, all of that is staying the same. My friend was saying that it is an irony that people who want to be so welcoming to people coming in to join their church are also, relatively, so unwilling to make the changes necessary to welcome those people. For example, the "home folk" are being asked to change maybe 20 percent. A new person is being asked to change 100 percent of their Sunday morning or otherwise religious experience.

Part of the reason why the church is dying is that we have become like an ancient lobster growing inside of its shell that cannot find a new shell and is suffocating inside of the old edifice from which we are afraid to part. That same friend, who had an uncle that was a professor at the divinity school where I went, also said that he lived with the grim realization that if Christianity kept going the way it was then we could be extinct in a couple of generations. He and I both agreed that the church triumphant and that the movement of the kingdom of God would continue in the world, but in the United States we face annihilation.

Looking at the possibility of no longer existing, it becomes easier, at least for me, to look at the acute death that we are now experiencing. Some people are afraid of losing their individual legacies: that the church named after their family will have its name changed; that the pew that they paid for, with their little brass nameplate, will be uprooted to make space for something else. But we also face the loss of our collective legacy.

But remember, my beloved, that we do not face this terrifying future alone. We are in community. And remember that these same storied structures of the church that have given us hope, that have accidentally excluded the ones we wished to include, are also dying. We may not have much of a tangible, physical home into which to invite people but we still have a spiritual home. We pray in the Lord's prayer, "Thy kingdom come . . . On earth as it is in heaven." We pray for the movement of the work of God that is much more than a physical kingdom with geographic boundaries. That movement, which will extend into the heavenly cosmos alongside our spiritual bodies after this corporeal home has died, will still incorporate and include us. That is our home. It is the same home that followers of Jesus Christ called their own in the first and second centuries before they were given palaces and cathedrals from the Roman Empire.

Now that this space of our physical home is dying we should definitely lament it, but we can also find reason to celebrate, because those who once were excluded now will find their place. And we will find that we, once insiders in church institutions, are no less insiders than the ones who lived on the streets, who were once excluded by accidental social clubs.

Now that the systems and methods of the church are dying we can ask if they can be repurposed and used in new and more holy ways that reflect the action of the Holy Spirit in this millennium. We will no longer have to be beholden to the paperwork that once marked so much of our time, but we may yet find ways of rehoming that paperwork and automating it in a way that it finds its rightful place albeit in service to the church with the church not being in service to it.

With the unknowing idols of our institutions taking precedence we can see community reflected in others who are beyond the bounds of what we first understood as ourselves, and we can leave our secret space to find the sacredness of church existing as an action verb, as a movement with people who we once saw as competition.

If we are to be faithful followers, we cannot circumvent the valley of the shadow of death, but we will find ourselves as people who experience new life after having reckoned with new deaths. We will also realize, as we start to name the death of all that we once knew as community, that what we understand to be new death is, in fact, old death. That is, so much of what we lament and mourn died long ago. We are only coming now to name it.

As a pastor, I have officiated dozens of funerals. I have seen a phenomenon where some people, who may only be tangentially connected to the deceased, come into the space and start wailing and crying for everything that they are worth. It is because they have closed off real grief for so long that when they open their hearts to it the flood of tears that have dammed up behind their red-hot eyes burst forth in a tidal wave that they do not think will ever stop.

When we start to mourn the death of one thing in the church we may find ourselves mourning a lot of things that died a long time ago that we should have cried about. But, also, as we grieve the community that used to be we will find new people, a new community that is more adept at lamentation, more accustomed to crying. When we become vulnerable again, maybe for the first time, we will find others who are adept at speaking the language of pain, maybe others who have made their home there. And when we lament the brokenness and loss that death brings to our communities, the act of lamentation brings us toward noticing resurrection. Like the two travelers lamenting on the road to Emmaus, we may, in some way, be walking and talking with the risen Lord, one step closer to seeing the power of resurrection revealed.

Consider at least one of the implications for "death and resurrection" with respect to our communication. Think about young people: that group of society constantly reminds us of the need to update our "methods" of church to be able to communicate with the world around us. In 2022 I became the director of youth ministry for the regional body of the United Methodist Church where I served. Before our schism we had somewhere around 780 churches. As I write this the schism has claimed more than a third of these. Historically, we have relied on events to communicate the message of Christianity to young people assuming that local churches are doing discipleship on an ongoing basis through youth fellowship. However, this way of communicating the idiom of our faith relied on sustainable youth ministry in local churches. It relied on people in the local church being able to afford to get to those events. It assumed that people already spoke much of the basic language of the church. As we continue into an age when a majority of young people are outside of the church, or any consistent religious organization, we need new modes of communication. I'm not saying to get rid of our old ways of communicating, but we need to realize if these methods have already died.

In 2007 a campus minister friend shared an alarming observation: a significant portion of incoming college students grappled with mental health challenges, notably anxiety and depression. Some young individuals have admitted to feeling out of place in church spaces that haven't evolved to resonate with their generation. If our churches appear out of touch or unwelcoming to young people, why should they darken the doorway, seeking community?

The decline in older church traditions' and youth ministries' effectiveness provides a window to innovate and communicate in novel ways. By mourning the loss of event-centric youth ministry we can pivot our focus toward fresh avenues of engagement. Instead of clinging to past paradigms we should prioritize the insights and aspirations of the youth still connected to our faith. Let's invest our resources in nurturing the innovative ideas they sow, drawing from the church's rich heritage to cultivate a fertile environment. Embracing change and mourning what's no longer effective can pave the way for vibrant future growth. It's a matter of recognizing and acting upon the opportunities.

You Are the Place to Be: Embracing a Community-Centric Faith

In a previous chapter, I talked about the death of the centrality of place—how either the literal or metaphorical termites were coming. At a time when church buildings are crumbling and our sacred spaces seem to be disappearing, it's crucial to remember the words of 1 Cor 6:19 (NRSV): "Or do you not know that your body is a temple of the Holy Spirit within you, which you have from God, and that you are not your own?" This verse reminds us that our faith is not confined to the walls of a building; rather it resides within us, in our relationships and communities.

The work of Alexia Salvatierra and Brandon Wrencher offers an inspiring perspective on the idea of base Christian communities. In *Buried Seeds*, they posit that these communities—whether they were the base Christian communities of Latin America amid crumbling governments or "hush harbors" where enslaved Africans gathered for worship and community on Southern plantations—are not merely geographic locations but are instead the very places where we, as believers, gather and connect.[7] Denominational churches in the United States have long provided shelter from the storms of injustice that rage outside their doors. But the decline of the church building as a central fixture in our lives offers a unique opportunity for renewal—a chance to create spaces that welcome not only the faithful but also the lonely sojourner and the placeless people seeking refuge.

Looking back at the pilgrimage paths of Jesus, the apostle Paul, and the circuit riders of early Methodism we see that the Holy Spirit has always been on the move. These examples demonstrate that the power of our faith lies not in the sanctity of any single location but in the connections we forge as we journey together. As Archbishop Desmond Tutu says, "Our humanity is bound up in one another, for we can only be human together."[8] Now is the time to rectify old mistakes by embracing a community-centric and not building-centric faith which transcends physical boundaries and embraces the potential of the Holy Spirit within all of us.

To truly become a people who are the place we must recognize the importance of self-care in preparing ourselves for this new journey. As we move away from the confines of traditional church buildings and embrace a more fluid, community-focused faith, we must prioritize nurturing our own spiritual well-being.

One way to foster self-care is through regular engagement in spiritual practices such as prayer, meditation, and reflection. By grounding ourselves in these practices we can create an internal sanctuary that serves as a refuge from the world's tumultuous landscape. Additionally, seeking out opportunities for fellowship with other believers can provide the support and encouragement needed to sustain us as we venture into unfamiliar territory.

Another essential aspect of self-care involves fostering a spirit of gratitude. Thich Nhat Hanh, a renowned Vietnamese Zen Buddhist monk, teacher, author, poet, and peace activist has inspired people from many religious traditions to live in gratitude. He says that we should live in "gratitude,

---

7. Salvatierra and Wrencher, *Buried Seeds*, 1–47.
8. Dalai Lama and Tutu, *Book of Joy*, 127.

and we can do this by generating the energies of mindfulness, peace, stability, and compassion in our daily lives."[9] By recognizing and ritualistically celebrating the blessings in our lives we cultivate an attitude of thankfulness that permeates our relationships and communities making the "place" where we gather more holy. This gratitude can serve as a powerful force in shaping a community-centric faith that is both resilient and transformative.

Ultimately, becoming a people who are the place requires a shift in perspective—a recognition that the true power of our faith lies not in the grandeur of any physical structure but in the relationships and connections we forge as we journey together. As we embrace this new vision for the church, remember that we are "temples" where the Spirit dwells. And as places we have given the deed over to the Spirit who will move other people needing shelter toward us.

Ahead of us is both a challenge and an opportunity. Even if, like me, you inherently think that you are more community-centered than building-centered, you may find yourself reevaluating that when the building gets threatened. If we are historically white churches, most of our wealth has been historically tied to physical locations. Part of the movement away from these is also admitting that they have been idols. In moving toward people as place instead of geography as place we also move toward solidarity with those historically dispossessed. White churches in the South in the early 1800s were almost certainly tied to the plantation economy. Moving away from addiction to place also moves us one step toward allowing the logic of the plantation, that still emerges sometimes, to further die so that we might be resurrected as a more equitable community of faith.

Following this thought out toward its end will help us inevitably to have more hope for life, but in the immediate future it might also cause us collective heartache. Are we saying to get rid of the buildings? Are we saying to share them? Are we saying to repurpose them for the community around us? We need to be in healthy places to ask these questions.

By prioritizing self-care we can ensure that we are prepared for the journey ahead. And as we embrace this new vision of the church—one that transcends physical boundaries and focuses on the power of the Holy Spirit within the temple of us—we can be confident that we are, indeed, the place to be.

---

9. Thich Nhat Hanh, *Love Letter to the Earth*, 110.

Self-Care in Crisis

In times of calm, the practice of self-care can be a soothing balm, a moment of respite in our otherwise busy lives. But when the world around us is engulfed in crisis, self-care takes on a new urgency, becoming an essential tool for navigating the choppy waters of turmoil and uncertainty.

A crisis is a significant event or series of events that threaten the stability and well-being of individuals, communities, or even entire societies. In our world today, we are faced with a multitude of overlapping crises and pandemics: COVID-19, political polarization, systemic racism, economic disparity, and ecological upheaval, to name just a few.

The temptation for many in times of crisis, particularly within religious institutions, is to turn inward, focusing solely on the survival of their own communities or organizations. However, this narrow perspective often neglects the broader social context in which these crises unfold. In times like these, we are called not just to look inward but also to consider our role in the wider world and to engage with the challenges that face us all.

So what does self-care look like in the midst of crisis? It begins with nurturing our own spirit through time spent alone with ourselves and with God. This can be a challenge for many, but it is an essential practice for sustaining our strength and resilience during difficult times.

Another vital aspect of self-care during crisis is to seek out and spend time with people who strengthen and support us. These connections provide a much-needed sense of stability and belonging when everything around us feels uncertain.

But true self-care in crisis goes beyond merely seeking solace in familiar places. What happens if those familiar places have been part of the problem? In my personal life some of the voices that connected me most with myself and God in the past—whether preaching, singing, or as conversation partners—have been the cause of my problems. Even the act of praying has been difficult, because the ground has been so shaken in my spiritual life.

Self care in crisis also involves engaging with those who may challenge us or hold opposing views. By fostering relationships with people of peace who may be adversaries we can learn to navigate differences and disagreements without resorting to violence or hostility.

One example of this kind of relationship is the man I call Jones, named in the last chapter. Though we hold different beliefs and he may be trying to convert me, we've reached an understanding. We are able to discuss our disagreements without animosity, allowing us both to grow and learn from one another.

In times of crisis, self-care is about more than just tending to our own needs. It is about finding the strength and resilience to engage with the world around us, even when that world is fraught with challenges and upheaval. By cultivating a deep sense of connection with ourselves, with others, and with the divine, we can navigate the crises of our time and emerge stronger, wiser, and more compassionate than before.

Care for the Caregiver

Regardless of the various tales and myths we encounter throughout literature, there are certain symbols and characters that capture the essence of despair and fear in a deeply resonating way. Think of those ancient legends where shadows or chilling winds represented omens, signaling a foreboding sense of doom. These stories often describe an overwhelming sensation of cold, as if all warmth and light are being drained away.

Such chilling allegories serve as apt metaphors for the emotions that surround us in moments of intense grief or anticipation of loss.

Sometimes caregivers for the terminally ill encounter such spirits wafting through the air. It's more than the angel of death, more than the stealing of life. Even though I have not experienced this with my own family I have noticed how the open wound of death deferred can rob the soul of hope—a feeling that *you may never be happy again, like all the warmth has been taken from the world.*

One of the biblical proverbs says, "Hope deferred makes the heart sick" (Prov 13:12). So what do you do when you intuitively know that your next dose of hope will not come from a cure of someone but will come when they have died? What do you do when you believe that someone's healing will come in heaven, but they are stuck in the muck of suffering in a broken body? Death deferred can make the heart sick too.

Throughout our culture we see so many sickened hearts, caregivers holding the hands of people whom they believe are already but not yet dead. Our culture has a fixation on keeping the heart pumping even when the brain function has ceased. "The body knows how to die," hospice chaplains have told me, "and our job is to make it comfortable as this transition happens." Sometimes we hold on too tightly to it because our identity has become wrapped in the deferral of death. *Acceptance* is a challenge for more people than the twelve-step recovery program-goers.

I've seen sickened hearts that have wilted like the leaves on my hot pepper plants after the first frost. The culture in which I live, in addition to not knowing how to let the body die, treats people as if they are already dead when they cannot produce anymore. Being thrown out of sight and mind, like a broken cog from an industrial machine, long-term care facilities run full with people who are unloved and unappreciated by the society to which they gave their lives.

Some of the people who work at these are wonderful. My father, a career nurse, has volumes of stories in his head of joy he has given to and received from patients in these facilities. He also talks of how worthless many of them are made to feel, like a caged, aging tiger that is placed out of sight at the zoo. Memory care units can feel like places that will never see happiness or brilliance again.

We have a hard time appreciating what is old and dying simply for its own sake. We may appreciate what was, or we may dream of what may be. When we see a human, made in the image of God, who used to pray and teach Sunday school—teaching people about the life-changing love of Jesus Christ—who cannot change their own diaper, who has forgotten the name of Jesus . . . the experience can make finding peace a challenge.

Whether it is in the presence of a person whose memory is fading like a 2:00 a.m. campfire, or whether in the presence of a person whose brain has already been declared lost, being a caregiver can be exhausting. Perhaps that is why we call custodians of real estate "care*takers*" and custodians of human lives "care*givers*." We know that offering part of ourselves to people who have lost themselves is a giving of part of ourselves.

The broader culture in which I live has forgotten or perhaps never known how to appreciate people who seem to exist without ability to give back, whose presence exists to be served or they will die. The obligatory response we give almost feels like a paltry attempt to say, "Hey, don't worry, you who are still able-bodied, we will have a landing place for you when you wear out." But we do not appreciate the presence of God within them, the image of God into which we Christians say they have been made. This larger societal trend of what we believe it is to be human—*I am because I have utilitarian value*—is just as much what sucks the soulfulness as the facts of death themselves.

Whatever the cause, if you agree that caregiving for those near death costs a lot of soulfulness, happiness, and brilliance, then perhaps you find it easier to agree on another premise. *What gets poured out must be refilled.*

Care for the Caregiver: My Dad's Witness

My father, a seasoned nurse and educator in Bladen Community College's nursing program, has often shared with me a crucial lesson that he imparts to his students: "Care for the caregiver is what enables us to continue in the giving professions." He sees little difference between his work as a nurse and my work as a pastor, and he has always offered me his care and encouragement.

In reflecting on my father's wisdom, I have been contemplating the despair that can arise when we bear witness to the transition of institutions like churches as they evolve from their centuries-old forms into something new and different. This process can feel akin to the experience of supporting someone nearing the end of their life.

When a person is brain dead, their body remains but their spirit is absent. Similarly, when a church is "brain dead," congregants may attend worship services but the essence of the community seems to have vanished. Churches, like individuals experiencing memory loss or Alzheimer's disease, may struggle to remember who they were and who they are.

In the final years of life people in the United States often spend more on medical care than they have throughout their entire lives. As institutions we must ask ourselves: How can we survive and connect with others if we approach our existence like a terminally ill person?

As caregivers the stress and challenges faced by our institutions can weigh heavily upon us, whether we are spiritual leaders, pastors, or ministers. Understanding the "soul of an institution," as Susan Beaumont discusses in her book *How to Lead When You Don't Know Where You're Going*, can help us define the parameters for our own self-care. Understanding the soul of the institution helps us understand what the institution is putting on us and might not exactly be from us.[10]

When people die there is a certain finality to their existence, at least from a modern perspective. However, the death of an institution can simultaneously represent both an end and a new beginning. Consider the metaphor of a tree in the forest: when a tree dies it falls, but in doing so it becomes a hub of life. Moss grows on it, saplings sprout from it, and rabbits nest beneath it.

As caregivers we must consider how we can remain resilient and alive, much like the saplings that grow from a fallen tree in the forest. The tree that fell left a gap in the canopy for the sunlight to fall, allowing new life to grow. Teaming lives of different entities are possible through the space of what once existed. New life yearns to learn how to flourish.

To care for ourselves in the face of institutional change, we can draw on several strategies:

---

10. Beaumont, *How to Lead*, chap. 3.

1. Establish boundaries: Recognize the limits of your energy and capacity to support others. Be mindful of the need to balance your personal life with your professional responsibilities.
2. Seek support: Surround yourself with a network of peers, mentors, and friends who understand the unique challenges you face as a caregiver. Share your experiences and draw on their collective wisdom.
3. Cultivate a practice of self-reflection: Regularly engage in activities that encourage introspection such as journaling, meditation, or prayer. Use these moments to reconnect with your sense of purpose and reaffirm your commitment to your vocation.
4. Pursue personal growth: Embrace opportunities for learning and growth both within your profession and in other areas of interest. This can help you stay engaged, inspired, and adaptable in the face of change.
5. Embrace change as an opportunity for growth: Recognize that change is a natural part of life and that it can offer valuable lessons and opportunities for renewal. Approach change with curiosity, openness, and a willingness to adapt.

By caring for ourselves as caregivers we can better support our institutions as they navigate the transitions and transformations that lie ahead. In doing so, we can ensure that we remain resilient and adaptable, like the saplings that grow from a fallen tree, and contribute to the flourishing of our communities in the face of change. We don't just need ideas or beliefs for self-care. We also need a spirituality for it.

Awake, Thou That Sleepest

The cry of Charles Wesley in his sermon "Awake, Thou That Sleepest" resonates in our hearts today with even more urgency and necessity. The Wesleys' call for spiritual awakening and renewal reverberates through the annals of Methodist history, from the revivals during the First and Second Great Awakenings to the very need for revival in our contemporary world.

The schism of 1808 over enslavement within the Methodist Episcopal Church stands as a stark reminder of our collective history, a challenge to our spiritual slumber. In the birth of the African Methodist Episcopal Church under Richard Allen we see a powerful response to this challenge—a vital awakening that continues to guide and inspire us.

The Fundamentalist/Modernist split, the Azuza Street Revivals, and other pivotal moments in the history of the Methodist Church bring us back to the core question: Revived to what?

In our times we witness a divide within the church. On one side, we find conservative Christians, grounded in individual transformation, embodying the Methodist tradition of "personal holiness." On the other side, we have progressive, justice-centered Christians who commit to societal transformation, embodying the principle of "social holiness."

This divide poses a profound question for our spiritual revival. What does it mean to be spiritually alive in today's world, where personal transformation and societal justice seem to stand at opposite ends? The answer may lie in seeking revival, not as an isolated personal or societal experience but as a unified pursuit of the kingdom of God, on earth as it is in heaven.

In this regard Jonathan Wilson-Hartgrove's book *Reconstructing the Gospel: Finding Freedom from Slaveholder Religion* offers a crucial perspective. Several places in the work, he asserts that the white church in the US needs to become a disciple of the Black Church.[11] In the prayer for revival I think this is also important, because the Black Church is a place that since its inception has struggled for both personal and social holiness, both for liberation of the body and soul.

In the face of death and burnout, let this be our encouraging, uplifting message: As individuals and as a church, we are called to awaken, to stir from our spiritual slumber. The stirring is not easy, but it is the path to true spiritual life. We are called to respond to the work of Jesus Christ through the Holy Spirit, through the kingdom of God coming "on earth as it is in heaven," not to a comfortable slumber but to an awakening. For in this pursuit we will find ourselves moving closer to the heart of God, the source of true life and renewal. As I consider the need for awakening, and as a member of a mostly white church, I invite us now to take some spiritual notes on self care from voices outside of the white church.

Spirituality of Self-Care

Self-care for me is intensely spiritual. It is mystical, and by that I mean it is marked by a real connection with the Holy Spirit—with what is greater than me that my eyes cannot see. In this twilight of Christian dominance in the United States there are so many things that we just cannot see. To "walk by faith and not by sight" means a whole lot more than it did when we reasonably knew what we believed.

11. See Wilson-Hartgrove, *Reconstructing the Gospel*.

I have so many doubts—doubts in certain ways of connecting to God, in the methods of practicing my spirituality, and in what I've been taught is and is not allowed. I have not come to doubt the saving grace of Jesus Christ. In some ways I have added a lot to my spirituality even while so much of it feels suspicious to me.

A sociologist might look at me and say that, as a postmodern Christian, I am trying on all of the things. In this world where everyone decides what their personal truth is, what their "thing" is, I am seeing where the truth of the love and grace of Jesus Christ resonates with me through all of the "things." Let me share a few:

- I still speak in tongues like I did while part of a Pentecostal ministry, because I have found incredible liberation in this act of worship where part of my brain feels freed up to allow a divine prayer language to inhabit my vocal chords. But I am also deeply suspicious of the exclusionary language that many Pentecostals use like gatekeepers of the Spirit.

- I still read the Bible, but I am deeply pained when I see ancient patriarchal customs that have been used by the church for sexual and racial domination. I still believe the "Word" became flesh and dwelt among us, even while I am pained by how many people think their English translation contains the entirety of the divine *Logos* and wisdom of God in its "common sense" understanding.

- I have begun connecting with my ancestors, much in the same way that the Roman Catholic Church has always advocated for connecting with God through the saints who have gone before us, and part of me struggles, having had a colonized imagination, having heard anti-ancestral rhetoric from Christian histories that demonized Native American theology for its connection with ancestors (and justified oppression over them).

As we hold on to different practices and exercises for and of spirituality, we need to be told that it is OK to do so. It is OK to find meaning while in transition. As I journey through change, I think of my ancestors. My mom's ancestors were English, Scottish, and Irish. They came to these shores amid troubles in their homelands in Europe.

My dad's ancestors were half European. The Villegas family was likely a Sephardic Jewish family that came around the year 1500 in a pogrom from Spain. Some of his ancestors were French, coming to receive a land grant in Mexico as the government tried to make the country more European. And some were Chichimecas—an indigenous tribe that lived north of where the Aztec Empire once stood, labeled with this name by the Spaniards who could not subdue them. Reminding me of the two Seminole Wars that Andrew Jackson fought in Florida trying to kill and subdue the Seminole Tribe, the Spaniards had to fight two Chichimecan wars to subdue this nomadic people who did not have villages that could easily be destroyed. Thinking of the transformation and borderlands in my family history, my mind travels to the idea of "*nepantla.*"

Amid spiritual liminality, a sense of *nepantla*, a term central to Gloria Anzaldúa's seminal work *Borderlands/La Frontera*, becomes particularly relevant. *Nepantla* refers to a spiritual state of being "in between," a space that exists in the "borderlands" between different realities or ways of understanding. It's a dynamic space that, much like Anzaldúa's borderlands, is fraught with confusion, growth, and transformation. When we embark on the journey of self-care, we step into this liminal space, daring to question established norms and embracing a new spiritual consciousness that includes a divine regard for the self.[12]

Anzaldúa tells us that we inhabit "borderlands" not just in geographical terms but also within the realms of our identities, spiritual beliefs, and personal histories. Our spiritual transition, like Anzaldúa's borderlands, involves crossing and recrossing the cultural, theological, and ideological borders we've been conditioned to abide by. This is an act of radical self-love that finds common ground with Audre Lorde's vision of self-care.

For Anzaldúa, these borderlands are the sites of a metamorphosis where the old and the new, the known and the unknown, are in constant negotiation. This is where we find our own "*mestiza* consciousness," a term Anzaldúa uses to describe a state of being that embraces multiplicity, fluidity, and hybridity. As we learn to navigate the wilderness of our own spirituality we embrace a *mestiza* consciousness, expanding our understanding of God's love and grace beyond the boundaries set by traditional religious institutions.[13]

Just as Anzaldúa discovered a new sense of self and identity in the tension-filled in-between, we too find our spiritual self-care in this liminal season. It is in this *nepantla* where we muster the bravery to question, the strength to love ourselves, and the faith to believe in a God that exists beyond the confines of language and doctrine. I have tried to meet God beyond these confines, and it is scary and sometimes lonesome work.

I was talking with Fatimah, a pastor friend with deep wisdom, about all of the transitions in my spirituality, and she said that she's going through

12. Anzaldúa, *Borderlands*, 11–13.
13. Anzaldúa, *Borderlands*, 102.

her own. She said that one of her friends told her, as she was in flux with her own spirituality, "Your bravery does not scare me." Don't get me wrong, I still love to connect with God in traditioned and practiced ways. And yet sometimes the Spirit, like a wind that refuses to blow through my open window, moves elsewhere and I want to go searching.

When practiced and traditioned methods of encountering God's Spirit have not helped us, the Spirit is big enough to find us in new ways, to be brave in doing so. Even Jesus said, "I have other sheep that do not belong to this fold. I must bring them also" (John 10:16 NRSV). As Jesus talks about being the Good Shepherd and makes the connection of coming later as the Holy Spirit, I interpret this to mean that the Lord works in mysterious ways and can reach us with different methods.

Some people would argue that there's nothing wrong with the methods and it is the way they are practiced that leaves us feeling devoid of God's goodness. In a spiritual sense, I agree. A ship may have the practiced method of unfurling its sails, and yet in the doldrums where no wind is blowing those methods do not serve. The situation then longs for those on board to break out the oars.

Right now, I think many of us are between methods. The ways through which we have encountered God have been wounded and broken by the church's oppressive marriage to the sinfulness of empire and through other ways we have "missed the mark." And so we are transitioning. In one sense, the church is like a sailboat without wind. In another sense, we are in a free fall right now. In this liminal season, as we seek a spirituality to hold us, I have a few thoughts about the idea of free fall.

Have you ever jumped off of a cliff into water below? I remember the first time I did so, at Smith Mountain Lake in Virginia. It must have been forty feet up, but it felt like a hundred. It took four or five seconds between when my feet left the rock and when they hit the water.

So many things marked that feeling of free fall. Fear gripped my throat, both before and after I leapt. The in-between threw my body into an animalistic sense of awareness, my nervous system taking control—the heart speeding up and time slowing down. Free fall is an in-between. It is a borderland. It is liminality. Free fall is when the gravitational forces of inevitability take you from the perch where you were to where you will be. It is when your potential energy gets thrown into full speed, and you hope that your inertia will have some good outcome and not a disastrous end.

Free fall reminds me of time in the wilderness. Wilderness time can feel like the unknown, where gravity grabs us and pulls us. We begin moving so quickly through the unknown that the body and nerves take control. All of the automatic sensitivities and bodily functions go into effect. We can't see, because it is all a blur. We have not mapped out the unknown space that zips past us.

Wilderness is a space of decentering the ego. Father Richard Rohr talks about the wilderness as liminal space and the importance of it. In *Adam's Return*, he talks about how the wilderness and liminal season was used for rites of passage in pre-axial civilizations. It was a time when young people, usually young men, would go into the wilderness and experience the fragility of their own lives, young women often learning this intuitively in puberty by having to contend with seeing their own blood on a monthly basis. For young people who intentionally went into the wilderness, it took them from being lost in the feeling of free fall to being found. It took them from speeding through a blurry landscape to knowing it and themselves. In learning through the liminal season of their own mortality these young people, in their rites of initiation, would be able to return to the community transformed, knowing that life was not all "about" them.[14] In lieu of this type of experience, I find the liminal season to offer a similar holy decentering.

Especially for people who have been raised in a wilderness space, we must find in the wilderness a space for radical self-love. Minoritized people have been taught that who they are is problematic. Black, feminist, lesbian author and activist Audre Lorde talked a lot in her life about the importance of learning to love yourself in a world that demonizes who you are. People with privilege will need to learn in the wilderness not to be self-centered in a prideful way. Those without privilege will need to learn not to be self-centered in a self-deprecating way. All of us should learn to love ourselves and choose ourselves, because only in doing so can we be obedient to Jesus who told us, "Love your neighbor as yourself."

As with Jesus in the wilderness, the liminal season for us also is marked by hunger. We have a hunger for encountering the Holy Spirit in the in-between. Charismatic Christian author Tommy Tenney, in *God Chasers*, talks about the hunger for the Holy Spirit as the bread of heaven.[15] I remember reading his book and hearing him talk about "the manifest presence of God" and wanting to be where God is as opposed to where God was. So much of institutional religion is the practice of where God was.

I am reminded, for example, of Jesus' experience on the Mount of Transfiguration. As Jesus was transfigured and his clothes became dazzling white Peter saw him conversing with Elijah and Moses—two long-dead heroes of the Jewish faith. In his astonishment, and perhaps thinking to honor the moment, Peter proposed to build three shelters—one for Jesus, one for

---

14. Rohr, *Adam's Return*, 1–5.
15. See Tenney, *God Chasers*.

Moses, and one for Elijah. It was while he was still speaking that a cloud enveloped them and, from within the cloud, God's voice declared, "This is my Son, the Beloved; listen to him!" (Mark 9:7 NRSV). As I mentioned in the chapter on the prophetic, spiritual care in liminal space is about stopping, looking, and listening. And while this can sometimes occur in remote and individual settings, it is most effectively accomplished in harmony with others.

The profound wisdom of bell hooks, celebrated scholar and social activist, guides us deeper into understanding liminal space in the context of community. In her groundbreaking work *All About Love: New Visions*, hooks stresses the importance of love as an active verb rather than a passive feeling, an intentional choice and commitment to mutual growth, respect, and shared vulnerability.[16] This understanding can bring clarity to our shared sojourn through the liminal spaces of our spirituality.

In the liminal space, the practice of love as hooks describes it is an antidote to the isolation that often comes with spiritual transformation. She describes love as a combination of care, knowledge, responsibility, respect, and the act of creating and maintaining spaces of mutual trust and affirmation. When applied in our spiritual transitions, we not only provide these for ourselves but also extend them to others navigating their own spiritual "borderlands."

In hooks's vision, this mutual support and validation are central to cultivating a community in the liminal space. Love, as she describes, is the act of reaching out to others, honoring their experiences and truths, and creating space for shared exploration and understanding.[17] As we navigate our individual spiritual uncertainties, we also remain interconnected, tethered to each other in our shared endeavor to redefine faith and spirituality. This is exactly what I meant when I talked about Pastor Fatimah quoting, "your bravery does not scare me."

With love—I would say, God's love acted out through our deep relationships—we are able to find out a few things about ourselves. In the in-between we find out who we deeply are. When we do not have the things that we once identified ourselves with, we find that we are not those things. When we lose technology, whether it is cellular technology or social technology, we realize that we have overidentified ourselves with it. We also build new relationships, because we've come to rely on people who are on the journey with us. We realize that no person is an island, as Thomas

---

16. hooks, *All About Love*, chap. 1.
17. hooks, *All About Love*, x–xv.

Merton wrote about. Even though some of us may live as hermits, we need each other.

We may also find new relationships with Mother Earth in the wilderness of liminality. I remember when I first heard Patowatomi author and spiritual leader Kaitlin Curtice speaking at a conference. She talked about relearning the indigenous wisdom of connecting with the earth. Some plants that she had wanted to kill as weeds, it turned out, were medicinal. My sister Tirzah taught me the same thing about the broadleaf and longleaf plantain, known to some indigenous people as "white man's footstep," which contains both vitamins and antioxidants. In the liminal space, we may realize that what we would resist on this earth is actually a gift.

Of course, after having been taught this about the plantain plants, I was asked to mow the lawn, making me realize how challenging it is to stay in our space of connecting. More broadly, the challenge to being in in-between space is staying there. Like surfing a wave we balance and try not to fall off. What we find in the wilderness is beautiful, but the world around us is designed not to allow us to stay there, much like the mountaintop's very essence makes it difficult to stay on it.

I realize that in-between space is often connected with suffering, and I have immense privilege even talking about it. But, also, it is where growth comes. I heard a neuroscientist say that one of the main reasons that elders in the United States struggle with memory loss is that they settle into such an immovable pattern that a lot of their neural pathways in the brain die off. Liminality keeps the brain strong.

And so each of us must develop a posture for being in liminality. Being trauma-informed, we should realize that it is difficult to stay in in-between spaces, because past wounds push us toward something solid. Being destabilized in liminal space triggers our trauma. We ought to develop and cultivate practices of healing our nervous systems if we are to stay in liminality. The ability to do so is often determined by our proximity to home or place.

Willie Jennings talked about place and habitation in the Bampton Lectures at University Church in Oxford in May 2023.[18] He talked about the Western fixation with owning place and being territorial, and how it is at odds with Jesus' own words—moving the disciples from seeing the temple as a building to the Lord's own body. Even though that idea was bastardized by colonial Christians who told Native people they could not have the land as a sacred place, Eurocentric practice has been obsessed with place and land.

---

18. Jennings, "Jesus and the Displaced."

Modernity has mixed territoriality with hypercapitalism; more and more land is being bought up by the ultrawealthy leaving less and less available for medium- and lower-income people. Fearing another great depression, many US citizens have left and bought land in other countries that offer digital nomad visas causing gentrification to start occurring in less wealthy European Union countries like Greece and Portugal. The struggle is worldwide. So many people are without houses at this moment.

And so I don't want to merely say "look for the silver lining" to those who are without a roof. Rather I want to say that when the powerful have taken control over most of the land, as they did in the time of Jesus, we may begin to find our place among people and not land. As I said earlier, "You are the place to be."

Whether we have homes or not, the in-between space creates a lot of stress which adds a layer of complexity to our spirituality in this moment. In most places of life stress is going to promote growth. If you prune a plant, it will grow. During exercise we strain our bodies causing the breakdown of muscle fibers which, combined with adequate nutrition and rest, means that they grow stronger. Thinking of all of the stressors we encounter, I want to take a few moments to address stress as part of our strategy for spiritual self-care in a liminal season:

When stress levels get high, we have a few different options for responding.

Option one: We can do nothing. And if we don't do anything, we will probably end up getting stressed out. Some of us implode, which might be more dangerous, because we may not see when our own demise is coming. Some of us explode, and it is evident to the world around these people that they are getting stressed.

Option two: We can medicate. Official medicine exists for stress and anxiety: passive medication, like Lexapro, which brings down a person's systemic anxiety, and fast-acting medication, like Xanax, which quickly mellows the nervous system during panic and acutely anxious moments. People also medicate with drugs, alcohol, and things that will give them dopamine release, things like video games and the magic mirror of powerful cellular devices that show us whatever we want to see. When we medicate, sometimes it prevents us from connecting with the beauty of the world, because, in addition to damaging the pain, sometimes it numbs our feeling receptors for joy. However, having been medicated for depression and anxiety I am a firm believer that it helps.

In *The Myth of Normal*, Gabor Maté talks about the destructive nature of what our Western culture deems as "normal."[19] Most people are suffering from some stress-related mental illness, and many people have heart disease and diabetes. I remember watching *The Onion Movie* around fifteen years ago, and they were making a satire about the obesity epidemic. This one man is labeled in this farce as "a formerly obese" man, and he says that it is high time that the government did something about obesity. The government's reaction, in this make-believe episode, was raising the definition of obesity from 55 percent body fat to 90 percent body fat.[20] Even though we medicate so many people, and the healthcare industry is quickly becoming the largest industry in the United States, we do not have an issue that we can medicate ourselves out of. I would argue that we need to have a revolution of values in our culture so that we can have a society with less stress on everybody. Because even though stress promotes growth, too much stress can kill.

Option three: Growing in resilience. I have been on a journey to grow in resilience for the last six years since I was diagnosed with anxiety and depression. As I mentioned elsewhere, mindfulness-based stress reduction is one of the key practices for me. Building resilience means changing our physiological relationship with stress, moving from it being something that hijacks our sympathetic nervous system to something that we can observe and decide whether or not we will respond to. It moves us a step back from the automatic reaction.

When we build resilience, it creates more ability for us to experience joy. This is one of the most spiritual experiences in life. Joy is a surprising encounter with what is larger than ourselves. Reflecting on *The Book of Joy* by the Dalai Lama and Desmond Tutu, it becomes clear that true joy isn't just a fleeting emotion; it's a profound realization of interconnectedness, a celebration of life's inherent beauty despite its challenges. Their shared wisdom reminds us that in the face of suffering and adversity choosing joy becomes an act of defiance and hope, a testament to the enduring human spirit.

For being able to show up spiritually, to "stop, look, and listen" in liminal space, we need to know how to handle stress. Maybe we are all a mix of these three ways—doing nothing, medicating, and building resilience. Whatever avenue we take, may we find ourselves able to handle our stress. Dealing with stress is so important because of the ongoing nature of liminality and change in our lives. It is not a temporary game, like going to play

---

19. Maté and Maté, *Myth of Normal*, chaps. 19–24.
20. Hanson and Siegel, *Onion Movie*.

two halves on a sports field. Life is an eternal game that we must always be training for.

This is the paradox in the idea of liminality. It is the space between two points. But, also, I think it is true that it can always be the process of arriving at something, never to have fully arrived. It is important for us to chase something so much bigger than ourselves that we will never get there.

A lawyer and Duke Divinity School student named Travis, who served as an intern with my wife and me, said that the only thing appropriate to dedicate your life to is a problem that will take at least one hundred years to solve. Most of us want to be in either year one or year ninety-nine, but the reality is that most of us are inextricably tied up in the middle of struggles that have gone on before us and will continue on after we are dead—for example, the struggle to make the United States an antiracist nation, as opposed to a "not racist" nation (see Ibram X. Kendi's amazing book *How to Be an Antiracist* on the difference between the two).

I have seen this long-form struggle evident in the lives of some of the greatest spiritual and prophetic leaders. More than one hundred years ago Walter Rauschenbusch wrote the book *Christianity and the Social Crisis*. He talked about the gross inequality in the country and used the Old Testament prophets to imagine another way. Implicitly, he had a theology of "postmillennialism," a belief that we could Christianize the public order and make the world better and better until Jesus came back. His ideas were largely ignored after two world wars and people coming to believe that the church should not try to take control of the government (and also realizing through the twentieth-century phenomenon of fascism how bad of an idea this could be). But at the root of it his spiritual idea lived in this same struggle that he knew was bigger than his own life. He said, "The Kingdom of God is always but coming."[21] Basically, we keep trying to live into what we pray in the Lord's prayer, "Thy kingdom come, thy will be done, on earth as it is in heaven."

The spiritual paradox also lives in the words of a prayer of Saint Oscar Romero: "We are prophets of a future not our own."[22] Like Moses standing on the mountaintop and looking into the promised land, but not able to be there; like Martin Luther King Jr. doing the same and preaching from that text right before he was assassinated; we stand in a liminal space almost able to taste what is yet to come, but not quite. We continue seeking the "foretaste of Glory Divine"[23] so that we will not fall back into the sinful patterns of self-gratification. And so, in this way, you can see that the spirituality of

---

21. Rauschenbusch, *Christianity and the Social Crisis*, 338.
22. Wrights, *Oscar Romero*, 162.
23. Lyrics from "Blessed Assurance" by Fanny J. Crosby (1873).

liminality connects with what I talked about in the chapter on the prophetic. It is a posture that holds us, through which the Spirit holds us, through which we hold and behold others, and through which we call the world around us to be accountable. In this spirituality of the in-between, may we always be encountering God in movement, and may we always be ready to give an account for the faith that drives us forward. Even if we are in free fall, we name what we experience. Even if we struggle with which methods we will practice, we practice. And however we live into our encounter with God's Spirit in the world, may it be with brave people and with love.

Conclusion: Self-Care as Targeted Incompetence

Finishing this conversation on self-care, I want to share a thought giving you permission to be imperfect and human in the work we do. I have been thinking about the idea of competence a lot the last few months. This is my first attempt to really talk about it, but I think it a spiritual discipline of sorts. Usually when I think about competence it is in regards to getting work done. But there's also a fiscal metaphor in there, like having competence and being able to pay for whatever you need for your way of life.

Until 2023 I had not considered competence as a discipline, but in doing so I realize the weight and stress of trying to do it all. So, to counter this, I have begun practicing "targeted incompetence." To wade through all the work that people think they want servants of the church to do one would need to burn the candle at both ends. I remember the damage that did to my mental and spiritual health back a few years ago.

Therefore, I've deliberately begun finding time to stop, to resist emails on my two-day weekend, to retreat from the chatter of social media. It's a clumsy dance with incompetence, a safeguard for my competence, for my energy. I long for enough to cover everything, but I know that I don't have enough. I remember the words of the apostle, "Therefore I am content with weaknesses, insults, hardships, persecutions, and calamities for the sake of Christ, for whenever I am weak, then I am strong" (2 Cor 12:10 NRSV).

Finding time to become stubborn like a mule who refuses to take another step is also a way of obeying the fourth commandment of Sabbath, that word which can be translated from Hebrew as "stop." To me, protecting myself and stopping in my tracks resembles the "quiet quitting" phenomenon, a whispering rebellion against the capitalistic structure that invades corporate life and even the church. And yet I still want to offer excellence in what I do. It's a paradox. I am going to appear incompetent and quit when I need a break. But I'll do my best when I'm working, when I re-engage.

For years I've used the language of "boundaries." Yet those who enforce boundaries are often so institutionalized. Institutions, like living organisms, fight against their own demise, hungering for sustenance they consume any resources given to them. Right now the church and many institutions starve and yet their bylaws and rules remain voracious, like a hungry pet barking as if to yell, "Feed me!"

The starving church asks more of its members, in most cases relying on the generosity of shrinking, interconnected stores of resources. It mirrors a body that, depleted of its fat stores, begins to consume its muscle tissue in desperation.

This paradox is that the church aims to respect boundaries and personal well-being yet it also craves nourishment, feeding itself on paid and volunteer labor. Did the heart disease prevalent among the older generation of pastors serve as an unheeded systemic alarm? In the face of starvation, values become compromised. It reminds me of sitting with my wife and son who were watching the show *Survivor*, and watching a vegan man on an island crying while he ate fish, driven by his immense hunger to violate his own personal boundary, which otherwise would have prevented him from consuming animal products.

On a societal level, I think of the book *Collapse* by Jared Diamond who talks about societies like Easter Island that collapsed. As that society starved, having cut down all of the trees on their island, the strong literally killed the weaker and ate their bodies. In a sense this happens in industrialized societies too. To prevent being digested, we must retreat from the belly of the beast if we have to work therein.

When I have sought good boundaries with powerful leaders (my present boss, who supported me having two weeks to finish this manuscript, excluded) some have succumbed to the familiar tune of, "Yes, good boundaries . . . but here are 150 tasks due tomorrow." Unwittingly those in power feed the ravenous beast, using the disempowered as fuel. Thus, if I must wear the label of incompetence, I shall do so with intent. I say all of this as a MethoBaptiCostal, multiracial, ADHD pastor who often struggles to fit within the "competent" label. I long to do my job well, but, also, I long to challenge myself and others to "be on when we are on and off when we are off."

During times of scarcity, achieving competence in both work and personal well-being seems an impossibility. My move toward what may be perceived as incompetence is intentional, not a retreat but a reallocation. I choose greater competence in mental and spiritual health (including plenty of play time) so that I can come back later with competence in church work.

The institutional demand for supercompetence is a question that lingers, a question I continue to explore—whether competently or incompetently. But whatever I bring to the table will be grounded in self-care, born of radical self-love, carried through the practices that I have shared. I invite you to do the same, to bring what you can from a place of deep, profound self-care and love, so that you can care for and love others as God loves you.

9.

Holy Saturday Silence
Waiting in the In-Between

In the hushed silence of Holy Saturday, we dwell,
In the belly of waiting, trauma throughout our cells.
Hidden behind doors, shadows casting truth aside,
Executions echoing in the air and, it seems, inside.
A panorama of patience, grief and loss intertwined,
And yet hope clings like a mother—nearness Divine.
Unseen resurrection whispers in the morning light,
Yet in this sacred in-between, we have little sight.
In between death and life, Holy Saturday unfolds,
An offering of Sabbath where true Strength takes hold.

Holy Saturday as Waiting:
The Witness of the *Latine* Church

The Latino people in the United States live in the space of Holy Saturday.

On the first Holy Saturday, the disciples, swathed in the blanket of trauma, cowered in a hidden crevice of existence. They had walked shoulder to shoulder with Jesus, their hearts and souls imbued with his teachings, only to bear witness to his ghastly execution upon the cross—a sight they were no stranger to given the grisly historical accounts of such crucifixions. The Romans had elevated this torturous demise to an art form, an obscene spectacle of naked, dying bodies strewn across the landscape, a grotesque testament to the Empire's might. Crucifixion became a nightmare in broad daylight, corpses left to be scavenged by buzzards and beasts.

Though Jesus' prophecies of death and resurrection had permeated their ears, the disciples found themselves paralyzed, rooted to the ground by the sheer weight of their trauma. John's Gospel tells how they hid in a locked room, a terror-filled cohort continuing even into Sunday morning. The shadow of Good Friday's trauma lingered, binding them like psych patients in straightjackets still on Holy Saturday.

The space of Holy Saturday is not often talked about, but I want to present to you at the beginning of this chapter the witness of many living in its metaphorical presence. The Latine communities in the United States are living an extended Holy Saturday, trapped within societal confines that stretch far ahead the very possibility of resurrection. The COVID-19 pandemic, too, has left many marooned on the shores of Holy Saturday, abiding in the eerie limbo of loss.

Many marginalized communities live in Holy Saturday. We can hear the space away from crucifixion but not yet at new life echoing through countless Latine tales of migratory aspirations and waits at the Southern border. If we learn what has happened, we see that US history is filled with many military interventions, the corrosive influences of multinational corporations, and the CIA-trained militants that have all contributed to the systemic trauma and disarray in Latin America, crucifixion triggering mass exodus.

The United Methodist Church, historically predominated by white folk, is being swept by the winds of change. The church is learning to recenter, stepping away from its Eurocentric narrative to encompass the vibrant blooms of the gospel of Jesus Christ in diverse cultures. Power is no longer a fortress to be guarded, but a resource to be shared. A once singular, authoritative story is learning to harmonize within the symphony of other stories. This is what Duke Divinity School Dean Edgardo Colón-Emeric often talks about as "theology *en conjunto*" or "theology together." More broadly, doing things "in conjunction" or together is a hallmark of the Latinx church.

In the waiting room of Holy Saturday a sign of resurrection might be the sharing of power as illustrated by my own journey within a diversifying church. Pentecostal life, as we see in the book of Acts, bears witness to the communal sharing of resources, while the apostle Paul's letters to the Corinthian church demonstrate the necessary and challenging task of working together despite diverse backgrounds. For those of you in white churches, remember that those from marginalized communities have lingered longer in the doldrums of Holy Saturday, yearning for a glimmer of resurrection.

As we wait, let us look within and see what needs to change as we wait for new life.

Specifically, I want to consider the linguistic landscape and challenge us to think about the way we use words. The language of our faith and our traditions is akin to the muscadine wine from Duplin County in North Carolina—the home of the world's largest muscadine winery (also the home of the first church I served). Words can be sweet and even intoxicating. The muscadine wine, not having the necessary chemical compounds to age, transforms into vinegar when aged too long. This is the fate of our religious language if it fails to evolve and connect with the diverse people surrounding us. Jesus warned us against pouring "new wine into old wineskins," a caution to make sure that both content and container are considered. If we are not careful, what we give people to drink will be bitter and indigestible. If our words are aged too long, and if they lack a certain quality to age well, they become acidic and acrid.

Let me share a specific example about using language. The evolution of terminology representing Latin Americans—from Hispanics to Latinos to Latinx to Latine (pronounced ⊠l⊠⊠ti⊠.ne⊠)—showcases this growth. Yet we must remember that growth does not mean assimilation into white Christianity or US culture, nor should it limit us to hoisting only the US flag within our churches to the exclusion of people from other countries. In this holy hiatus, the holy *and* allows us to hold space for both death and resurrection. It encourages us to hold the tension of coexisting realities—a difficult task in our polarized *or* world.

The witness of the Latine Church in living through Holy Saturday teaches us about sustainability. We mourn the death of our church buildings aware of the resources it took to erect them and the ecological consequences. Yet many among the Latine communities hail from resource-scarce environments. When I worshiped at the border and in small towns in Mexico, the church was not a majestic edifice, but often a simple structure without windows. Or sometimes the church was just a congregation, their shoulders forming the church's walls. Our current way of life, built upon the ruin of ecosystems and exploitation of workers, is spiritually and physically unsustainable. As we witness the tireless labor that keeps our food systems running, we realize the inherent inequity that prevails. We need to envision a different way of living, to allow ourselves to be impregnated by the Spirit with a new perspective on welcoming people.

As we consider the posture of waiting and the witness of the Latine Church, I am reminded of Colón-Emeric's book *The People Called Metodista: Renewing Doctrine, Worship, and Mission from the Margins*. It is a compelling exploration of the Methodist faith as lived by Latin American communities who have navigated their faith through much disempowerment.

In the midst of a schismatic divide within the global United Methodist Church, Colón-Emeric's book serves as a wake-up call. He reminds us that it was not to the religious elite that Jesus Christ ministered but to those at the edges of society. This book therefore encourages readers to draw from Latine Methodists' experiences of individual salvation that give rise to liberation, calling our attention back to what I mentioned in chapter 5 about living the mission of Jesus Christ through the church with both personal holiness and social holiness.

Colón-Emeric prompts us to consider what evangelism and ecumenism (working with other Christian traditions) mean in the context of liberation. He shares the story of the ecumenical heart of the Methodist movement as it continues to beat within the *metodista* community. The book inspires us to explore the unique ways in which different Christian traditions inform the lives of Methodists around the world, suggesting that we can find opportunities for renewal through these shared practices.[1]

Colón-Emeric further emphasizes the importance of worship and celebration, even amid adversity. He illustrates this through the practice of fiesta, a form of worship rooted in joy and celebration, common among the *metodistas*.[2] When he was teaching a class of mine in my doctor of ministry program, he added on to Archbishop Desmond Tutu's, "There is no future without forgiveness," by saying, "There is also no future without fiesta." And he told stories of serving a Latine immigrant community in Durham where impoverished *campesinos* and blue collar workers would spend lavishly on birthday parties and holiday celebrations, because fiesta gives life.[3] This resonates with my own experience of leading an ecumenical group of Latine migrants in the last United Methodist Church I served. The love and grace of the communion table overflows into the celebration of life together where everyone's voice is given dignity and everyone's presence is seen as participation in bringing hope.

In discussing the historical shadows cast by Christianity's introduction to the Americas by colonizers, Colón-Emeric suggests that the current situation of dwindling Christian church membership could offer an

---

1. Colón-Emeric, *People Called Metodista*, chap. 3.
2. Colón-Emeric, *People Called Metodista*, chap. 4.
3. The course was XTIAN 890: Practicing Justice and Reconciliation in Community taught by Edgardo Colón-Emeric and Ryan Juskus at Duke Divinity School during the summer of 2021. Specifically, this was from the intensive week sessions, May 18–21, 2021.

opportunity for renewal and reconciliation, mirroring past struggles and eclipses.[4] In our Service of Death and Resurrection we see the light of our life eclipsed by the stone rolled in front of the tomb.

Colón-Emeric urges the church to look beyond its internal divisions and instead focus on reconnecting with marginalized communities, by extension reconnecting with an essential part of the church's own identity.[5] This call to renewal by learning from the *metodistas* stands as a beacon of hope and a reminder that the church's salvation always comes from Jesus Christ's actions at the margins.

"What do I have to gain?" many people will ask about learning from an ethnically different church. Specifically in learning from *metodistas*, the church can encounter the power of the gospel and mission of Jesus Christ as learned and spoken through a different language. Even if people do not speak Spanish, they can learn these lessons through exposure. Let me share one tangible example close to our heart. Methodist movement founder John Wesley's life was changed when he said his heart was "strangely warmed" by the Holy Spirit convincing him of God's grace. When that phrase is translated into Spanish, it is "*el corazón ardiente*" or "the burning heart." Colón-Emeric has said, "So the temperature turns up in Spanish."[6] This sentiment is so true in many of my experiences. I don't want to put pressure on *metodistas* to be on fire, but, also, I will say that the experience of living in Holy Saturday, and the need to stay close to the fire of the Holy Spirit, has a way of heating a people up.

In the interim of Holy Saturday the white US church, the institutions, and majority groups need to learn the patience and worshipful practice of minorities. We need to wait with intention, like a waiter attending tables, being active and living out our responsibilities while bringing sustenance to others. We ought to also remember that, in the active waiting, we take shifts, resting and recharging while others take up the task. We need to evolve from being the overbearing majority to being humble minorities open to learning from the experiences of the Black Church, the Latine Church, the Asian Church, the Indigenous Church, and all minoritized churches. Let us learn how to wait and have faith, even when it seems like all is lost.

---

4. Colón-Emeric, *People Called Metodista*, chap. 7.
5. Colón-Emeric, *People Called Metodista*, chap. 8.
6. Colón-Emeric, "El Corazón Ardiente."

Holy Saturday as Sabbath

I am going to move toward talking about Holy Saturday as an occasion for Sabbath and rest. But to do that I want to elaborate a bit more on part of my own story:

"It was a short two years," pastors and church folk have said to me many different times, thinking about a certain season. It could have been the amount of time they spent at a certain house while in college, serving at a church they once knew, or how long it took them to get ordained. Even if the years were hair-pullingly difficult, with enough time passed, they may seem shorter.

Jesus accomplished a lot in three years, and the world has been changed as a result of his ministry even as we do so many different things in his name, having been changed into many different traditions. We may leave profound roots growing in different places, the ripple effects of our short presence extending out beyond the borders of our imaginations. And yet two years can feel so short, especially in church work.

I have jokingly said to many people, "I am on the frequent-flier plan" with respect to my appointments at different churches. My first appointment as a full-time pastor out of my master of divinity degree program was at Rose Hill UMC, a small church in rural southeastern North Carolina It lasted for two years. From there I moved to be an associate pastor at First UMC Morehead City, what I considered to be a large, beach church on the coast of North Carolina, again for two years. Then I moved inland to Murfreesboro, a rural town of under two thousand, the place where I received my undergraduate degree and met my wife, and stayed for two years. The next pair of years saw me move to be "half-time" serving this congregation and half-time on the other side of the county at Ahoskie UMC—both of which could not remember having to share a pastor in their 207- and 116-year histories respectively. That was 2019.

"I'm cursed," I thought to myself several times, as I pondered the possible reasons for my two-year stints in churches. A voice of shame in my head asked, "What's wrong with you that you can't remain anywhere for longer than *a couple short years*?" My heart longed to stay at these two appointments even while I did not know how to be a pastor to two different groups of people who did not know or want to spend time together. (I learned in that season that almost all congregations can be insular. Nobody is foaming at the mouth with excitement to share a pastor and get to know the new would-be sibling down the road even if they have both been churches in the same denomination for over one hundred years.)

For two years I worked diligently to foster connections between these two churches and split myself to be in two places while also not splitting my soul or overworking myself. I think, as we call them, "splitting headaches" come from trying to be in too many places at once. "Lord, help me to keep my head where my feet are," I would hear my old friend Cynthia tell me. Many leaders know the struggle of walking the tightrope, balancing presence and hard work. Especially if you have ADHD like me you might struggle with rejection-sensitive dysphoria and executive function, both of which can be monumental challenges to being present to work hard on a specific task that does not provide dopamine to the reward centers of your brain. With all these challenges, I struggled on for two short years on both sides of Hertford County, North Carolina.

A global pandemic has a way of drastically changing our plans. In 2020 when COVID-19 hit us like a tsunami it drastically affected life, and ultimately led to the closing of one of my two congregations. However, it laid bare what was already present. Let me tell you about some other pandemics that were already playing their way out in Murfreesboro and Ahoskie prior to 2019 when the two congregations came together.

Both of the congregations I served had experienced immense challenges of different kinds: long-term decay from political polarization, racism, classism, the sin of greed, the mindset of militarism, the rural-urban divide brought on by rapid industrialization, secularism, and mental health disparity. Throughout my doctor of ministry studies, which started in the 2020 quarantine, my cohort talked about some of these phenomena as being different types of social pandemics. They were all in play before we were sent into quarantine with the COVID-19 pandemic in March 2020.

In both the lives of Murfreesboro UMC, where I'd been serving as a solo pastor, and at our counterpart congregation in Ahoskie we saw precipitating events where several of these pandemics came together like the waters of a flood encircling a small wooden edifice on a hill surrounded by small sandbags. It was just a matter of time before the waters would ravage the two congregations and cause severe damage.

An old mentor, Pastor Marty, talked with me a lot about "narrative theology." He said it was important to know the history of congregations and where they saw God in their history because cycles repeat themselves.[7] Let me lay some narrative out for you, my dear reader, a story of pandemics—before the COVID-19 pandemic—at each of the two churches I served.

---

7. In the life cycle of the church, he thought a lot about our history but worked most noticeably in evangelism—in showing the church how we still held "good news" to be shared with the world.

At Murfreesboro UMC

I enthusiastically welcomed people from the migrant, Latine community in Murfreesboro in 2017, something which coincided with my praying for things that were happening to the nationwide Latine community—deportations. As I have mentioned earlier in the book, some white, English-speaking church members said that I was being too "political," and in a few weeks four families who believed that had left. That was the event that spurred the church on to be a "half-time" church, with half of my time as their pastor being in another place.

At Ahoskie UMC

In the same year that the families left MUMC a similar exodus occurred at AUMC, some two years before I would go on to be its pastor. They welcomed a gay couple to be part of the church. It was not a big issue at first, with one of them singing in the choir and helping with the community garden. But as soon as they were announced and recognized before the church as husband and husband, conflict erupted. Behind the scenes people organized and eventually left the church. It went from between seventy-five to ninety in attendance to only having around twenty in attendance in a matter of about two weeks. That spurred them to move from having a full-time pastor to sharing one with MUMC.

The events that flooded both of these little churches were also like tips of icebergs. You can look back and see what happened on the surface, but below the precipitating events are systems that are set up in a specific way, pieces of culture that operate in a certain way, and, the most challenging thing to move, patterns of thinking and assumptions about the way things are.

These events were like the Good Friday of the churches. They both occurred in 2017, and in 2019 I took on the leadership of both congregations, which felt like they were bleeding out. After many people left, I found myself in a Holy Saturday silence, waiting with the remaining members.

With both churches we went through the conference's "Office of Church Transformation" together, as the two churches came together with the hopes of doing things with one another. We talked about being a "Cooperative Parish," a group of two distinct congregations on mission together. We worked, through a coalition of the community health center called "Farm to School to Healthcare," in the Ahoskie Community Garden and with the AUMC produce trailer. We worked together in the AUMC industrial kitchen. MUMC had a growing ministry with the Latine population. The churches tried to have Bible study together a few times. It was awkward but beautiful.

We knew that holding something new meant letting go of the past. As I planned worship, the Holy Spirit led us to the idea of the funeral service and our current moment. I had no idea at the time that the virus spreading across the world, which had zero infections in the United States, would permanently change the face of how we lived in "church."

As March 2020 rolled around I began preparing for a worship series to preach at both rural congregations I served. I had been working with my friend Dusty, a pastor and carpenter, to make a coffin as a sermon illustration, as we preachers often do. It was about five feet long, looked like a large marionette could fit inside, and had that oblong look that Dracula's coffin had.

The bottom half of it went to Murfreesboro and the top half went to Ahoskie as we began that worship series. I used some words from a funeral service, saying things like, "We believe that death is not an end but a transition, a passage through death to life. This service is a marker on our pilgrimage, a journey we make in solidarity with our brothers and sisters. As John Wesley observed on his deathbed, 'The best of all is, God is with us.'[8] To which we add, 'Our brothers and sisters are with us, too.'"

The United Methodist Church is called a *liturgical* church. That means a lot of things, but most noticeably, we see *liturgy* as the written out order of worship, complete with who is saying what and when. Growing up in more Pentecostal space I did not see this type of order, and so when I first came to the UMC it felt to me like the Holy Spirit was absent. I have since found out that She is present in the preparation, knocking on the hearts of people in the service, and comes out in the practice of worship—in the sights and sounds.

The Greek term translated as *liturgy* means "the work of the people." In the way that my church defines this it is usually more restrictive than my preference for improvisational and spontaneous acts of worship. The liturgical church still sees me showing up, because it was created to involve people. It was created to allow a space for people, even for people to belong when they don't know if they believe. But whether in preplanned or improvised worship, the Holy Spirit pours herself out through the work of the people.

During our Service of Death and Resurrection worship in early 2020, we had a liturgical moment in which we asked people, "What things have died?" In the process of worshipfully responding, people were invited to

---

8. Southey, *Life of John Wesley*, 255.

leave their seats, pick up a sticky note that was included in their worship bulletin, and write down things that had died.

Slowly, over the course of two weeks, the coffin halves began to be filled with neon-colored sticky notes. They bore names like men's Sunday school class; women's circle; youth group; day care space; community garden; food ministry with other churches, and many more. The sticky notes let us know that people were still grieving things that had died a long time ago. Some of them were grieving things that had disappeared since I had been there. Some of the things named were less material like people who had left because of conflict.

We continued the practice during the next church council meeting, both at Murfreesboro and in Ahoskie at the United Methodist Churches. In Murfreesboro, we held a service at a council meeting where we named things that had died, which connected to the things named by the congregation during the worship service.

This practice taught me that oftentimes people are silently grieving. It taught me that when people act out in the church, it might be because of the huge pain of loss they are experiencing—like a child whose unnamed pain comes out in a tantrum. Sometimes church folk, too, will overreact to things, not because of the situation but because they do not know how to voice the grief they are experiencing.

Just after we had named the things which had died, the COVID-19 pandemic quickly shut the world down and let us slowly burn, like pressure cookers, holding all of the pain that was inside. I don't know if it affected what would come next—talking about the death we had experienced in church. But I would like to think it did.

In Murfreesboro, the pandemic coincided with the Latine ministries actually growing. When we had talked about starting worship in the parking lot, I was preparing to preach that week on Acts 8 where Philip is sent by the Holy Spirit into the desert and meets a man from the queen's house in Ethiopia. Philip shares how Jesus is present in the scroll of Isaiah he's reading, and the Ethiopian man says, "Look, here is water! What is to prevent me from being baptized?" (Acts 8:36 NRSV).

In that same week Alejandra, a foreigner and first Latina member of MUMC said to me, "There's a parking lot here where you will preach in English. What is to prevent us from worshiping in Spanish?" I asked, "Who will preach?" (My Spanish was relatively weak at the time.) She said, "You are our pastor! And the Holy Spirit will continue to lead you." And that's how our Spanish worship service started in about two weeks.

Around that same time, in Ahoskie we brought back the Church Transformation Ministries (CTM) people, who helped us talk through the ideas of realignment (slight change), redirection (huge change), and legacy (permanently closing the doors of the congregation). Over the course of many meetings held virtually and in person the church decided, first in the small group that met with CTM, then at a church council, and then at a church conference vote in which the whole membership of the church voted, to become a legacy congregation. Specifically, they decided that the church would do so by merging its membership and assets with Murfreesboro UMC.

It was only in the process of starting to move forward, with one church in the grief of the process of moving toward death and with another church in the process of starting a new church service, that I came to realize that I never took the coffin halves out of the sanctuaries. For six months we had tried to implement new worship paradigms. We had tried worship on Zoom, on Facebook Live, pre-recorded on YouTube with premier and live chat on Sunday, and finally in the parking lot with radio transmitters. And for six months the coffins had remained untouched, like bones in whitewashed tombs. "Can these bones live again?" I found myself being asked. "Lord, you know," I would respond, like Ezekiel.

As Murfreesboro began to grow, Ahoskie began the work of transitioning, of dying and merging with Murfreesboro. I took a lot of pauses as the church died. It felt like I was the captain of the *Titanic* going out to smoke a cigarette or take a nap as the ship took on water.

I had not heard back from a lot of the people who had stepped back as the church moved toward closure, but I had made up a lot of self-blaming stories in my head extrapolated from some of the critical feedback that I did receive. And the ones who came were super grieved, at the end of the day. They were going through a tragic death—displacement and exile. My final sermon was about being people who went out, as if into exile, but still having a church home because, even apart from this building, their baptismal vows hadn't changed. Through all of this, I knew that whatever the future held would be a long haul. So I took a lot of time to myself.

In Murfreesboro, things began to grow and thrive, at first. Shortly before the pandemic, I had begun applying to be in the pilot Rural Ministry Fellowship Doctor of Ministry cohort at Duke Divinity School. I had long wanted to continue my schooling, and this was the perfect opportunity. My coursework took place as I was overseeing Ahoskie UMC becoming a legacy congregation and merging with Murfreesboro UMC. The aim of my doctoral work began to be focused on understanding what was needed from a rural, historically white congregation that was moving to be multicultural and multilingual.

As we started the parking lot worship services in Spanish and English, I learned that MUMC was the only rural congregation in a geographical conference of around eight hundred churches that had gone from being all white to both multiracial and multilingual with worship services in both languages. This type of maneuver typically happened in suburban or urban churches, but the Spirit had found a way to take this congregation formed in 1810 and change its direction after a couple of centuries. How did that happen?

The answer? Death and resurrection.

I mentioned in earlier chapters that people had left rather than help the congregation integrate—their leaving being because of "political reasons." (The gospel is always political, but it should never be about "partisan politics" in our neoliberal, individualistic democracy.) Where they left created a space for the multilingual growth that happened.

Murfreesboro would go on to receive more than half a dozen small grants helping it grow cross-culturally and be a part of two different cohorts of churches working for change. But I also learned that just because a change happens doesn't mean it's permanent.

The parable of the sower that Jesus tells (Matt 13:1–23, Mark 4:1–20, Luke 8:4–15) is such a good witness about faith growth in community. Sometimes the seeds grow up quickly and sometimes they get gobbled up and sometimes they get choked out. I don't know what the situation has been at MUMC, but I do know that seeds sometimes need a lot of attention. The more foreign a seed is to a certain ecology, the more love and nurture it will need as it tries to grow in that ecology.

The main takeaway from my doctoral work is that whenever two cultural groups grow together they need three types of spaces: a separate and sovereign space for the first group, a separate and sovereign space for the new group, and a shared space for them to grow together. (The sovereign spaces should have a "semi-permeable" membrane that allows people from the other group to come in, even if they are not in control.) In telling different church folk about this sometimes they have disagreed with me. Since the civil rights movement of the 1960s the practice has been to integrate people and focus on the shared space, the assumption being that whenever two people groups are together they will strengthen that space. In many places, that type of reconciliation has not worked.

Listening to people in radically white, radically Black, and radically Latine spaces, I have heard the same thing. People need a space to be honest and speak their truth if they are going to come together and continually practice reconciliation. I assume that every context is different, but in northeastern North Carolina, this proved to be the best idea.

However, after roughly a year of having worship in Spanish, we started to struggle. I became increasingly unable to handle all of the things needed to be a pastor in both separate spaces and the shared space. I knew a lot of what was needed, but I suffered from analysis paralysis.

The nature of the Spanish-speaking members of the congregation was that they were long-term migrant workers, and several who had attended worship either went back to their home country or moved on to other jobs. I had not done a good enough job at empowering laity to invite new people in, and I had not built good systems.

So in June 2022, as I was preparing to become the director of youth ministry for the North Carolina Conference of the UMC, a bilingual team of people at the local church I served in Murfreesboro agreed it was best to have a combined worship service, being 80 percent in English and 20 percent in Spanish, the percentages reflecting the demographics of the active worship attendees.

At the time of my writing this, May 2023, I am preparing to be reappointed to a different ministry outside of Murfreesboro and the MUMC continues to work diligently trying to understand what it means to minister to people of different ethnic and linguistic backgrounds. As I write this, I look at both what has gone well but also what has not worked. "Can these bones live?"

The space of watching a church institution die, of watching ministries grow and die and not knowing what would be next has been like Holy Saturday. Only now, after some painful time, have I been able to start to think about what resurrection looks like. Holy Saturday is a space that cannot be rushed through. It is painful, and it seems like death has won out.

I was talking with my friend Pastor Malinda who runs a program for rural faith leaders out of Barton College. She said that as she has seen "death and resurrection" in the rural areas, she thinks of it in light of the drama of Jesus' death and resurrection. It's easy to see where Good Friday is, that hellish day when everything goes sideways and the world closes down.

Then we are stuck in the space of Holy Saturday. She said that it's like the stone or boulder is rolled in front of the tomb, and, even if there is the possibility for new life, we cannot get the stone out of the way.

If you have been in church work, or even more broadly, if you worked in a social institution during the first couple of years of the COVID-19 pandemic, you probably have felt the pain of something dying, of a longtime well of wisdom drying up, of ancient expectations being untenable, or of a forest of wisdom seeming to burn down. This type of loss definitely feels like a death.

The church has long used the image of Holy Week—that week in which Jesus died and rose from the grave—as our characteristic paradigm for thinking about death. This is not to say that all of us who have experienced death have been crucified as disempowered revolutionaries by a powerful empire.

That said, we still feel the offering of the framework of Holy Week to move through our feelings of loss. When we experience great loss, we are in Good Friday. Then, when we cannot see the possibility of new life, we are in Holy Saturday. This can be a sincere time of waiting, as I talk about in the other part of this chapter.

For we who have spent far too much time being busy, it can be a time to reset. It can be a time of Sabbath. As Malinda says, sometimes on Holy Saturday, we are stuck in the tomb. We might even be like Jesus, stuck in the tomb having experienced new life and resurrection. But without someone to "roll the stone away" that blocks the entrance to the tomb, we are just stuck there, unable to exercise new life.

For many of us, the space of Holy Saturday means being stuck behind a wall, in the shadows of unknowing, unsure if new life will ever come, and feeling alone. We don't like to be alone, sure that we have been abandoned. We don't like to be away from busywork, sure that if we stop moving, our worth will also dwindle. And we don't like to be restricted, walking around the maze of our lives like rats looking for cheese.

When we experience all of these things, we can feel really anxious. However, it can also be a gift. Waiting, like many of us did during the "lockdown" of COVID-19, can be the gift of time. Much like a prisoner, to whom we say, "you've got time," we wait behind the walls of the way things actually are.

During my time, I kept working. Some people might be mad that I didn't work harder to keep the church going the way they wanted it. Some people thought I was working myself too hard. But I used the time like Sabbath. I had to—similar to the "targeted incompetence" idea that I shared earlier.

In the future, time to stop may not be as available as it was during the quarantine, but I have learned this lesson that I pass on to you. Whenever you experience death, take some time. Make some time. In Greek, two words exist for *time*. One is *chronos*, and it talks about chronological time as we experience it in hours, days, and weeks. The other is *kairos*, which is God's time. God comes to us, disguised as ordinary things, breaking into the minutes and hours of our day. If we do not take time, we may not notice the Divine presence. We may not notice the seeds of resurrection during Holy Saturday, when everything feels dead.

As I think about the death that we are experiencing in the church, I remember what Phyllis Tickle wrote, that every five hundred years or so there is a great change in world religion, and we are experiencing one now.[9] The change we are experiencing is as big as the Reformation started by Martin Luther and as big as the great schism between the Catholic and Orthodox Churches. It is an end, and a beginning. We need to take Sabbath time to experience what our place in it will be.

To ask, "Will I be here for the resurrection?" is the wrong question. Resurrection happens in parts, much like new growth in plant life happens in parts. Give yourself permission to rest and hope, even if nobody else does.

This moves us to the importance of the next chapter. I wanted to have this chapter to talk about the importance of Sabbath and rest (connecting with the last chapter and self-care) and waiting before going to the next one.

If you have never practiced "holy waiting and pause," I want you to prepare yourself to be in a place where you can be led into it. It's like going swimming, but you've never stepped into the water before. You can be told about it, but until you get there, you won't know what it's like. Also, you don't know what you're missing out on until you rest. So find someone who can help lead you into rest, to practice it, as you wait to see if new life can come, and wait. Pause. Rest.

When you do rest, it's a weird thing. It creates some anxiety, because the hyperfocused, productive part of you will want to be working. But when you have silence, stuff starts to arise. When you stop, something else starts. When you wade into the reality of death, as in Holy Saturday, you get ready for the dawn of resurrection.

---

9. See Tickle, *Great Emergence*, introduction and chap. 1.

10.

Resurrection's Dawn
A Step Toward Renewal

In the afterglow of execution,
Among dying embers, lies the seed—
Of resurrection, in the cradle of our hearts
Where love and faith are braided.

Do we not sprout from the soil
Touched by the death of past seasons?
In our veins, the carbon of forebears,
Life's cyclical dance beyond reason.

The echo of the Divine in our chest,
Pulsing with the rhythm of grace,
Like dormant seeds under fire-licked earth,
Awaiting the rain's embrace.

Through corridors of hurt and healing,
We came, patient here, ears tuning
To the mouth of God, for whispers,
In the language of loving pruning.

We say our truth, Jesus resurrected,
rises like the climbing of the morning sun,

Yet some, eyes turned away, hearts locked,
Resist the miracle that has begun.

We are all unfinished melodies,
Humming in our flawed existence,
Yet the choir of God sings within us,
Resonating Their persistence.

To be loved is to let go, to surrender,
Our false claim over life's crests and troughs,
In the humbling act of release, we find
God's signature on our hearts embossed.

Resurrection lies not in distant realms,
But deep in soul and world terrain,
A testament of agape, unyielding,
In the face of life's pain.

In the story of the church, in society's gaze,
We trace the arc of resurrection's grace,
The return to self, to the divine within,
In each face, God's face.

We are scribes of resurrection,
In the art of our existence,
In the pulse of love, in the act of faith,
God's work bears constant witness.

In this dance with life and death,
We learn the rhythm of ebb and flow,
In the steady beat of love's refrain,
Resurrection's song comes to show.

A symphony of faith in each heart,
In the silence of our soul,
May God, the composer of our lives,
Conduct us toward love's final goal.

The Startled Disciples

The shock expressed by Jesus Christ's disciples at his resurrection on Easter Sunday is indeed ironic, yet simultaneously it's entirely comprehensible. Individuals don't return from death—except Jesus did. Similarly, we often find ourselves unable to grasp the extent of the decay we are experiencing, or we become complacent in it, living as if God won't bring forth a novel chapter.

In tethering ourselves to a particular way of practicing church, we confine our imagination within man-made walls, forgetting that God's actions aren't bounded by our constructs. This is a quintessentially human predicament. Jesus' unanticipated actions, whether in life, death, or resurrection, break these boundaries, pushing us to envision beyond.

In this concluding chapter, I want to share a few final insights about resurrection. In order to encounter resurrection we must admit that we are addicted to our old way of life. Getting unstuck can happen in a posture of worship and singing. In the United Methodist Church, our mission is to make disciples of Jesus Christ for the transformation of the world. To get a good look at what exactly that might look like in the United Methodist context, I encourage y'all to consider resources like the *Fresh Expressions* books by Audrey Warren, Bishop Kenneth H. Carter Jr., and Michael Adam Beck (I appeared in the *Fresh Expressions of the Rural Church* volume) or perhaps *Don't Look Back* by Bishop Will Willimon. In my witness to the resurrection, I am going to speak about ways that we can try to agree amid tribalism, nurture new life, talk about truth, and choose love.

Surrendering to Be Embraced

When an addict embarks on the journey to recovery, they seldom realize how close they are to resurrected life. Breaking free from the chains of their brain's bondage could reveal a fresh realm of possibility. Many addicts I've known possess the elements needed for a resurrected life: a loving family, a roof over their heads, and a job opportunity—yet their addiction and the unresolved pain that fuels it obstruct their path to recovery.

The church clings to its time-worn ways, viewing them as the only way, the only truth, the only life. What if we navigated through a twelve-step program instead? The first step would be admitting our helplessness in resisting our inclination to do things as we've always done and acknowledging that our lives have become unmanageable.

Part of acceptance and transitioning to a new life involves shifting from expectation to expectancy. We must evolve from a pretentious posture of expectation, where we assume things ought to unfold in a particular manner, to expectancy, a state of hopeful anticipation where we await God's resurrected action. Sometimes we get in our own way, and it causes us to get in the way of others. As Shelby says in the movie *Steel Magnolias*, "Daddy always says, 'An ounce of pretension is worth a pound of manure.'"[1] Usually, others see our pretentious ways and our need for recovery, how we have strayed from the mission and need to come back before we do.

When we begin living in recovery and resurrection, we'll discover that God's ways differ significantly from ours. Many of us are torn between the red and blue divide, convinced that only two political paths exist. The politics of Jesus, of the kingdom of God, represent an entirely different approach. Pledging allegiance to Jesus signifies that we are transient visitors and "aliens" in this world, our true citizenship lies elsewhere (see Heb 11:13 and Phil 3:20).

This means being "in this world and not of it." Reflecting on our country, we see that we've established an ecosystem where, according to the Federal Reserve, as of 2022, the wealthiest 1 percent of US citizens possess more wealth than the entire middle class combined.[2] Gun violence is the leading cause of child mortality in the US.[3] We've deregulated our food industry to such an extent that nearly half of the adults suffer from metabolic dysfunction. Obesity affects over 40 percent of adults,[4] yet it's become so commonplace that it's no longer seen as abnormal. Despite healthcare being the fastest growing industry, health outcomes continue to decline as costs skyrocket.[5] To say we've "missed the mark" or fallen into sin is to understate the gravity of our situation.

As a church, we cannot compel the nation to enter recovery, but we can embark on this journey ourselves. A hundred years ago, after World War I, most of the church learned that Christianizing the public order would not really be feasible. (Some Christofascists are still trying to take power.) Despite the numerous issues plaguing our country, I see immense potential in its people. Historically, US systems have been manipulated by elites rooted in ideologies such as white supremacy and exclusion. Heather McGhee's compelling book *The Sum of Us* illuminates how these systems, initially designed to harm minority populations, now affect everyone in the

---

1. Harling, *Steel Magnolias*.
2. USAFacts, "Wealth Distribution."
3. Roberts et al., "Firearm Deaths Among Children."
4. CDC, "Adult Obesity Facts."
5. Papanicolas et al., "Health Care Spending."

middle and lower classes.⁶ Despite these grim realities, I see many working tirelessly for resurrection and recovery. The church has significant opportunities to join the Holy Spirit's transformative work in our world.

One of the church's challenges in its journey toward recovery and resurrection is its mission to evangelize a younger generation that, in many respects, surpasses the church in morality. Aspects of personal holiness provide valuable lessons. Movements like #MeToo asserting personal dignity and holding powerful men accountable have arisen outside the Christian world at the same time that reports of sexual misconduct within the church have surged. The church can also learn social holiness from initiatives like #BlackLivesMatter, which spotlight violence against marginalized bodies.

While millennials like me may stay to help the church rectify its issues, Generation Z seems unwilling to endure the burnout experienced by their predecessors. Gen Zers (20 percent) are almost twenty percentage points less likely than members of the silent generation (38 percent) to attend religious services at least once a week.⁷ If the church continues to resist recovery and resurrection, they will simply leave.

As a relatively new youth ministry director, I'm frequently asked why young people won't stick around in the church. One study suggested that millennials, eager to change the world, didn't see the church as a viable platform for their mission, so they left. The lavish structures of our churches, the lifestyle disparities between baby boomers and younger generations, and the harsh economic realities faced by young people all contribute to a bitter sentiment toward a church that refuses to seek recovery.

So, as we enter recovery, let us break free from the shackles of our old lives, welcoming the power of resurrection and the embrace of God's presence. One of my favorite ways of feeling God's embrace is in worship, in the communal pursuit of God's presence, in singing.

A Hymn of Promise

Death is exhausting and so also is thinking about life in the midst of death. In church work we have a delicate balance to dance. My mental feet are moving in that dance even now while writing these words. Given the heaviness of everything that I've said up to this point, some of you might think that it has been a catharsis—me getting it off my chest to make myself feel better. My joy is in the hope that others also might live into this hope.

---

6. McGhee, *Sum of Us*, chaps. 5, 8.
7. PRRI, "Generation Z's Views."

Weighing the formidable reality of death with the hope of life has been one of the most arduous tasks of my life. In the twenty-first century, at a time when we are hyperpolarized, how does one try to write to a mixed group of people? How do we write about death and resurrection in a way that brings people's attention without alienating them? That's the million-dollar question.

The beauty of resurrection, victory, and the divine mystery of life unseen until its destined moment can stir a soul deeply. Silently, tentatively, I sat and listened to a songbird in human form singing about death and resurrection and the unknown timing of new life—hanging on the precipice of each syllable like an eager eagle waiting to dive off the edge of its eyrie, off the face of a cliff. With my body silently quaking from tremors of tears that longed to come out of dry eyes, I simply sat and observed the musical majesty of it. Why can't I just fall flat on my face and cry it out? The question hung in my mind as I longed to let these words move my body as they were moving my soul.

Some pastors will push back against having too much "emotionalism" in worship. "How do we prevent this from devolving into sentimentality?" I remember one seasoned pastor asking. These questions and cautions could go to hell for all I cared at that moment. God's beauty, like the outline of galaxies unknown faintly twinkling on the edge of our eyesight at midnight, was just outside of the grasp of my listening—close enough to create an infinite longing for more of it. In a world of wildfires, earthquakes, and rampant hurricanes, God's beauty breaking into this plane of existence will save us—if we are able to be embraced by it.

The song that gripped me that day was Natalie Sleeth's "Hymn of Promise." As it enfolded me, I had been unable to embrace God's beauty for quite some time. In this moment I'm saying "God's beauty," but really we cannot separate God's beauty from God's reign, or from God's "kin-dom"—which makes us move from being strangers to kinfolk. It all works together, sometimes one piece in the front and sometimes another. When those words pierced my heart of stone and cut to my heart of flesh, I realized what part of the problem was. My heart of stone was really a heart covered by calluses. In the words of my friend Jordan, "Maybe it was first my feet covered in calluses for trying to follow Jesus." In the humdrum of having too much to do, I had gotten so busy working for the church that I had forgotten to experience the Lord. When Mrs. Pat sang "Hymn of Promise," she sang from the depth of a soul that saw the need for resurrection. Even as she sang that word *resurrection*, chills reverberated down my spine, like an alarm clock at 5:30 a.m. It wasn't just ecstasy but a reminder that the resurrection is a promise that is wholly outside of my control.

As I sat and listened to "Hymn of Promise," I was an associate pastor at the large, multi-staffed church at the beach that I thought I wanted to go to after divinity school. Things were going so well. In the two years I served the church the average worship attendance of the contemporary service that I helped lead went from 150 to 250, and the Holy Spirit seemed to be on the move. And yet the Holy Spirit spoke a convicting word to me through that hymn. I had forgotten the prophetic sentence spoken to me from a magnet on my fridge, given to me by a young Southern Baptist pastor at my first rural church appointment. I had forgotten the warning: "Don't get so busy making a living that you forget to make a life."

The song reminded me of both the reality of death and its entanglement with the effervescent hope of resurrection that bubbles up within our lives. It sang to me, but not only as a word of hope. In some ways it haunted me even as it uplifted me. I began to know that something would have to change if I was going to be apprehended by the resurrection.

In some ways that song helped to awaken me to myself, to the needs to which I had fallen asleep. I mentioned in a previous chapter the Charles Wesley sermon "Awake, Thou That Sleepest," which talks about the need for spiritual awakening and kindling connection with the Holy Spirit. How could I be pointing others in that direction when I was not there? I realized just how complex my current reality was, that I was helping people to be awakened, but that I had fallen asleep to so much.

In our Methodist methods are the power of resurrection and the threat of creeping death. If we fall asleep to ourselves, we can't merely be like Rip Van Winkle, imbibing the wine of the world and then awakening much later with a funny story to live. If we fall asleep, our energy stores will be depleted and we will accidentally die the death of stagnation.

On that day, I heard Mrs. Pat's beautiful voice, like the first bird of spring, saying that verdant life would soon break through the oppressive dryness. As I observed the stagnation in my own life, I came to work through it with psychotherapy and with medication for anxiety and depression. Depression is like a persistent threat of numbness, of feeling nothing, a threat that feels like death only when you're just starting to come to the other side of it, with nerves reeling in fresh pain. Anxiety is the twin of depression, the constant fear that every bump in the road will send you over the precipice into oblivion.

As I heard "Hymn of Promise" that day, I started to recognize the death from which God was bringing me. Coming through severe anxiety and depression at the same time slows down your life and speeds it up. For me, it gave me a kind of superpower. I came to realize other people who were depressed, something intuitively connecting me to them on a deeper level. We read in the Bible that "deep calls out to deep," and likewise deep pain calls out to deep pain.

In my own life, I started making time in the middle of the day for meditation as medication, for contemplative prayer as a "divine therapy," as I've heard it called. And as I did this, I slowed down. This made me a worse pastor, at least as the corporate system measured it, but it helped me to be able to sense the slow infringement of death and the need to long for the resurrection. This became true not only in my personal life but also in the life of the church.

"The present form of this world is passing away," we read in the Bible (1 Cor 7:31 NRSV), and in some ways, we are locked in an inescapable cycle of death and resurrection. The completion of this will be when that vision in Revelation is realized, when the old heaven and earth pass away, because, behold, God has made a new heaven and new earth, having come down to be with God's people.

I have begun to recognize the things that cause death in the structures of the church. Looking around, my mind realizes that we are in a moment of revelation when we can see clearly the inadequacies of humanity's attempts to perfectly love a God who perfectly loves us. In some ways this is grace, because in seeing where we've gotten it wrong we see where we can go from here.

I'm reminded of the words of a poem by Walter Rauschenbusch. He said that in prayer he realizes that the best of human achievements seem "as full of infernal iniquities as a carcass is full of maggots."[8] I have begun to recognize a number of the human inadequacies within our systems and structures, but it is only as a part of the larger whole of seeing God's glory that longs to break in.

"Dying is not the worst thing that can happen to your church," I have said to one of the congregations I served. "The worst thing that could happen is that your church refuses to change (or plant seeds for the future) and dies, without the hope of resurrection, from all your work and toil."

In this book, I have mentioned many places where death encroaches—both things that are dying and things that cause death. Our method of church dying is not the worst thing. Worse would be closing the door to the tomb, as if to say that we do not believe what is dead can be resurrected. What is worse than death is dying without trying to work against the forces of wickedness that work against God's reign of shalom and love on earth as it is in heaven.

---

8. Rauschenbusch, *Christianity and the Social Crisis*, xvi.

This book has for me been a ballad of lamentation—a long song of sorrow and grief that has tried to move toward hope. And so this final chapter is a hymn of promise, a tune of longing for what might be possible. But even more broadly, I invite you to find your own tune of longing, your own song of resurrection and hope. Whether this is literally singing, listening to others sing, or worshiping in another way, act like the psalmist—admitting to what has died and crying out unto the Lord in new life.

In these last couple of sections, I will share a few thoughts about what I think resurrection will look like.

Traditioned Tribal Innovation and Christ's Mission

Picture the fantastical scene from the book of Revelation's conclusion: every tribe, tongue, and nation bowing in worship before Jesus Christ. In the times of yore, tribal identities were distinguishable, each proudly carrying their distinctive colors. But as the planet shrinks into a global village, it seems like these vibrant tribal hues are washing out into a uniform gray.

Now don't get me wrong: I'm not against moving past harmful tribalism. But there's something primal, something deeply human about having a tribe, a group that resonates with your quirks, your ideas, your you-ness.

The might of colonizing powers tried to erase these tribes, thinking them primitive or unnecessary. But I would say being a part of a tribe isn't inherently bad. In fact, it can be quite comforting. It's like sitting at the familiar corner of your favorite coffee shop, the barista knowing your order by heart. But the real problem is getting these tribes to play nice, to learn from one another.

In *The Persuaders* Anand Giridharadas talks about finding overlaps with others, seeking common fronts, and united fronts. Do you remember my friend called Jones, the self-proclaimed eighteenth-century man, also a racist member of the League of the South? Even with him I found shared grievances with the government. In political theory it's called the "Horseshoe theory," where the opposites are closer than we think.

It's this same logic that led me to advocate for language groups to have a "sovereign" place in the church I served. Recognizing the tribal nature of people, I envisioned a healthy coexistence of our respective tribes. We should not just accept but celebrate our differences. Remember the day of Pentecost? Everyone heard the disciples in their native language, and, as Edgardo Colón-Emeric says, they knew they were Galileans because they still had their accents.[9] The Spirit allowed them to communicate with each other but let them keep what made them special!

A resurrected life isn't about a domineering power, but a shared table. It's about acknowledging the multicolored tapestry of humanity. The "Word" became flesh and moved into different neighborhoods, taking on different shades.

The tricky part is in reconciling the tribes with the kingdom of God. There's no denying that a lot of folks identify more closely with their non-Christian tribes. In his book *Traditioned Innovation* Greg Jones suggests working within these tribes, becoming part of their traditions. It's like visiting a friend's house: you don't just barge in and start rearranging furniture; you respect their space, their rules.

The idea is to go local, to start at the ground level. You work with the existing tribal customs, traditions, and virtues, and from there you push for innovation, for transformation. Resurrection, after all, is not just about the *me* but about the *we*.

There will be bumps in the road, spots where our tribes just don't see eye to eye. But that's the thing about love; it doesn't insist on its own way. It's respectful; it's patient. Remember, as the saying goes, "The enemy of my enemy is my friend." And our enemy—it's not flesh and blood. We should be fighting against spiritual evil, an idea that consumes everything, concentrates wealth, and makes us think that all we are is consumers.

As long as we're not trying to erase each other's existence, we can find ways to work together. This collaboration is key in a crisis; it's often the very thing that triggers innovation. Tribes may be distinct, but in the face of a common threat they're forced to come together, to innovate.

Living the resurrected life means recognizing that God's work is bigger than us, that it spans across our tribes, and, yes, it even includes our enemies. Loving our enemies is not about feeling warm fuzzies for them; it's about acknowledging their humanity and their place in the world we share. Whether inside or outside the church, we can draw from our traditions to innovate and explore new possibilities—together.

From our different ideological silos, we can work together. In my work with the TENx10 collaborative,[10] I helped create a resource called "The Relational Discipleship Kickstart," which was designed as a ten-step process through which adults, working with youth, could grow in their work of accompanying youth and trying to form disciples. This resource is available to

---

9. Colón-Emeric, "El Corazón Ardiente."

10. You can find more information about these resources on the TENx10 webpage "Personalized tools for: Youth Leaders" available at https://www.tenx10.org/youth-leader-tools.

the more than one hundred partners who gather through TENx10, trying to make faith matter more to the next generation. Yet each of these many denominations, networks, and organizations see our mission in a slightly different way. This is what I call "traditioned tribal innovation." We live with the dynamic presence of the Holy Spirit, which takes the different flavors we embody, and tries to invite us together.

We are all tribal. Sometimes I wish we were not, but we are. Even in the church. Back around the time I was born, Willimon and Stanley Hauerwas wrote a book called *Resident Aliens* in which they talked about the church as a Christian colony. If that is so, we have different neighborhoods or tribes within the colony.

In the United States, I have not seen where people will stop being their tribal selves. But if we see that as part of a larger identity in God's reign in the world, we can work together. We can acknowledge and celebrate the diversity of God's creation while pursuing a shared mission of love and reconciliation. This fulfills Jesus's mission in two distinct ways. Firstly, it embodies the love Jesus commanded us to have for one another, a love that is not weakened by differences but is actually strengthened and enriched by them. Secondly, it engages in the work of reconciliation, a central element of Jesus's mission.

Connecting with the work of Jesus Christ, whether on earth or in heaven, whether by myself or with others, is salvation. It is simultaneously personal and communal. In the work of that salvation, we ought to have no room for division or animosity. Even though we are separated by our subgroups, we need to perpetually find or make ways to innovate and work together! The church is called to reflect that reconciliation, to bring together many groups under the banner of Christ, and to allow the diverse languages, cultures, and customs to enrich our understanding of God's word and the mission of Jesus Christ.

The challenge for the church, therefore, is to adopt this perspective of traditioned tribal innovation, to see the value in our diverse identities, to become the living body of Christ that doesn't just tolerate differences but embraces them as essential for its mission.

God gives to the church and also through the church, graciously giving without the need for merits to prove our worthiness. So this gift, imbued with many different voices and identities, becomes an embodiment of the diverse, inclusive, and reconciling love of Christ.

As we step into the fragility and promise of new life, we must remember that it is the Spirit that breathes life into our tribes, nudging us toward innovation and collaboration, pushing us to uphold the mission of Jesus Christ. We must embrace our differences, not as a source of division, but as a shared language of love, respect, and mutual understanding. In doing so we carry forward the mission of Jesus Christ, bringing the kingdom of God closer to earth, one collaboration at a time. Working together shows signs of new life, signs which are as beautiful as they are fragile. The resurrection is fragile, yet full of boundless potential, much like new life. So as we take the next step, let's discuss this fragility of new life.

Nurturing Seedlings of the Church

Lately my thoughts have been preoccupied with the question of what comes after death. The premise of this exploration is life following death, the promise of resurrection. While it's tempting to regard this as mere consolation amid the agony of death, simply restating it feels like a hollow echo of religious sentiment. We know resurrection follows death, but what form does it take? Can we provide any more precise directions?

When I first wrote this section, I was in the sacred season of Advent, a period dedicated to celebrating the divine coming closer, God making Their presence felt. This leads me back to a different perspective on the cycle of death and resurrection, an idea Valerie Kaur introduces in her book *See No Stranger*. She asks, "But what if what if this darkness is not the darkness of the tomb but the darkness of the womb?"[11]

Kaur speculates on whether our society is at the precipice of demise or on the cusp of a new birth. I propose that these two notions aren't mutually exclusive. What is old, decrepit, and necrotic needs to perish to create room for new life. But this emerging life won't likely resemble the resurrection as embodied by Jesus' return with a heavenly body, scarred yet healed. Our hope for something that retains its former appearance while showcasing signs of healing and transformation is optimistic.

The evolution we'll witness, though sharing the same DNA as what was before, will take an embryonic form. We might wish for it to burst forth fully formed and charismatic, much like the dinosaur baby from Jim Henson's television show, but what's coming could be far more delicate. Jesus' arrival in the world wasn't about abolishing the past, but about building a new movement of faith rooted in the Jewish story, the narrative of God and the people of Israel. This is the tradition I've pledged my allegiance to, my story, my song.

Yet it's crucial to acknowledge that this transformation didn't occur rapidly. The divine chose to incarnate through a humble, unwed mother, not a powerful warrior or a wealthy king. We encounter Mary, ripe with

---

11. Kaur, *See No Stranger*, xiii.

pregnancy, in her elder cousin Elizabeth's home. Both women, removed from the patriarchs of their family, prophesy about God's grand plan during their pregnancies. God works through these women, the powerless, and brings Jesus into the world under seemingly scandalous circumstances.

These divine operations contradict our expectations, and we're quick to find faults in others' plans while promoting our own. From Mary's womb to Jesus' public ministry, it took nearly thirty years for the seed of God's kingdom to sprout. Jesus began not with a high priest but with his rugged cousin in the wilderness, not in a temple but amid the desert's rocks and spirits.

This history serves to remind us of the patience required for God's work to unfold. Even when Jesus chose to act he didn't gallop on a chariot but strolled at a humble three miles per hour. He didn't impose truth on people but laid it before them, allowing them to embrace it when ready.

So why should the transformation of the institutional church be any different? We shepherd churches that clamor for results, for novelty, but somehow resist the loss of methods that are often already dead. Working through this dance is arduous. It's not the task of a few years but of several lifetimes. I can already spot signs of the new emerging, not because the church has started to disintegrate, but because people, a generation or more ago, recognized the dying church and started sowing seeds for a future revival.

The sparks of resurrection we see now didn't ignite because the church has just started to perish or because a part of the church was sealed behind a tombstone for a brief period. They're burning because the church died a long time ago, and people endeavored to follow God's work.

The infantile instances of the gospel we see today need protection. If we had a garden serving as our sole source of sustenance, we wouldn't recklessly mow it down for having weeds. Neither would we dump weed killer over a neighbor's weed-infested garden. It's more constructive to encourage virtuous farming and ecological practices while disregarding the harmful ones.

Despite this we often find it easier to eliminate the budding movements of the church around us. Cancel culture has done much good, calling many to justice, but it can also lead to the indiscriminate extermination of burgeoning churches for their dissimilarities.

When I witness the church stifling young congregations for being different it feels akin to ecclesiastic infanticide. I can hope for a church plant that adheres to 90 percent of the same gospel principles as I do, but in reality, we will probably differ on a few things. Even if you think someone's church is full of problems, look for a few places you can agree.

This isn't to say we should overlook our disparities or ignore the damage we've inflicted on each other. I concur that in many cases a schism or separation within parts of the church might be the most pragmatic course. But just as many divorced families manage an amicable split, we can aspire to want the best for each other, even if our commitments have altered.

Unity through division and reconciliation from a distance could be our shared goal. We work toward a future where no single church holds the majority in our secular society. As the last vestiges of Christendom wane in the West and the maturing youth's generation becomes predominantly unchurched, it's time to cease our disputes and begin loving one another deeply.

In Matt 18 Jesus discusses church conflict and suggests that unrepentant individuals should be removed from the church and treated as nonbelievers. And how should the church treat nonbelievers? With the utmost love. So why not extend the same love to one another?

When we encounter theological offspring in young church plants, our words possess the power to heal or destroy. I fervently hope that we choose to heal. The power of the resurrection, the power of life and death, live in our words. The biggest challenge is about truth. And that is where I am going to end, with a conversation about truth.

Encountering Truth Along the Resurrected Way

After being so immersed in problems, how can we possibly move toward resurrection? Living as Christians in a secular society, how can we find the courage to proclaim our faith? Living as people who have witnessed the death that has not only come to the church but has been propagated through it, how can we expect a different form of resurrection when Christians often refuse to accept accountability for repair?

I cannot offer answers in the form of solutions, but I do believe that solutions often emerge in the drama of living out the Christian life. Like the disciples of Jesus Christ who walked along the road to Emmaus and had their hearts strangely warmed while talking to the stranger they did not know was Jesus, we often encounter the sacred through journeys that carry us away from crucifixion and into an uncertain future.

I believe that we can find answers along the way, and thus it is more crucial to consider our disposition on the journey than rushing to a solution. Along the road to Emmaus Jesus opened the disciples' eyes to God's work in the Holy Scriptures. They walked and listened, allowing their pent-up energy to be exercised step by step. They learned something new about the truth of God's work and their own story. This transformation happened as the crucified and resurrected Lord taught them something they apparently could not have learned from a Lord whose resume did not include "been to hell and back again."

Before Jesus' death, before the crucifixion, he was brought before the Roman governor, Pontius Pilate. In John's Gospel, Pilate asks Jesus, "What is truth?" Nowadays, truth seems to be relativized. Instead of talking about ultimate truth, most people say "This is my truth" as a way of expressing their subjective understanding of truth. We do not look at truth as a society as being a universal truth applicable to everyone.

Perhaps this is why we have a hard time speaking and being heard. I do not wish to say that resurrection means combating others' narratives of truth. But I do think we need to explore what a resurrected Lord has to say to a church whose method of church has died and may be resurrected. What does a resurrected Lord have to say to a congregation and a denomination that has experienced demise and wonders if their collective bones can live again?

I would suggest that we start with the truth of our story. When I say this, I'm not referring to the scientific facts. I'm talking about the truth by which we live. My thoughts turn to the words of Jesus Christ: "And you will know the truth, and the truth will make you free" (John 8:32 NRSV). I have suggested that resurrection involves rediscovering the truth of our story, and for me this is grounded in Jesus Christ. We must examine our stories, and the church's stories, and reevaluate them in light of where Jesus is and was—and where Jesus was absent.

What types of spiritual truth and lived religious expression of truth has brought us to freedom, and what has imprisoned us? This is one of the most difficult questions to ask precisely because sometimes the answers seem to contradict what immediately surfaces. For example, it may seem like having lots of rules could be confining. But what do these rules and regulations actually do? In the United Methodist Church we have a *Book of Resolutions*—a list of articles that might seem to curtail our individual liberties—but when we look more closely we realize that they align with the lived truth of Jesus Christ, the movement of God's reign, and the kinship of God's kingdom, which seeks to set the captives free and offer recovery of sight to the blind, to proclaim the year of the Lord's favor.

Conversely, it is also true that some things which may seem to give us liberty can be confining. Many churches that have disaffiliated from the United Methodist Church in our recent schism might look at the donations they used to give to the United Methodist Church and think, "My years of being taxed by the overreaching structure of the church are over. Now I can use my money however I want." But whenever a global pandemic occurs or whenever they face financial hardship and they find themselves constrained by being disconnected from the larger community, they will see that the short-term gain was indeed restricting. If these churches consider the money that they have withdrawn from the international work of the church, the universities for pastors in African countries, and the finances offered to start churches in the Philippines, they may realize that what seems like freedom to them is constraining the liberation of their sisters and brothers who they cannot see. This is much like the spirit at work in free market capitalism, which seeks to give consumers ease of access and freedom of choice yet is built on the constriction and deprivation of people they may never see. So again, the question is, What does our truth in action look like? What does this resurrection look like?

We live in what some call a "post-truth society." It is a society that confuses what truth and fact are. The truths by which we live may or may not be scientifically verifiable. Many people deny the fact of significant political events like the Holocaust or what happened at the January 6, 2021, insurrection attempt at the US Capitol by claiming it is their truth.

Undeniably, we can read a biology textbook and agree on certain facts. We can look at the stars and the images from the Webb Telescope and agree on the vastness of the cosmos. We can look under the microscope at the smallest living beings and find facts about life at the cellular and DNA levels.

But even unlocking secrets of the human genome has not given us enough truth to ensure a thriving survival. The facts do not equal the truth of what we need. Our species is draining the world of its resources. As the Christian church, we are more divided than ever with Christian extremists on one side advocating for a specific nationalist ideology through violent means, and on the other side Christians so open-minded that they cannot tell you definitively what they believe. There is beauty in the umbrella of Christianity being so broad, but we must also acknowledge that we all have access to the same abundance of truth. We have access to the earliest existing manuscripts of the Bible, and we can examine Christian history from numerous angles if we wish. But having all these verifiable facts has not led us to agree on a truth that would unite us.

So I would contend that truth involves not only examining where Jesus has been in the past but also asking what Jesus is doing right now, in this moment. This approach can challenge us toward repentance and having a new mindset, opening the door for new possibilities and a new world of existence in the future.

Truth is not merely about examining facts or even the piece of fact that we hold on to with all our might, condemning everyone else. Truth is about looking at the way things are going right now and asking, "Is there something that the Lord Jesus Christ might be doing right now that can bring me together with others?" We can disagree with people about many doctrinal issues or interpretations of the Bible, but if we can look at the number of species going extinct, we might be able to imagine what healing and resurrection look like together. If we can look at the increasing division between the impoverished and the superwealthy, we might be able to join the resistance to injustice, together. If we consider the potential loss of lives if nationalist terrorist warfare broke out in our country, we might agree that sharing our resources and daily bread is preferable to engaging in a conflict that would probably destroy the supply chain for all of us.

When we have too many options about what truth might be, we risk spreading ourselves too thin in an attempt to embrace them all. And when we scatter our focus, we run the risk of getting off track. If we can slow down and understand what the truth of our Christian experience looks like, we may come to a place where we think about one or two things that healing might look like, one or two places where we can live expectantly and hope for the resurrection to peek out like a delicate flower through a crack in the pavement. Another way of saying this is we might rediscover our purpose for being, and in so doing we might be able to elevate it above continuing to keep certain dead methods on life support in programs that struggle to make people feel connected.

Resurrection, insofar as it is the work of God Almighty in Jesus Christ, is a natural process. God is everywhere in nature, and it is in God's nature to work toward holistic healing and resurrection. Whether or not the church I serve may be resurrected remains unanswered, but the question of whether God is still in the business of resurrection is one that, to me, has already been answered. I believe that just as surely as a small tree will grow in defiance of the drought around it, oblivious of the wildfires that threaten it, the resurrection power of God at work in the world will not be shut out.

The question for us as individual Christians is much the same as the question posed to the institutions we serve. How are we going to position ourselves in light of the deaths we are experiencing so that either we or our successors may be in a place to respond to the resurrection when it begins to happen? Will we be open to the new way that Jesus teaches us the story that we thought we already knew—in light of what resurrection looks like around us? Are we willing to accept the possibility of reformation? I hope so, not for my sake but for the sake of those who come after me.

Conclusion: Choosing Love as a Testament to the Resurrection

In this conversation about our sacred spaces, we've journeyed through the landscapes of death, the demise of our methods, and the curiosity about the coming of resurrection. Especially the death and resurrection of our methods, within our church and across broader society. We cannot negate the death that has come, but we do have a say in our way forward. Our forebears' mistakes may not be undone, but we can commit ourselves to the fundamental rule—"do no harm." We can seed new systems of healing, minimize the damage done, and initiate a ripple effect that extends beyond our lifetimes. In this work, we serve a purpose greater than our individual existence.

We must realize that resurrection, akin to sunrise or the awakening of dormant seeds after a wildfire, cannot be coerced into existence. However, our relationship with resurrection can be transformed. Jesus was resurrected, yet not everyone saw or believed it. Similarly, the divine spark of new life surrounds us, and we can position ourselves either as self-reliant beings untouched by the intervention of a benevolent God in our flawed lives and systems, or as observant witnesses, keenly seeking God's work in progress. The beauty of resurrection is in its ceaseless recurrence. The affluent white denomination that I am part of is grappling with death and yearning for resurrection. Yet the marginalized communities around us have existed within this cycle too. By choosing to see resurrection we enable ourselves to be transfigured by its existence, which affects not only our disposition but also the healing of our spiritual, physical, and collective bodies.

We need to make a conscious decision to consistently relinquish our hold over life's boundaries. Whether that involves surrendering our decision-making authority over full inclusion of members or relinquishing control over our finances, the most profound choice is the decision to love others.

So how does love intertwine with the concept of resurrection? It involves love for neighbors—and love for enemies. If I am a witness to the resurrection, then my love for others must burn with the intensity of that perspective.

And how does resurrection shape our re-imagination of the church? Healing implies a return to our roots, not in a historical context but by uncovering the profound truths nestled deep within us. The essence of our past selves, the core of our being, is what needs resurrection. We are called to witness the divine that abides deep within us and our community.

As we consider the resurrection, let's choose love—a testament to our faith and our witness to God's perpetual resurrection. May the divine that abides deep within us find us, guiding us to shape our church and community in the likeness of Christ's transformative love. This, I believe, is the greatest testament to our faith in the resurrection.

Bibliography

Anzaldúa, Gloria. *Borderlands/La Frontera: The New Mestiza*. San Francisco: Aunt Lute, 1987.
Baldwin, James. "The Fire Next Time." In *The Price of the Ticket: Collected Nonfiction 1948–1985*. Boston: Beacon, 2021.
Barber, William J., II. *The Third Reconstruction: How a Moral Movement Is Overcoming the Politics of Division and Fear*. With Jonathan Wilson-Hartgrove. Boston: Beacon, 2016. Kindle.
Barna Group. "Three Spiritual Journeys of Millennials." Faith Formation Learning Exchange, May 9, 2013. www.faithformationlearningexchange.net/uploads/5/2/4/6/5246709/the_barna_group_-_three_spiritual_journeys_of_millennials.pdf.
Beaumont, Susan. *How to Lead When You Don't Know Where You're Going: Leading in a Liminal Season*. Lanham, MD: Rowman and Littlefield, 2019.
Beck, Michael Adam, and Tyler Kleeberger. *Fresh Expressions of the Rural Church*. Nashville: Abingdon, 2022.
Berg, Manfred. *Popular Justice: A History of Lynching in America*. Chicago: Ivan R. Dee, 2011.
Bowler, Kate. "Sunita Puri: The Uncertainty Specialist." *Everything Happens with Kate Bowler*, season 5, episode 1. Apr. 20, 2020. Podcast. https://podcasts.apple.com/us/podcast/everything-happens-with-kate-bowler/id1341076079?i=1000472157440.
Brown, Brené. *Daring Greatly: How the Courage to Be Vulnerable Transforms the Way We Live, Love, Parent, and Lead*. New York: Gotham, 2012.
Bruce-Lockhart, Anna. "Who Are the 1%? The Answer Might Surprise You." World Economic Forum, Oct. 14, 2015. https://www.weforum.org/stories/2015/10/who-are-the-1-the-answer-might-surprise-you.
CDC. "Adult Obesity Facts." CDC, May 14, 2024. https://www.cdc.gov/obesity/adult-obesity-facts/?CDC_AAref_Val=https://www.cdc.gov/obesity/data/adult.html.
Claiborne, Shane. *The Irresistible Revolution: Living as an Ordinary Radical*. Grand Rapids: Zondervan, 2006.
Cleveland, Christena. *God Is a Black Woman*. New York: HarperOne, 2022.
Colón-Emeric, Edgardo. "El Corazón Ardiente for Renewing Doctrine, Worship, and Mission." Webinar, Center for Leadership Excellence, Feb. 15, 2023.
———. *The People Called Metodista: Renewing Doctrine, Worship, and Mission from the Margins*. Nashville: Abingdon, 2022.
Cone, James. *The Cross and the Lynching Tree*. Maryknoll, NY: Orbis, 2011. Kindle.

Curtice, Kaitlin. *Native: Identity, Belonging, and Rediscovering God*. Grand Rapids: Brazos, 2020.

Dalai Lama [Tenzin Gyatso], and Desmond Tutu. *The Book of Joy: Lasting Happiness in a Changing World*. New York: Avery, 2016.

Diamond, Jared. *Collapse: How Societies Choose to Fail or Succeed*. New York: Penguin, 2011.

DiAngelo, Robin. *White Fragility: Why It's So Hard for White People to Talk About Racism*. Boston: Beacon, 2018.

Douglass, Frederick. *Narrative of the Life of Frederick Douglass*. New York: Dover, 1995. https://archive.org/details/narrativeoflifeooodoug/page/n7/mode/2up.

Duke Clergy Health Initiative. *Clergy Health Trends: Findings from the Statewide Clergy Health Survey of North Carolina United Methodist Clergy, 2008–2021*. 2022. https://clergyreligionresearch.duke.edu/sites/default/files/ClergyHealthTrends.pdf.

Duplin Times. "CHURCH FIRE—A fire destroyed much of Rose Hill United Methodist Church this morning. More information as we get it." Facebook, Jan. 1, 2018. https://www.facebook.com/share/1F5uAZ9LEy/?mibextid%3DWC7FNe&source.

Epstein, David. *Range: Why Generalists Triumph in a Specialized World*. New York: Riverhead, 2019.

Giridharadas, Anand. *The Persuaders: At the Front Lines of the Fight for Hearts, Minds, and Democracy*. Narrated by the author. Random House Audio, 2022. Audible audio ed., 12 hr., 21 min.

González, Juan. *Harvest of Empire: A History of Latinos in America*. New York: Penguin, 2000.

Hanson, Todd, and Robert Siegel. *The Onion Movie*. Directed by Tom Kuntz and Mike Maguire. 20th Century Fox Home Entertainment, 2008.

Harling, Robert. *Steel Magnolias*. Directed by Herbert Ross. Culver City, CA: TriStar Pictures, 1989.

Hart, Drew G. I. *Who Will Be a Witness? Igniting Activism for God's Justice, Love, and Deliverance*. Harrisonburg, VA: Herald, 2020.

Hauerwas, Stanley, and William H. Willimon. *Resident Aliens: Life in the Christian Colony*. Nashville: Abingdon, 1989.

hooks, bell. *All About Love: New Visions*. New York: William Morrow, 2000.

Human Rights Watch. "US: Lasting Harm from Family Separation at the Border." Dec. 16, 2024. https://www.hrw.org/news/2024/12/16/us-lasting-harm-family-separation-border.

Irving, Debby. *Waking Up White: And Finding Myself in the Story of Race*. Cambridge, MA: Self-published, Elephant Room, 2014.

Jennings, Willie James. *After Whiteness: An Education in Belonging*. Grand Rapids: Eerdmans, 2020.

———. "Jesus and the Displaced: Christology and the Redemption of Habitation." Lecture presented at the University Church 2023 Bampton Lectures, Oxford, UK, May 23, 2023. https://www.youtube.com/live/yq3fFwQ7a8c.

Jenson, Matt. *The Gravity of Sin: Augustine, Luther and Barth on* homo incurvatus in se. London: T&T Clark, 2007.

Jones, L. Gregory. *Traditioned Innovation: Finding the Good in Change*. Grand Rapids: Brazos, 2016.

Jones, Robert P. *The End of White Christian America*. New York: Simon and Schuster, 2016.
———. *White Too Long: The Legacy of White Supremacy in American Christianity*. New York: Simon and Schuster, 2020. Kindle.
Kagge, Erling. *Silence: In the Age of Noise*. New York: Pantheon, 2017.
Katz, Bruce, and Jeremy Nowak. *The New Localism: How Cities Can Thrive in the Age of Populism*. Washington, DC: Brookings Institution, 2018.
Kaur, Valerie. *See No Stranger: A Memoir and Manifesto of Revolutionary Love*. New York: Random House, 2020.
Kendi, Ibram X. *How to Be an Antiracist*. New York: One World, 2019.
———. *Stamped from the Beginning: The Definitive History of Racist Ideas in America*. New York: Nation Books, 2016.
Kim, Young. "Trauma and Church." Medium, July 8, 2020. https://medium.com/@jamesyounghan/trauma-and-church-739584979acd.
Kimmerer, Robin Wall. *Braiding Sweetgrass: Indigenous Wisdom, Scientific Knowledge, and the Teachings of Plants*. Minneapolis: Milkweed Editions, 2013.
King, Martin Luther, Jr. "Beyond Vietnam: A Time to Break Silence." Speech delivered at Riverside Church, New York City, NY, Apr. 4, 1967. https://archive.org/details/MLKBeyondVietnam.
———. "On Being a Good Neighbor." In *Strength to Love*, 16–24. New York: Harper and Row, 1963.
Knight, Paul. "Quote from Humphrey, Not Gandhi." Letter to the Editor. *Columbian*, Nov. 11, 2016. https://www.columbian.com/news/2016/nov/11/letter-quote-from-humphrey-not-gandhi.
Lamott, Anne. *Bird by Bird: Some Instructions on Writing and Life*. New York: Anchor, 1995.
Lewis, C. S. *The Great Divorce: A Dream*. New York: HarperOne, 2001.
Lorde, Audre. *A Burst of Light: Essays*. Mineola, NY: Dover, 2017.
Luhrmann, T. M. *When God Talks Back: Understanding the American Evangelical Relationship with God*. New York: Knopf, 2012.
Lupton, Robert D. *Toxic Charity: How Churches and Charities Hurt Those They Help (and How to Reverse It)*. New York: HarperOne, 2011.
Maté, Gabor, and Daniel Maté. *The Myth of Normal: Trauma, Illness, and Healing in a Toxic Culture*. Narrated by Daniel Maté. Penguin Audio, 2022. Audible audio ed., 18 hr., 12 min.
Mayo Clinic. "Complicated Grief." Dec. 13, 2022. https://www.mayoclinic.org/diseases-conditions/complicated-grief/diagnosis-treatment/drc-20360389.
McGhee, Heather. *The Sum of Us: What Racism Costs Everyone and How We Can Prosper Together*. New York: Random House, 2022.
Menakem, Resmaa. *My Grandmother's Hands: Racialized Trauma and the Pathway to Mending Our Hearts and Bodies*. Las Vegas: Central Recovery, 2017.
Merton, Thomas. *No Man Is an Island*. Boston: Shambhala, 2005.
NAACP. *Thirty Years of Lynching in the United States, 1889–1918*. New York: NAACP, 1919. https://www.google.com/books/edition/Thirty_Years_of_Lynching_in_the_United_S/Ujo6AQAAMAAJ?hl=en&gbpv=1.
National Park Service. "Sojourner Truth." Sept. 2, 2017. https://www.nps.gov/wori/learn/historyculture/sojourner-truth.htm.

NETWORK. "Sister Simone Campbell, SSS." https://networklobby.org/about/srsimonebio.

Noah, Trevor. *The Daily Show*. Season 26, episode 10, "The Daily Social Distancing Show/Wilmer Valderrama." Aired Oct. 14, 2020, on Comedy Central. The Daily Show, YouTube video. https://www.youtube.com/watch?v=MlYQqHXBhaE.

North Carolina Conference of the United Methodist Church. "Vision Statement." https://nccumc.org/about.

Office of the Surgeon General. *Our Epidemic of Loneliness and Isolation: The U.S. Surgeon General's Advisory on the Healing Effects of Social Connection and Community*. Edited by Julianne Holt-Lunstad. Office of the Surgeon General, 2023. www.hhs.gov/sites/default/files/surgeon-general-social-connection-advisory.pdf.

Papanicolas, Irene, et al. "Health Care Spending in the United States and Other High-Income Countries." *JAMA* 319 (2018) 1024–39. https://jamanetwork.com/journals/jama/fullarticle/2674671.

Parsons, Mikeal C., and Cody J. Sanders. *Corpse Care: Ethics for Tending the Dead*. Minneapolis: Fortress, 2023.

PRRI. "A Political and Cultural Glimpse into America's Future: Generation Z's Views on Generational Change and the Challenges and Opportunities Ahead." PRRI, Jan. 22, 2024. https://www.prri.org/research/generation-zs-views-on-generational-change-and-the-challenges-and-opportunities-ahead-a-political-and-cultural-glimpse-into-americas-future.

Rauschenbusch, Walter. *Christianity and the Social Crisis in the 21st Century: The Classic That Woke Up the Church*. New York: HarperOne, 2007.

Reynolds, Kevin, dir. *The Count of Monte Cristo*. Featuring Jim Caviezel, Guy Pearce, and Richard Harris. Burbank, CA: Touchstone Pictures, 2002.

Roberts, Bailey K., et al. "Trends and Disparities in Firearm Deaths Among Children and Adolescents." *Pediatrics* 152 (Sept. 2023). https://doi.org/10.1542/peds.2023-061296.

Rohr, Richard. *Adam's Return: The Five Promises of Male Initiation*. New York: Crossroad, 2004.

Root, Andrew. "Why Are They Leaving? Youth Ministry in a Secular Age." Keynote address presented at the 2023 Perkins School of Youth Ministry: Everyday Adventure, Dallas, TX, Jan. 9, 2023.

Rothstein, Richard. *The Color of Law: A Forgotten History of How Our Government Segregated America*. New York: Liveright, 2017.

Rowe, C. Kavin. *Christianity's Surprise: A Sure and Certain Hope*. Nashville: Abingdon, 2020. Kindle.

Ruiz, Don Miguel. *The Four Agreements: A Practical Guide to Personal Freedom*. San Rafael, CA: Amber-Allen, 1997.

Salvatierra, Alexia, and Peter Heltzel. *Faith-Rooted Organizing: Mobilizing the Church in Service to the World*. Downers Grove, IL: InterVarsity, 2014.

Salvatierra, Alexia, and Brandon Wrencher. *Buried Seeds: Learning from the Vibrant Resilience of Marginalized Christian Communities*. Grand Rapids: Baker Academic, 2022.

Southey, Robert. *The Life of John Wesley*. London: Seeley, Jackson, and Halliday, 1856. https://www.google.com/books/edition/The_Life_of_John_Wesley/xo86AAAAcAAJ?hl=en&gbpv=0.

Taylor, Charles. *A Secular Age*. Cambridge, MA: Harvard University Press, 2007.

"Technology." Dictionary.com. https://www.dictionary.com/browse/technology.
Tenney, Tommy. *The God Chasers: Pursuing the Lover of Your Soul*. Shippensburg, PA: Destiny Image, 1998.
Thich Nhat Hanh. *Love Letter to the Earth*. Berkeley: Parallax, 2013.
Tickle, Phyllis. *The Great Emergence: How Christianity Is Changing and Why*. Grand Rapids: Baker, 2008.
Tisby, Jemar. *The Color of Compromise: The Truth About the American Church's Complicity in Racism*. Grand Rapids: Zondervan, 2019.
Tutu, Desmond, and Mpho Tutu. *The Book of Forgiving: The Fourfold Path for Healing Ourselves and Our World*. New York: HarperOne, 2014.
United Methodist Church. "Mission Statement of the United Methodist Church." *Book of Discipline of the United Methodist Church*, 2016. https://www.umc.org/en/content/book-of-discipline-120-ff-section-1-the-churches.
United Methodist Publishing House. *The Book of Discipline of the United Methodist Church*. Nashville: United Methodist Publishing House, 2016.
———. *The United Methodist Book of Worship*. Nashville: United Methodist Publishing House, 1992.
USAFacts. "How Has Wealth Distribution in the US Changed Over Time?" USAFacts, Nov. 13, 2023. https://usafacts.org/articles/how-has-wealth-distribution-in-the-us-changed-over-time.
Warren, Audrey, and Kenneth H. Carter Jr. *Fresh Expressions: A New Kind of Methodist Church for People Not in Church*. Nashville: Abingdon, 2017.
Weems, Lovett H., Jr. "The Coming Death Tsunami." Ministry Matters, Oct. 5, 2011. https://www.ministrymatters.com/all/entry/1868/the-coming-death-tsunami.
Wesley, Charles. "Awake, Thou That Sleepest." Sermon preached Apr. 14, 1742. London: John Mason, 1832. https://archive.org/details/awake-thou-that-sleepest-charles-wesley.
White, James Emery. *The Rise of the Nones: Understanding and Reaching the Religiously Unaffiliated*. Grand Rapids: Baker, 2014.
Willimon, William H. *Acts*. Interpretation: A Bible Commentary for Teaching and Preaching. Louisville: Westminster John Knox, 2010.
———. *Don't Look Back: Methodist Hope for What Comes Next*. Nashville: Abingdon, 2022.
Wilson, Charles Reagan. *Baptized in Blood: The Religion of the Lost Cause, 1865–1920*. Athens: University of Georgia Press, 2011.
Wilson-Hartgrove, Jonathan. *Reconstructing the Gospel: Finding Freedom from Slaveholder Religion*. Downers Grove, IL: InterVarsity, 2018.
Wrights, Scott. *Oscar Romero and the Communion of Saints: A Biography*. Maryknoll, NY: Orbis, 2005.
Wuthnow, Robert. *The Left Behind: Decline and Rage in Rural America*. Princeton, NJ: Princeton University Press, 2019.

www.ingramcontent.com/pod-product-compliance
Lightning Source LLC
Chambersburg PA
CBHW062036220426
43662CB00010B/1528